Dr Lindsay Simpson is the author and co-author of nine books including the bestselling *Brothers in Arms*, co-authored with Sandra Harvey, the subject of a the television mini-series *Bikie Wars*. Her 2014 book *Where is Daniel?* written with parents Bruce and Denise Morcombe dealt with the disappearance of their son Daniel and the subsequent police investigation. Her novel *The Curer of Souls* was shortlisted for the Colin Roderick prize in 2007. That year, she also won with Sandra the Lifetime Achievement Award in the Australian Crime Writers Association Ned Kelly Awards for her contribution to crime writing.

Lindsay was an investigative journalist for *The Sydney Morning Herald* from 1983 to 1995. She spent 13 years as an academic as the inaugural Head of Journalism and Media Studies at the University of Tasmania and headed the multimedia journalism degree at James Cook University. She started postgraduate writing degree programs at both universities. She now writes fulltime and lives in the Whitsundays with her husband Grant. They have their own tourism business running two sailing boats, *Providence V* and *MiLady* around the islands.

T0294258

Also by Lindsay Simpson

Fiction
The Curer of Souls (2006)

Non-fiction
Where is Daniel?
    with Bruce Morcombe and Denise Morcombe (2014)
Honeymoon Dive,
    co-written with Jennifer Cooke (2010)
Fatal Honeymoon Dive,
    co-written with Jennifer Cooke (2010, ebook)
The Australian Geographic Guide to Tasmania (1997)
To Have and To Hold,
    with Walter Mikac (1997)
The Killer Next Door,
    co-written with Sandra Harvey (1994)
My Husband My Killer: The Murder of Megan Kalajzich,
    co-written with Sandra Harvey (1992)
Brothers in Arms,
    co-written with Sandra Harvey (1986)

Adani,
Following Its Dirty Footsteps

A Personal Story

Lindsay Simpson

Spinifex

First published by Spinifex Press, 2018

Spinifex Press Pty Ltd
PO Box 5270, North Geelong, Victoria 3215
PO Box 105, Mission Beach, Queensland 4852
Australia

women@spinifexpress.com.au
www.spinifexpress.com.au

Front cover concept: Elliot Miller, DigitallyBlessed
Cover design: Deb Snibson
Typesetting: Helen Christie
Typeset in Utopia
Printed by McPherson's Printing Group

A catalogue record for this
book is available from the
National Library of Australia

Paperback   9781925581478
ePub   9781925581508
Adobe PDF   9781925581485
Kindle   9781925581492

Acknowledgements

I would like to acknowledge firstly my husband, Grant Lewis who has patiently supported me in the writing of this manuscript. Thanks, too, to the people who cannot be named who put themselves on the line to help the cause on the ground in India. Their assistance and knowledge was invaluable. Without them, doors would not have opened.

I would also like to acknowledge all of the hard work from the following organisations: Australian Marine Conservation Society (in particular Imogen Zethoven and her dedication to the cause), the Australian Conservation Foundation as well as all of those courageous supporters of Stop Adani and the small group of committed people in the Whitsundays who fight so hard for the reef that they love. Individuals such as Libby Edge and her group of dedicated followers from Eco Barge make all the difference to looking after our reef and caring for our turtles.

I would especially like to thank Cherry Muddle whose invitation to attend a local Christmas party for the dynamic WRAD (Whitsunday Residents Against Dumping) two and a half years ago led me on this journey.

Lastly, thanks to my Dad, Charles Simpson, and the many passionate discussions we continue to have. He is always there as an inspiration.

Contents

Chapter 1

The Courting of a Mining Magnate

The Indian businessman next to me in the window seat is crunching coated chickpeas just before takeoff at the Indira Gandhi International Airport in New Delhi. It is 15 March 2017 and we are heading for Gujarat in India's far northwest. Gujarat is India's most lucrative industrial state and home to the US$12 billion multinational Adani Group – the largest port operator in India and India's largest trader and importer of coal.

"It's foggy out there," I gesture at the impenetrable mist outside. "Why is that?"

"Madam," the businessman replies still crunching. "That's the morning."

How could I have forgotten the density of the pollution in India? For four months in 2015, while researching my new novel, I had lived in Chennai in southern India. I'd forgotten the way it clogs the nostrils. Hugs the throat. Makes breathing an obvious rather than involuntary motion. Every breath signs a death warrant.

Tomorrow, on 16 March 2017, the Queensland Premier, Annastacia Palaszczuk, and her eight regional mayors will begin their descent into Mumbai from London passing through the liquorice-allsort layers of impenetrable pollution. I don't know whether any of them have ever visited this continent. Representing eight regional areas across Queensland, they have secured ratepayer-funded budgets of up to $10,000 for a few days' visit to India. Their mission: to ensure that Australia's largest coal mine and potentially the biggest in the world – the Carmichael coal mine to be built by Adani Mining Pty Ltd – goes ahead. If successful, Gautam Adani, billionaire chair, one of the wealthiest

1

men in India and founder of the Adani Group whose close friend is none other than India's Prime Minister Narendra Modi – will be the first to open the rich seams of thermal coal housed deep underground in the Australian outback previously never accessed because of the remoteness of the location.

The proposed mine is to include six open cut pits and five underground mines across an area that is 30 kms long. The company's regulatory permissions are all but in place. A mining lease, already granted by the Queensland State Government will permit the company to mine 60 million tonnes of coal every year for 60 years. If the mine goes ahead, the groundwater from the Great Artesian Basin, home to the country's ancient well – an area occupying about 22% of Australia – will be under threat. Adani is also about to be granted a free unlimited 60-year water licence by the Queensland Government (this happened on 4 April 2017). The mine will use 250 litres of freshwater for each tonne of coal produced. All the company needs to do, under the conditions of the licence, is to monitor and report the amount of water it extracts under this permit that runs until 2077. Its water usage will not be subject to public submissions or appeals.

While Adani is paying nothing to access the water, Australian farmers and graziers in the arid land surrounding the mine, who heavily rely on water for their livelihood, will still have to pay for that resource.

Adani, at this time in March 2017, is also poised to gain a $1 billion loan funded by Australian taxpayers to build a 388 km railway line to transport the coal to the coast where the world's largest coal terminal will be built only 19 kms away from the world's largest living organism – the Great Barrier Reef. The expansion of the coal port to accommodate the mine will require dredging an estimated 1.1 million cubic metres of spoil right next to the Great Barrier Reef marine park. Dissecting Indigenous spiritual land as well as thousands of hectares of agricultural land, the proposed rail line will transport the coal to around 500 ships waiting at anchor to ship the coal through the Great Barrier Reef to India.

But perhaps worst of all, the proposed Adani mine and proposed rail link will open up the massive Galilee coal basin, which straddles the Great Dividing Range covering an area of around 250,000 square kms, to a host of other mega mines including projects backed by Gina Rinehart, one of Australia's richest people and one of the world's richest women, and Clive Palmer, whose company bought the now defunct Yabulu nickel refinery north of the North Queensland city of Townsville and was later accused of environmental degradation. The refinery fronts on to the Coral Sea.

Blinded by promises of thousands of jobs, these Australian politicians are hastily visiting India to carve up what they perceive is a lucrative future for regional Queenslanders as well as shoring up their own political future. The mayors are already at each other's throats. Unseemly headlines shout how they will divide up imagined spoils.

Later, there will be promises from two of the mayors to build a $30 million airport (which their councils will never own) to hand to Adani as a gift for fly-in fly-out workers to work in the mine – all with ratepayers' money. Free office space is to be offered to Adani by the Mayor of Townsville, the North Queensland capital, while the company searches for suitable offices for its headquarters. The Mayor of Whitsunday Regional Council has been told to offer a parcel of land in the township of Bowen near Adani's coal port of Abbot Point.

There is something unseemly about this scramble. By March 2017, there has been limited debate, even in the Australian media, about the massive scale of global environmental destruction this project will entail. The largest source of carbon dioxide is from the combustion of fossil fuels (coal, natural gas and oil) which produces 81% of human carbon dioxide carbon emissions. Burning coal is the biggest single source of carbon dioxide emissions from human activity. It generates less than 30% of the world's energy supply, while producing 46% of global carbon dioxide emissions. Coal is, quite simply, incredibly dirty and it carries toxic airborne pollutants and heavy metals including mercury and lead into the atmosphere.

The effects of these carbon dioxide emissions are forcibly felt. 2016 was the warmest year on record since record keeping began in 1880 (1.2°C above pre-industrial era) according to NASA and a separate, independent analysis by the National Oceanic and Atmospheric Administration (NOAA).[1] What is even more alarming, however, is that the change has proved to be consecutive – proof of continuing long-term climate change. Both organisations found that globally, 2013–17 was the "hottest five-year period on record."

Since 2015, the Great Barrier Reef has been subjected to some of the highest temperatures recorded. In the summer of 2016, two-thirds of the coral in the northern reef died through bleaching. In some reefs in the north almost all of the coral died. Heat stress from these record temperatures damage the microscopic algae (*zooxanthellae*) that live in the tissues of corals turning them white. Up until the 1980s, mass bleachings were unheard of. In 1998 and 2002 the reef experienced its first severe bleachings but nothing to match the back-to-back bleaching of 2016/17.

In the weeks following Premier Palaszczuk's visit to India with her assorted regional mayors begging for the country's largest coal mine to be built, Professor Terry Hughes from the Australian Research Council's (ARC) Centre of Excellence for Coral Reef Studies at James Cook University (JCU), and convenor of the national coral bleaching task force, will fly over the Great Barrier Reef as part of an annual survey. He will conduct a follow-up survey from October and November 2016 when he discovers that in the northern third of the reef, 67% of coral cover was lost across 60 reefs (the largest loss ever recorded) through bleaching events. In May 2017, Hughes tweeted that a further 19% had died in 2017. Worse still, the bleaching had extended a further 500 kms south. And this Hughes found after flying for eight days in a small plane and helicopter covering an area of 8000 square kms and surveying more than 1000 of the Great Barrier Reef's nearly 3000 reefs. Unlike the

Great Barrier Reef Marine Park Authority that also blames a strong El Niño for the bleaching, Hughes unequivocally blamed climate change for the reef's demise and points the finger squarely at politicians and a lack of leadership to redirect resources from coal to renewable energy.

The Australian public slumbers apparently unaware that they, as taxpayers, will be, at this point in March 2017, the sole investor in Adani's coal export plans, a company most have never even heard of. Their political leaders, however, are certainly acquainted with Adani both at the Federal and State level. One of his earliest supporters was then Labor Premier of Queensland, Anna Bligh, who was one of the first to declare the Adani mine a 'significant project' for Queensland, one that was suggested, at that time, to have an unbelievable lifespan of 150 years. She was also one of the first to propose that the construction of the mine and rail line would generate "around 11,000 jobs" according to a media release on the Queensland Government website in November 2010. So enthusiastic was she that she officiated at the opening of Adani's Australian headquarters in Brisbane. She had met Adani earlier during a trade mission to India.

Since Gautam Adani's entry into the Australian scene in 2010, he has made donations across both sides of politics and across various levels of local, state and national politics. Campbell Newman, Bligh's Liberal National Party (LNP) successor, promised that taxpayers' funds would help establish the mine. After leading a 76-strong business delegation and touring the Adani power plant and port in Mundra in 2012, he was given a lavish reception.

Tony Abbott, when he was Prime Minister, had been due to be seated next to Mr Adani at a luncheon in Mumbai for business leaders in September 2014, but Adani failed to show. Abbott was, the newspaper claimed, presented with a silver Indian vase and a pashmina wrap.[2] A troop of other Australian politicians followed: a former Deputy Premier of Queensland and two former New South Wales Premiers were hosted by Gautam Adani. Adani, the master of business relations, was the perfect host. After the trip of the Queensland mayors to Mumbai and the Mundra power plant, Rockhampton Mayor, Margaret Strelow, and Townsville Mayor, Jenny Hill, publicly declared $1600 and $1400 respectively for gifts bestowed on them by Adani including airfares and meals while in India.[3] Prime Ministers have also been steadfast supporters of Adani. Former Prime Minister, Tony Abbott, once described the Adani mine as a "poverty-busting miracle that would put Australia on the path to becoming an energy superpower" according to an article in *The Sydney Morning Herald* on 30 June 2015. Nothing or no one, it seems, could stop the hype.

Abbott continued to inflate the number of jobs the Carmichael mine would produce. In his pursuit of promoting the building of the Adani mine, he used the number that is commonly bandied about by politicians and the media: 10,000. Adani had used the figure of 10,000 jobs in its Environmental Impact Statement and said the mine would bring $22 billion in royalties according to an article in *The Age* in December 2015. However, in April 2015, Adani's own expert witness, Dr Jerome Fahrer in the Land Court of Queensland at a court hearing for objections to the proposed mine, declared in his affidavit there would be "an average of 1464 full-time employees (FTE) direct and indirect" jobs a year. At that time, the Land Court President, Carmel MacDonald, found that Adani had significantly overstated its job figures in court evidence as well as to the State Government. She rejected the company's modelling, accepting instead Fahrer's evidence that Adani would "increase average annual employment by 1206 FTE jobs in Queensland and 1464 FTE jobs in Australia."

Three weeks after Premier Palaszczuk's visit, the current Australian Prime Minister, Malcolm Turnbull, is poised to fly to India to provide a 'ringing endorsement' of the mine. At that time, he tells the media that the mine will generate "tens of thousands of jobs," according to David Crowe writing in *The Australian*. Turnbull will tell Adani that any legal hurdles to do with Native Title (the legislation that recognises the traditional rights and interests to land and waters of Aboriginal and Torres Strait Islander people) will be amended according to *The Australian Financial Review*.[4/5] Up until 1992, Australian law did not even recognise that Indigenous people had *any* rights to Australian land or waters. Indigenous people are still not recognised in the Australian constitution, the founding document of the nation, nor recognise pre-existing Aboriginal rights as the Canadian constitution does.[6]

The God Adani has miraculously managed to convince the Queensland Government to waive the usual rigorous environmental State Government scrutiny that might challenge the mine. The Queensland Government, with unseemly haste, in October 2016, invoked critical infrastructure powers to fast-track Adani's requests, powers given to the Premier to invoke in times of famine, drought and catastrophe. Palaszczuk's Government will later in 2017 agree to a deferred royalties scheme for the entire Galilee Basin which will offer a deferral of mining royalties for the first four years of operation; a move the Australian Greens, at that time, estimated would cost Queensland taxpayers $253.3 million in net terms over five years for the Adani mine alone.

Federally, too, there is a lack of scrutiny in the scramble to approve the Carmichael mine. When seeking Federal environment approval for the mine, Adani failed to disclose the background of its CEO and Country Head of Adani Australia, Jeyakumar Janakaraj. Janakaraj had been Director of Operations at a copper mine in Zambia which was prosecuted for serious environmental charges involving major pollution of a river in Zambia, a fact revealed by Mark Willacy on the ABC-TV in December 2015.[7/8]

The environmental history of companies' executive officers is relevant when assessing the environmental history of a company in determining whether that company should be entrusted with potentially risky operations in Australia according to *The Adani Brief*, an investigation by Environmental Justice Australia into Adani business practices.

In February 2018, following a decision by the Federal Government *not* to prosecute Adani for the omission about Janakaraj's past history, Samantha Hepburn, writing in the *The Conversation*, questioned the viability of our environmental laws to protect the environment, when falling between Queensland State and Federal legislation. According to Environmental Justice Australia (EJA), the Environmental Protection Act 1994 (Qld) is woefully inadequate. The public is supposed to be able to have access to copies of environmental authorities. But, in Adani's case, when EJA filed a right of information application to obtain it, it discovered that in August 2011, the type of environmental authority Adani Mining Pty Ltd held was changed. Then in March 2012, the environmental authority number was changed again apparently due to an administrative error resulting in the original authority having three different numbers in two years. EJA pointed out that the Queensland Auditor General in 2014 found that the Department is "not fully effective in its supervision, monitoring and enforcement of environmental conditions and is exposing the state to liability and the environment to harm unnecessarily."[9]

EJA also pointed out in its report that in March 2013, the Act was amended to require a company to be registered as "a suitable operator" before being granted an environmental authority. But it deemed anyone with an existing environmental authority to be "a suitable operator." As Adani Mining Pty Ltd held an environmental authority, it did not have to go through a statutory process to assess its suitability to operate. For example, when being assessed, a company "must disclose information about its environment record" which includes executive officers working for the company "and any other corporations of which the executive officers are, or have been, an executive officer." EJA states that Adani Mining Pty Ltd had received four more environmental authority permits all without having its environmental record assessed.

Adani's track record of environmental pollution has also seemingly been ignored, the brief noted. In 2011, an unseaworthy ship carrying Adani coal sank off the coast of Mumbai causing a massive oil spill of 60,054 metric tonnes of coal which devastated beaches, tourism and marine life. Five years later, the company had still not cleaned up the mess according to *The Adani Brief* and was fined AU$975,000. The Federal Environment Minister did not consider this "because Adani Mining Pty Ltd failed to provide that information, even though it was specifically requested to do so," the Brief noted. It continued: "With this international track record, the Adani Group's plan to ship Carmichael coal out of Abbot Point port and through the fragile Great Barrier Reef World Heritage Area is of serious concern."[10]

Nor was Adani's track record in handling coal at its ports in India without blemish. In 2015, according to the *Indian Business Standard*,[11] the Goa State Pollution Control Board (GSPCB) issued notices to Adani and one other company for allegedly causing an environmental hazard after dust pollution emanating from coal dust was found to have increased in the Port of Vasco near Goa. Data had been collected from an air ambient monitoring station which showed the number of suspended particles was above the permissible level.

In addition to the environmental accusations, there has been disquiet for several years about the Adani Group's financial state. According to Tim Buckley, Director of Energy Finance Studies, who prepared an Institute for Energy Economics and Financial Analysis (IEEFA) 2017 Report,[12] India's Adani Enterprises is one of four listed companies majority owned by the Adani family. Alongside Adani Enterprises (75% owned by the Adani family) are Adani Power (72% owned), Adani Ports and SEZ (64% owned), and Adani Transmission (75% owned).

In August 2010, Adani Enterprises acquired the Galilee Basin Carmichael export thermal coal deposit for a total of AU$680 million via its Australian subsidiary Adani Mining Pty Ltd. At the time, the Adani Enterprises had a US$10 billion market capitalisation, making it one of the largest conglomerates in India. However, a major corporate restructuring in 2015 saw a de-merger into four (now in 2018 five) independent, separately listed entities, albeit all still controlled by a single promoter. In 2017, Adani Enterprises was significantly downsized, with a remaining US$1.9 billion market capitalisation. More worryingly, according to the same report, the Adani Group has current capital expenditure proposals underway totalling US$36 billion in aggregate. Buckley states: "With the Carmichael coal proposal still well away from financial close to seven years after Adani Enterprises first acquired the coal deposit in 2010 for a collective AU$680 million, it is clear that the company is struggling to secure financing for the project."

As of May 2018, Tim Buckley wrote that Adani Power Ltd is in clear financial distress, with US$7.4 billion of debt against a shareholder equity of just US$133 million.[13] However, he notes, the rest of the Adani Group is "powering ahead." Adani Ports' full year results for 2017/18 proved that it is the largest and most successful port operator in India. And Adani Transmissions and Adani Green Energy (both only created as new business units just over three years ago) each now stand as two of the largest private grid and renewable energy firms in India. Adani Gas 2018 results forecast it continues to deliver an 18% annual growth rate in revenues and the company is set to become the largest private gas distribution firm in India.

For all its travails in Australia, Adani Enterprises is also on track to become the largest private coal mine operator in India, if it can deliver on its target to double output to 14 Mtpa (million tonnes per annum) in 2018/19 according to the report. The Carmichael mine, however, Buckley suggests, is "a stranded asset." The demise of the Mundra power plant, a project where Gautam Adani launched his career, has contributed. India is turning its back on thermal power plants and the Adani Group has admitted the Mundra coal fired power plant, where the Carmichael coal was destined for, is financially unviable.[14]

Writing back in June 2015, before the Carmichael mine was approved by Federal and State Governments and having accessed documents through FOI from the highest level of the Queensland Treasury, Lisa Cox from *The Sydney Morning Herald* wrote that the Queensland Treasury harboured grave doubts about the Adani Group's capacity to see the Carmichael project through to completion and believed that the project was "unviable."[15]

The documents, wrote Cox back then, identified the high level of debt within the company and labelled the mining giant as a 'risk' because of its unclear corporate structure and use of offshore entities. The project, principal commercial analyst Jason Wishart wrote to David Quinn, the Executive Director of Projects Queensland was, "unlikely to stack up on a conventional project finance assessment." Gautam Adani, he wrote, could argue the 'blue sky' on controlling the supply chain for development of new power stations in India but that made the Adani Group "an Indian energy market player not a coal project." Expansion would put Adani's financial position under 'increased strain'. Briefing notes also stated: "the group is highly susceptible to cost shocks."

Lisa Cox had already earlier scrutinised the operational setup of the complex web of international companies. This would later become the focus of other media coverage, including the Australian ABC's TV *Four Corners* Program, 'Digging into Adani'.[16] Company documents suggested billionaire Gautam Adani did not ultimately control many of the companies. Instead his eldest brother Vinod Shantilal Adani held pivotal positions. Vinod was also, according to *The Adani Brief*, the sole director of a number of Singapore companies which own nine of the Adani group entities operating in Australia.

But neither the financial investigations at that time nor the environmental status of the Adani Group appears to have made any difference to the Queensland Premier or Australian Prime Minister and their associated entourages in their exuberant bid for the Adani mine.

The hastily constructed local government budgets to fund the March 2017 trip for the mayors is buried in media coverage trumpeting Australians' nostalgia for yesteryear when times were good 'and the livin' was easy' when you lived off the fat of the land with no consequences.

Adani is the saviour on everyone's lips. Plastic bags swirl in the wind-blown, often deserted canyons in what were once shopping malls in the regional Queensland towns of Bowen and Townsville where unemployment has dramatically risen since the mining bust. Adani, everyone appears to be saying, will restore everything to how it used to be. A collective community sigh: the community's fearless leaders will provide. And the Federal Government will follow. Adani logos are creeping into the most prominent positions in the regional North Queensland cities of Townsville and regional towns and Adani is funding community events from powerboats to tourism awards. The saviour is here.

* * *

In April 2017, when Turnbull lands in New Delhi, he will discover that the last liquorice-allsort layer closer to the ground is faeces-brown as the oxygen is starved. The hue is puce grey. Turnbull is well aware of the catastrophic consequences of his Government soliciting a mine that, according to the Australian Institute[17] will spew about 79 million tonnes of CO_2 – three times the annual emissions from New Delhi, double those from Tokyo, six times those of Amsterdam and 20% more than New York City. If the mine goes ahead, it will leave a legacy of a 4.6 billion tonne carbon footprint in its proposed lifetime.

Back in July 2011, as Shadow Minister for Communications, at the Virginia Chadwick memorial lecture,[18] Turnbull defended the Great Barrier Reef and climate change scientists' claims, criticising anyone who was seduced by far-right anti-science propagandists. He warned that the effects of climate change would "be felt painfully and cruelly by the generations ahead of us." The people in the world who will suffer the most cruelly, he said, "would be the poorest and the people who have contributed the least to the problem. There is an enormous injustice here. When people suggest to you that climate change is not a moral issue, they are wrong. It is an intensely moral issue."

But, after being appointed Prime Minister in 2015, Turnbull joined the chorus of doubters of climate change and global warming, compromised by heading a political party of largely urban voters which clings to power only by forming a coalition government with a right-wing National Party whose leaders mostly debunk climate change. Since the election in 2016, after initially not even having enough seats to govern, the coalition held government by a one-seat majority after Turnbull negotiated with independent members. Yet, it is this government in particular, that is making the most catastrophic environmental decisions that will have an irrevocable outcome not just for Australia but internationally as well.

The Australian media, particularly its Murdoch-dominated newspapers, support anti-climate change sentiment. As my flight leaves the Indira Gandhi airport in New Delhi, the brown-coal power station, Hazelwood, in the Latrobe Valley, which had powered the state of Victoria for half a century and was known as 'Australia's dirtiest power station', is being closed down. Environment Victoria recorded that Hazelwood had accounted for 14% of Victoria's greenhouse gas emissions. Closing it down could cut emissions by 16 million tonnes. But the Murdoch press, far from praising such a move, leverages the news to spray caustic headlines privileging doomsayers and the climate change sceptics. Later, less than a year after the closure, in the dazzling heat of a Melbourne summer, *The Australian* runs a story on 18 January 2018: "A power supply crisis gripped southern states yesterday, forcing Melbourne's hospitals to dim their lights as several major companies in Victoria and South Australia were paid to reduce their electricity consumption."

The heat wave and dire consequences, particularly if it can undermine a move to clean energy, sells newspapers especially if it hits the moral panic button. Even better if it hits the hip pocket. A breakaway story on the front page focused on the price of electricity bills rising in Victoria due to the Hazelwood closure.

The spin of 'doubt' generates fear and after all is a lucrative business.

* * *

It was my father who presented me with the book *Merchants of Doubt* by Naomi Oreskes and Erik M. Conway (2010).[19] "Lassie, if you're going to research all this stuff about Adani, you'd better read this." Dad, now in his 80s and still an avid newshound, has forever been my fountain of knowledge. I have consulted him on my weekly current affair quiz questions for my undergraduate journalism students at JCU and asked for his assistance with historical research for my doctorate which included focusing on Canadian convicts in Port Arthur, Tasmania.

Merchants of Doubt showcases how the individuals who denied the links between smoking and lung cancer are the same type of people who now debunk the science of global warming. The book details how a deliberate counter narrative, similar to that which countered negative statements about tobacco, was constructed to deny global warming even though scientific research on carbon dioxide and climate change has now been around for at least 40 years. The book also documented how all too often governments focused on the fact that any changes under consideration were "beyond the lifetimes of contemporary decision makers." The old adage: "when in doubt, do nothing" could still be applied to many politicians' attitudes to the question of climate change today. Dispel doubt about the figures and pass it on to future generations as a problem.

Doubt, after all, even if it is 'fake' news, sells. Even Malcolm Turnbull in his Virginia Chadwick memorial lecture back in July 2011 noted the use of doubt criticising those "with vested interests" who "were trying to muddy the waters on climate science to prolong the export of coal" and compared their actions to tobacco companies discrediting the connection between smoking and lung cancer.

As far back as the mid-nineteenth century, the authors of *Merchants of Doubt* outline, Irish experimentalist John Tyndall first established that carbon dioxide was a greenhouse gas – meaning that it traps heat and keeps it from escaping to outer space. Human activities are responsible for almost all of the increase in greenhouse gases in the atmosphere for the past 150 years.[20] It wasn't until the early twentieth century, however, that a British engineer named Guy Callendar came across the consequences of how this would impact on the Earth's climate. That was plenty of time for us to have become prepared.

Seven years ago, Sir David Attenborough, an erstwhile climate change advocate, spoke out after making his 2011 documentary *Frozen Planet* and witnessing the effects of climate change on the North and South Poles. He has often said that if we had acted in the 1980s, we may have been able to cut greenhouse gases. Unbelievably, we only began measuring global temperatures on the ocean and land in the 1970s. What have we done about it since then? Clearly not enough.

Chapter 2
The Dirty Truth

In the plane's seat pocket in front of me in the *Delhi Times* a headline brags: "In past two weeks, Delhi city air is cleaner than Mumbai's according to the System of Air Quality and Weather Forecasting and Research (SAFAR)." In India, the media has long given up pretending that the air will improve. Instead, headlines revert to jocular, competitive ribbing - poking fun from one major city to another. The Indian businessman watches under sleepy eyelids as I take photos of the story on my phone.

What the newspaper story does not record, reported in *The Times of India* in January 2017,[21] is that from 1991 to 2017, deaths in India's largest cities due to air pollution have doubled. Mumbai's death toll has risen from 19,291 to 32,014. In Delhi for the same period there were 48,651 deaths in 2017 compared to 19,716 in 1991. While the reasons for India's air pollution are many, according to the World Health Organisation, such as indoor cook stoves and road traffic - including the ubiquitous auto-rickshaws that use a toxic mix of kerosene and diesel - fossil fuel burned by industrial plants is listed as a key contributor.

In May 2016, with 370 coal power stations planned and construction beginning across the country, it would have been all but impossible to meet, let alone exceed, India's commitment to the 2015 Paris agreement, the first ever global agreement to confront climate change.[22] The pledge is to get 40% of India's electricity from non-fossil fuel sources by 2030. Piyush Goyal, then India's Minister of State (Independent Charge) for Power, Coal, New and Renewable Energy and Mines, even pledged to end coal imports, repeatedly stating that he is committed to making

India a global hub for renewable energy. He is now the Minister of Railways and Minister of Coal.

Meanwhile, India's carbon emissions are rising. In 2016, they rose almost 5%.

But India is a developing country. Although as recently as May 2018, the Indian Government pledged that 100% of India's villages would be electrified; the definition of 'village electrification' is that a transmission line from the grid reaches a transformer in each village. Only 10% of homes in the village need to receive power for the village to qualify as 'electrified'.[23] In 2017, it was estimated 240 million Indians are living without electricity.[24]

Australia is a developed nation. As the rest of the world is turning its back on fossil fuel, the Doomsday Clock, set up by the Chicago Atomic Scientists after the bombing of Hiroshima and Nagasaki, monitors the likelihood of a man-made global catastrophe. Since 2007, the 'clock' has included climate change, along with nuclear threat, as a major catastrophic contributor. Meanwhile, in 2018, Australia remains the largest exporter of coal in the world with a clear lead in metallurgical coal[25] and an increasing share of thermal coal exports.[26/27] Over the past decade, it has doubled coal exports. Far from scaling back on coal as part of global efforts to reduce emissions, Australia plans to give public subsidies for new coal mines.

The Federal Government, under Turnbull's leadership, is also considering financing new coal-fired power plants. Like the other G20 nations, Australia is pursuing fossil fuel with a vengeance. Around $88 billion a year's worth of subsidies worldwide is being thrown at fossil fuel companies by 44 governments for the exploration of new oil, gas, and coal reserves with Australia providing $3.5 billion for the development of offshore and inland fossil fuel resources ahead of the United Kingdom and Russia according to a 2014 report 'The Fossil Fuel Bailout'[28] on G20 nations. Australia has cut the emissions intensity of its electricity sector by 15% since 2005, but it has still the highest emissions of *any* International Energy Agency (IEA) member country and double the average of any other member country according to an Australian Associated Press (AAP) account in *The Guardian* in February 2018.

The IEA was set up in 1974 in the wake of the oil crisis with the aim of ensuring reliable, affordable, renewable energy. In spite of pledging to cut emissions under the Paris climate agreement, citing the four-yearly review of IEA countries' energy policies, the IEA found that Australia had "not yet come forward with durable climate change policies after 2020," nor had it named a long-term goal. The IEA[29] also noted that wind and solar power still only represented 1% of total primary energy for the country as a whole.[30] It concluded that: "Climate change is an area where government leadership is critical to guide the transition from coal use in power generation to the integration of renewable energy."

In late 2017, the Turnbull Government came up with an energy and climate change policy entitled the National Energy Guarantee (NEG), which, Turnbull claimed, was to ensure Australia meets its Paris agreement obligations. The Finkel Review into Australia's National Electricity market from Chief Scientist Alan Finkel was released in June 2017 with a key recommendation[31] for the adoption of a Clean Energy Target (CET) that mandates that energy retailers provide a certain amount of their electricity from 'low-emissions' generators: sources that produce emissions below a threshold level of carbon dioxide.

Under the proposed NEG – which is not adopting the CET recommended in the Finkel Review – renewable energy will account for 28–36% of total energy generation by 2030. The old energy sources coal and gas, however, are still included under the banner of 'reliable' energy. The NEG has two pillars: 'a reliability guarantee' to ensure energy is always available and 'an emissions guarantee' to address international concerns about emissions. The NEG is yet to be implemented, as the policy has still to be approved by all of the States and Territories at the time of writing (June 2018). But even that step towards cutting emissions and developing an energy policy which focuses on climate change was undermined by Turnbull's own party.

In April 2018, former Prime Minister, Tony Abbott, and backbencher Kevin Andrews as well as Tasmanian Senator Eric Abetz joined the Monash Forum, a new internal lobby group challenging the NEG. The rogue MPs demanded new coal-fired power stations be built or they would boycott the NEG. The 'Monash' was named after General Sir John Monash, an Australian World War I military commander who was a pioneer of brown coal generation in Victoria. However, the idea backfired. In an article in *The Australian* on 4 April, Monash's descendants were scathing in the choice of name saying that their ancestor would have been a proponent of green energy including wind and solar power.

Chris Dunstan, a research director at the Institute for Sustainable Futures at the University of Technology in Sydney is heavily critical of the Australian Government's ineptitude at dealing with climate change. He wrote in *The Sydney Morning Herald* on 8 November 2017: "Apart from in matters of race relations, has Australia never managed to cock up an issue of major national importance as comprehensively and over a longer period of time than it has for energy and climate change? For more than a decade, our politicians, and to be fair a good share of the rest of us, have bitched and moaned but achieved little more than higher electricity and gas prices and rising carbon pollution."

He did concede, however, that an NEG's emissions cap from the electricity sector was "major reform."

Meanwhile, the approval of new coal mines continues. As already mentioned, it is not just Adani who is waiting in the wings for the Galilee Basin to open. Other mining companies have escaped scrutiny while the focus has been on Adani. Clive Palmer is one of the mining magnates lining up with proposed mines for the Galilee Basin. In May 2018, the mining magnate was on the *Financial Review* Rich List as Queensland's wealthiest man, which estimated his wealth at AU$2.84 billion. As recently as March 2018, he had stated that his $6.5 billion Alpha North mine proposed by

Palmer's Waratah coal company in the Galilee Basin would go ahead even if the Adani mine does not.

In May 2018, Peter Hannam from *The Sydney Morning Herald* reported that Palmer was seeking approval to develop a monster coal mine twice the size of the Adani mine and that it was separate from Palmer's proposal to develop the China First mine also in the region. The proposed mine would be about 27 times the size of Sydney Harbour, Hannam quoted Greenpeace stating, which had lodged a submission against the mine. The $6.4 billion GVK/Hancock Coal's Alpha and Kevin's Corner projects by Gina Rinehart and the wealthy Indian company, G.V. Krishna Reddy, has three proposed mines with the capability of producing 60 million tonnes of coal in full production annually for 30 years. In 2017, the project received environmental authority approval from the Queensland Land Court. The project was still working its way through the approvals process at the time of writing (June 2018), which, if granted, will guarantee the opening of the Galilee Basin whether the Adani mine goes ahead or not.

Little wonder that Fiji's Prime Minister, Josaia Voreqe Bainimarama, the leader of one of Australia's closest neighbours, in an article in *The Australian* in May 2015 has labelled Australia a prominent member of the 'coalition of the selfish' describing a group of industrialised nations who put the welfare of their carbon-polluting industries before the environment – actions which, he says, directly threaten the survival of Pacific Island countries because of rising sea levels caused by climate change. This fact too was recognised by Malcolm Turnbull in his speech in 2011 when he talked about the 'intensely moral' issues of climate change that by now, he appears to have forgotten.

Australia's continued promotion of coal is also clearly at odds with the 2015 Paris Agreement. The agreement, signed by 195 parties, aims to limit global ocean warming to well below 2°C above the pre-industrial average and indeed to limit temperature increases even further to 1.5°C. The reputable journal *Nature*[32] in January 2015 states that to have a reasonable chance of achieving that goal, there's little doubt that the vast majority of the world's coal reserves must stay in the ground. It states that a third of all oil reserves, half of gas reserves and over 80% of current coal reserves, need to remain in the ground to give us a 50% chance of avoiding a maximum 2°C global average temperature rise through the twenty-first century. Greenhouse gas emissions in fossil fuel reserves, notes the article, are around three times higher than should be burnt if the world is to avoid the worst impacts of climate change.

* * *

In 1997, Australia and the United States remained the only industrialised nations not to have ratified the Kyoto Protocol, a landmark treaty requiring a cut in greenhouse gas emissions. It was only ratified ten years later by a Labor Government under then Prime Minister, Kevin Rudd, who also, in 2008, introduced the idea of a carbon pollution reduction scheme penalising those who released too much carbon into the atmosphere saying Australia would cut its greenhouse gas emissions by 5% by 2020. But the scheme was rejected by the Senate in 2009 whereupon Rudd revised the scheme in the hope of appealing to the opposition to accept it.[33] Rudd did manage to convince then opposition leader Malcolm Turnbull to accept the revised scheme but on 1 December 2009, Turnbull was toppled and replaced by Tony Abbott.

Julia Gillard, Australia's first female Prime Minister and Rudd's successor in June 2010, introduced legislation for a carbon price scheme through the Clean Energy Act 2011 aimed at the big polluters. In July 2010, she had announced she would rule out a carbon tax as an interim measure but later Gillard *did* unveil plans for a carbon tax and in November 2011 the bill was passed by the Senate. From July 1, 2012 the tax raised $3.8 billion in six months. After a carbon price collapse in Europe, however, the Gillard Government deferred a $2.8 billion tax cut planned for 2015.

When he returned as Prime Minister in 2013, Rudd terminated the carbon tax saying his government was moving to an emissions trading scheme. But less than two months later, Abbott claimed victory in the federal election and all these plans evaporated.

A carbon tax is designed to create incentives for companies, businesses and individuals to change their behaviours, consumption patterns and products from being carbon intensive to low carbon alternatives. On 17 July 2014, a report by the Australian National University estimated that the Australian scheme, while in operation, had cut carbon emissions by as much as 17 million tonnes. It was the biggest annual reduction in greenhouse gas emissions in 24 years of records by 2013 as the carbon tax had helped drive a large drop in pollution from the electricity sector.

Rudd and Gillard's main opponent, apart from conservative politicians, was the mining industry. Opposition to the tax, especially by the Minerals Council, the industry's national body in Australia, focused predictably on job losses. Figures revealed by the Australian Electoral Commission on political spending were quoted in *The Sydney Morning Herald*[34] in February 2011 where Mark Davis posed the question: "How much does it cost to get rid of a prime minister?" He revealed that the industry spent a total of $22.2 million on the campaign which ran from the start of May until late June 2010 when Julia Gillard took over from Kevin Rudd and negotiated a compromise on the tax.

The amount of advertising dollars thrown at the debate was staggering: $17.2 million primarily on TV ads: BHP Billiton spent $4.2 million, Rio Tinto just over $537,000, and a smaller lobby group, the Association of Mining and Exploration Companies, just under $274,000.

Malcolm Turnbull, who in 2009 campaigned with Labor for a reduction of carbon emissions, lost his leadership bid that same year to Liberal Tony Abbott who is on the record as describing climate change as 'crap'. The message was clear: that Turnbull would never gain the prime ministership if he continued to promote climate change. In his 2017 book *Climate Wars*,[35] Mark Butler, Shadow Minister for Climate Change and Energy, writes that the Greens also helped destroy Rudd's Carbon Pollution

Reduction Scheme by voting with Abbott against it on Abbott's first full day as Liberal leader. Upon becoming Prime Minister, Abbott immediately withdrew support for the carbon pricing scheme. When Turnbull later succeeded Abbott in 2015 without an election after being elevated to Prime Minister by his own party, his political rhetoric had drastically changed to promoting the mining industry at the expense of climate change. His ministers, many of them National Party MPs, did everything they could to ensure he stayed on track.

Comparing Australia's attempts at redressing the climate change issues with the approach taken by UK politicians, Mark Butler writes that in the lead up to the UK 2015 general election, the leaders of the three major political parties sat down and signed a statement on climate change policy. These politicians undertook to work across party lines and to agree on carbon budgets pledging "to accelerate the transition to a competitive, energy-efficient, low-carbon economy and to end the use of unabated coal for power generation." The last coal-fired power station will be closed by 2025 at the latest. There were no battles and when the Committee on Climate Change recommended an ambitious carbon reduction target for the five-year period 2028–32, the budget was "quietly endorsed by both political parties shortly afterwards."[36]

* * *

How can a country like Australia, known for its pristine beaches and tracts of wilderness and distinctive marsupials, reptiles and insects, Gondwana-descended flora and fauna have such a treacherous heart? How can its leaders, elected by the Australian public, wilfully jeopardise these natural assets?

The answer lies in the way Australian politicians pay homage to the clout of the mining industry and its vocal workforce. The history of the country's white settlers runs parallel with white mining history: silver, copper, lead, gold, coal, diamonds, opals and natural gas. Slick campaigns of male working-class heroes in hard hats, promoting the larrikin national characteristic we enjoy, portray the mining sector as the backbone of the economy. The myth is that mining creates jobs and provides a foundation of prosperity – particularly for rural and regional Australia.

This prosperity rewards the individual over the nation; a get-rich-quick tagline used by advertising gurus and promoted by the media in prominent stories profiling our richest who own the mining leases. It's a licence to print money. We, apparently, will give leases to anyone who has the dosh. But mining, in reality, employs fewer than 2% of the Australian workforce according to a 2011 Report by the Institute, 'Mining the truth: the rhetoric and reality of the commodities boom'[37] by David Richardson and Richard Denniss. This has remained the case today with Australian Bureau of Statistics[38] figures for 2018 showing 1.8% of the total population is employed either full- or part-time in the mining industry.

Even in the USA, according to an article in Investopedia,[39] a US website focusing on investment and financial news, figures from March 2017 pointed to coal mining employment as representing 0.03% of the 160 million strong civilian workforce. How can that be when 'jobs' have been the main justification for soliciting the Adani coal mine?

Focusing on Australia, the Richardson and Denniss Report notes that the mining industry routinely includes figures for indirect employment in its mining employment figures, making the figures appear substantially larger than Australian Bureau of Statistics figures. Back in 2013, Lee Rhiannon, a Greens Senator from New South Wales, citing the Richardson and Denniss report, told parliament: "The mining industry practises deception – paying economists and consultants to estimate the size of their industry's multiplier estimating the number of indirect jobs mining will bring." The Australia Institute Report estimates that if the number of indirect jobs associated with every industry were totalled, then the number of jobs in the economy would exceed 30 million – almost three times the size of the Australian labour market. Interestingly, this multiplier effect is the same trick used by Adani to manipulate proposed benefits from the Carmichael mine for our nation through providing jobs.

Once the multiplier is applied to all other industries, mining returns to being a very small employer in Australia, Richardson and Denniss point out. Over the past seven years, the increase in jobs in the mining sector accounts for only 7% of the total employment creation over that period.

The coal industry has been the subject of this great myth. At the end of 2012, out of a national workforce of 11 million it only employed just over 45,700 workers. To put this in perspective, Rhiannon told parliament, employees in the coal industry represented a quarter of the number of those working in the tertiary education sector and a few thousand more than in the printing and publishing industry and the dairy sector.

Richardson and Denniss also pointed out that pre-tax profits from the mining industry amounted to $51 billion in 2009–10 and that in the next ten years they would be likely to exceed $600 billion. Citing an Australian Institute survey conducted in 2011, also quoted in the Richardson and Denniss report, out of 1370, the average response was that around 16% of workers were employed in the mining industry – instead of fewer than 2%. The same survey found on average respondents believed that 53% of Australian mining activity was foreign owned whereas the figure was 83% at that time. Out of the $51 billion mining profits from 2009–10, 83%, or $42 billion, accrued to foreign investors.

Expensive advertising campaigns, Rhiannon told parliament back in 2013, were "petty cash" for big mining giants and helped bolster the myth. In 2013, she said BHP Billiton brought in a profit of $12 billion. Rio Tinto's half-yearly profit for 2013 was $1.7 billion. Glencore Xstrata's underlying profit was $2.04 billion. Rhiannon raged that with 83% of mining companies being foreign-owned, the idea that they are all part of our national interest is an absolute myth. They already pay 7.1% less tax than the industry average, so the economy is not even gaining the benefit that many people expect comes from the mining industry, she said. Typically, the

Adani Group is fully foreign owned. Since Rhiannon's impassioned speech, the number of jobs in the mining industry has slumped further. In 2013 at least 26,000 people had lost their jobs in the coal mining industry. Apart from a slump in the industry, technology has played a major role in future job prospects by creating the 'digital mine'. Driverless trains can now be a kilometre long and driverless trucks are commonplace in the West Australian Pilbara region with Rio Tinto planning to run one mine by mid-2019 entirely with autonomous trucks.

In 2017, the ABC reported that mining accounted for nearly $9 billion of the $13 billion increase in profits over the December quarter.[40] The five big companies: BHP Billiton, Rio Tinto, together with West Australian companies Fortescue, Newcrest Mining and South32, reported a combined 13% increase in revenue and a 426% increase in profits as commodity prices and production picked up in November 2017.

* * *

Ironically, the first story ever printed under my own byline was about coal miners long before anyone dreamt of driverless trucks and an automated industry. Published back in August 1982 in *The Sydney Morning Herald's Good Weekend*, it was entitled: 'A coal miner's life: big money, small savings and dust, dust, dust'. I was a third-year journalism undergraduate at Mitchell College of Advanced Education, now Charles Sturt University, in the inland town of Bathurst in Central Western New South Wales. My South African lecturer, the late Peter Temple, famous author of crime fiction, winner of the Miles Franklin award whose books led to the television series *Jack Irish*, handed me a snippet out of *The Sydney Morning Herald*. Citing the Joint Coal Board, the brief proclaimed that Australian coal miners were the highest paid workers in Australia, higher paid even than doctors and architects, due, no doubt to the danger involved in their profession.

Temple had looked balefully at me through his coke bottle glasses. "There's a bigger story somewhere."

I went to the library and did some research handing back a page or two of copy. He hurled the pages across the room.

"You can do baiter than thet," he shouted all South African rage. 'Thea are no interviews whatsoever. Thees is NOT a story."

It was a turning point. Gathering what was left of my self-esteem, I went home to sulk. Temple's scathing comments, however, had inadvertently creaked open the door to my new career. He had given me three out of ten for my first writing assignment – one of the highest marks in the class. After that, though, we had been negotiating respect and friendship. Sadly, he died from cancer in March 2018 during the writing of this book. His legacy and support are lasting gifts.

The week after his dressing down in 1982, I drove to the coal-mining town of Lithgow. Stumbling into the local hotel, I discovered a wake for two miners in full throttle. Pulling out my notebook, I began using my rusty shorthand honed at secretarial college amazed at how candid these miners were. One even described how he had been working with one of the men who had died on a 'patchy bit of roof' when a big piece of rock crushed him: "... his spine was broken in two places, guts smashed, legs broken," I had written. The exchange at the pub and the harsh reality of the story empowered me. Unlike the theory in the university, *this* was a real story. What did they do with all the money they earned?

The photographer and I stayed for the weekend knocking on a few doors in the town. The Lithgow District Workmen's Club turned out to have the highest turnover in New South Wales. In 1981, it had grossed $1.6 million. What's more, half of the 5900 members were miners. The powerboat merchandiser and caravan saleyard in town was doing a roaring trade. The miners themselves lived in weatherboard shacks more like shanties and seemed to spend most of their money on consumables – video cameras (then a luxury item) and televisions. The head of the Lithgow Credit Union informed me that after payday on a Wednesday, the miners would withdraw the whole pay cheque Thursday. I had quoted Bill Smale from the Australian Coal and Shale Employees Federation who claimed the reason for the high pay was "the outcome of a class struggle ... The miners," he said, "and wharfies and seamen have been able to use their industry to get higher pay because it's a commodity industry and they can fight the bosses because they've got something to fight them with ..." And the bosses, I had written, all those years ago, had found them a force to reckon with. In 1981, 2 million tonnes of export coal was lost through miners' disputes.

The mining industry has a lot to lose if it fails to woo its workers, but it also must woo the politicians. The Australia Institute, in a recent report entitled: 'The tip of the iceberg: Political donations from the mining industry,'[41] reported the mining industry had disclosed donations of $16.6 million to major political parties over the last ten years (2006-07 to 2015-16). The Report found these donations had increased from a base of $345,000 in 2006-07 to a peak of $3,788,904 in 2010-11 (interestingly coinciding with the demise of the proposal on carbon tax). 81% of these donations went to the Coalition, including 71% to the Liberal Party. The Report noted that it was not until 2007-08 that the mining industry first disclosed donations that reached over $1 million: the first year that carbon-pricing policy was taken to an election in Australia. It also noted that mining company donors often made significant political donations in years when they pay no company tax. Chillingly, it revealed that these donations correlate with the election cycles, timelines on project approvals, and debates on key industry policies such as the mining tax and carbon price.

Thirty-five years after I wrote that article in *The Sydney Morning Herald*, we continue to encourage, applaud and grudgingly admire the bolshy characteristics of our cultivated egalitarian working-class identity: the hard-hat fighting heroes. The current Premier of Queensland, Annastacia Palaszczuk, takes every opportunity to don a hard hat, knowing mining royalties are a big source of income. The success of the select few who benefit from the huge surge in profits in the mining industry are applauded. Our grudging admiration for the wealthy is exemplified by how affectionately they are portrayed in the national media.

Clive Palmer, waiting in the wings for the Galilee Basin to be opened up, is a case in point. Media coverage of Palmer's escapades over the years has focused on the 55 Mercedes Benzes, 700 international holidays and 50 weekends to the Sheraton Mirage at Port Douglas he doled out to his best performing workers for Christmas presents when his Yabulu Queensland Nickel refinery north of Townsville, fronting on to the Coral Sea, was in its heyday. The refinery produced about 30,000 tonnes of nickel and 1500 tonnes of cobalt a year and employed around 1000 people. There were further humorous headlines over the 160 giant plastic dinosaurs Palmer put in his theme park in the Sunshine Coast – 'the world's largest dinosaur park' – which spectacularly failed in March 2015. Other headlines detail how Palmer evicted a guest who had questioned the theme park restaurant about whether they knew how to cook a blue steak.

The environmental fallout and the catastrophic legacy Queensland Nickel left Australia after the refinery collapsed was buried under headlines about the company's business dealings. Palmer had been telling the media the refinery had gone from strength to strength and production was 'going through the roof'. He was also one of the strongest critics of the carbon tax. Unbelievably, Australia had no legislation at that time to prosecute directors for what the company had done to the environment. Upon buying the refinery in 2009 from BHP Billiton, Palmer, according to Hedley Thomas writing in *The Australian* on 30 January 2016,[42] agreed that for three years after the 2009 sale, the refinery would not pay "any dividend ... permit or facilitate any return of capital, capital reduction, share buyback or any other form of distribution ... provide any financial benefit to a buyer or (Mr Palmer) or to any person or entity associated with a buyer or (Mr Palmer)." Thomas also quoted a BHP Billiton 2009 review of the site that warned: "groundwater is already high in ammonia. Post closure activities could go well beyond 2021."

In May 2018, the Brisbane Supreme Court approved an application by Queensland Nickel liquidators, who had started court proceedings against Palmer to recover money owed to creditors to freeze almost $205 million of Palmer's personal wealth.[43] But this was only a temporary direction as the court case is not yet finalised. Palmer's lawyers asked for a stay in proceedings to lodge an appeal but this was dismissed.

In June 2012, according to documents obtained by the North Queensland Conservation Council and published by *The Guardian*,[44] Queensland Nickel had indicated its intention to discharge sewage, through its ocean outfall pipeline, from its tailings dam into the Great Barrier Reef even though the Great Barrier Reef Marine Park Authority (GBRMPA) had stated that the company had no permit to do so. The company requested that the discharge continue for "at least three months." The documents stated the release would be 100 times the maximum level permitted for sewage discharge in the marine park and included heavy metals and other contaminants. The threat of another major discharge from the refinery ponds to the ecosystem of Halifax Bay in the World Heritage Area was described, in the documents, as "similar to the daily discharge of treated sewage from a city of seven million people."

The Guardian[45] later reported that the nickel refinery had also made unauthorised discharges of nitrogen-laden water into the world heritage area in 2009 and again in 2011 when 516 tonnes of nitrogen was released into the World Heritage Area. This represented a 14% increase in the amount of nitrogen into the Burdekin catchment.

At the time this book goes to print, Palmer was in the news again saying that QNI Resources, which owns the refinery, would re-open it.[46]

Not until April 2016 did the Queensland Government finally pass legislation to empower the Government to ensure resource companies meet their environmental responsibilities even if they go into administration after a venture fails. The Environmental Protection (Chain of Responsibility) Amendment Act 2016 (EPCR Act), ensures that Queensland taxpayers will no longer be left to clean up the mess of failed industrial ventures, and instead will hold executives responsible for the clean-up costs. The environmental damage caused, however, may never be repaired. The fact that it has taken this long to introduce such legislation shows how little regard our governments have for the environment and how willing they are to accept the mining industry claims all in the name of 'progress' and jobs.

There is another mining project that may also yet escape penalties for major pollution in Queensland. Adani secured its proposed Carmichael mine site in 2010 doing a deal with Linc Energy worth up to $3 billion over 20 years for its Galilee Basin coal deposits.[47] In the years since, Linc Energy has caused catastrophic environmental consequences following the collapse of its coal gasification site in Chinchilla, 300 kms west-northwest of Brisbane after the company went into liquidation.

After a 10-week trial which began in January 2018, the company pleaded not guilty but offered no defence to the allegations. It faces a record $4.5 million fine for causing serious environmental harm under the Environment Protection Act. Five directors of Linc Energy were also charged with five counts of wilfully causing serious environmental harm between 2007 and 2013 and are due to face a committal hearing in the Brisbane Magistrate's Court in July 2018. The company was liquidated in May 2016 with speculation this was to avoid fines from the Queensland Government.

The Queensland Government had to accept responsibility to clean up and secure the site even though the Department of Environment and Science served an Environment Protection Order (EPO)[48] on the former chief executive of Linc Energy, Peter Bond, in May 2016 to clean up the site. The site was ordered to be decommissioned and a $5.5 million fee be paid to secure compliance of the order.

Media reports from the court case revealed some alarming facts. In the opening address to the jury, Crown Prosecutor, Ralph Devlin, QC, told the jury that explosive and toxic gases had been released into the environment. Even though the alarm had been raised to the board in 2009, and former managers and senior figures at Linc Energy had been repeatedly warned about the risks of environmental harm over a seven-year period, 'commercial interests' were often prioritised by the company, an ABC report stated.[49] The soil of local farming families was at risk of being contaminated by dangerous levels of carbon monoxide and farmers had been advised not to dig deeper than two metres without contacting the government. This was after it was discovered that Linc Energy had fractured the rock beneath their land releasing toxic chemicals into the soil, air and groundwater for six years.

A statement by a gas operator, Timothy Ford, was read to the jury. Timothy Ford had revealed that workers had been told to drink milk and eat yoghurt to protect their stomachs from acid. According to a report from the ABC in February 2018, Ford had said that during his time working for Linc, he felt "the sickest he'd ever been" and that the gas burnt his eyes and nose and he would need to leave the plant after work to get fresh air. Ford died in 2015, too late to give evidence.

The prosecution noted that the company, especially its CEO Peter Bond, had allowed operations to continue because "it put commercial interests over environmental obligations." This included injecting air into underground combustion chambers that was too high causing the rock surrounding the coal seam to fracture and allow the escape of toxic gases.

Premier Palaszczuk described the venture as "the biggest pollution event probably in Queensland history." Environmental campaigner Lock the Gate spokesperson Vicki Perrin told the ABC[50] she was "deeply concerned" about the company's ability to pay the penalty given it was in liquidation.

"The Queensland Government needs to stop approving every mining and gas project that comes before it, and set higher standards in the early stages before we end up with another mess like this," she said.

As to who is responsible for the massive environmental clean-up, said to be worth $78 million according to an article in *The Australian* by Michael McKenna on 9 April 2018, the squabbles began in what the Queensland Government described as "the most complex environmental investigation in Queensland's history."[51] In April 2017, the Queensland Supreme Court accepted the Department of Environment and Science's (DES) argument that the liquidators were still responsible to comply with the EPO attached to the site as they were deemed executive officers of the company. Newspaper reports had speculated that the Queensland taxpayer is already paying around $6 million to prosecute the company.

But the most expensive issue, as it was in Queensland Nickel's case, is the massive clean-up left behind after these projects gain environmental approval from governments to go ahead. And this from a company who has been the subject of a so-called rigorous environmental process that includes public scrutiny. It is not even clear at this stage exactly what damage has been done underground through the gasification cavities according to the DES. On 9 March 2018, the liquidators for Linc were relieved of responsibility for ongoing statutory environmental obligations by the Queensland Court of Appeal.[52]

Our environmental regulations, both at the State and Federal level, are supposed to stop these major polluters from causing environmental harm. It is obvious, however, particularly when reviewing the number of legal objections filed in court to the Adani mine, that whether there are objections or not, the wealthy will continue to be supported by our legal system. Right back to the approval by our environmental gatekeepers, is there enough scrutiny about who we are letting through the gates? What consequences did the Linc experiment have on any ongoing coal seam gas extraction? Or will companies simply continue to get away with not enough transparency in their operations?

Meanwhile, even those who have committed massive environmental breaches continue to flourish on the back-mining-ventures-at-all-costs merry-go-round that the taxpayer funds. The personal wealth of Peter Bond, CEO of Linc, who initially made his money through coal, soared to an estimated $350 million when mining shares boomed.

Commenting on the guilty verdict against Linc, Bond, quoted by McKenna in *The Sydney Morning Herald*, said the trial was "meaningless and a waste of taxpayer's money."

Richard Guilliatt who profiled the businessman in *The Weekend Australian* Magazine, said Bond's $9.5 million mansion in Brisbane's Fig Tree Pocket featured parking for seven cars and its own cinema.

After a continuing history of environmental catastrophes where those who cause the environmental disasters walk away, it is time to create new headlines: to awaken the public to the kinds of decisions Australian politicians have been making over the past decade. Specifically, given the magnitude of the project and its consequences, we need to draw people's attention to the proposed Adani mine that has one of the longest of all mining leases.

* * *

Gujarat is our first stop on this journey in March 2017. Ahmedabad, the largest city in Gujarat and its former capital, is Adani's headquarters. Our aim is to cross Annastacia Palaszczuk's path – to throw an international spotlight on her dealings with Adani – casting further scrutiny on Australia's environmental reputation on the world stage. Our brief from the Australian Marine Conservation Society, that is funding this journey, is to tell the world, that the Queensland Government is "on a dangerous junket to promote a damaging project."

We are also carrying a letter for Gautam Adani signed by 90 prominent Australians including the cricket giants – the Chappell brothers, Greg and Ian – Booker prize winning author, Richard Flanagan and Pulitzer prize winning novelist, Geraldine Brooks. The letter is to be personally delivered by our group to Adani headquarters in Ahmedabad.

The letter urges Adani to abandon the Carmichael mine in Australia and invest in renewables.

The businessman next to me has finished crunching. As we head skyward, he pushes back his chair and closes his eyes. I gaze again at the headlines in the Indian newspaper struck by the preposterous situation with its Monty-Pythonesque skit-like proportions. I wonder, and it won't be for the last time, why no one appears to care.

Chapter 3
'The Custodians' of the Great Barrier Reef

This is my first time as an environmental vigilante, despite the fact I've spent more than a decade as an investigative journalist. For 13 years, I've taught students both at undergraduate and postgraduate level to adopt the principles of the fourth estate: urging them to consider the media's independence from the other three estates (which originally had a more anachronistic meaning but are more commonly referred to as judiciary, parliament and church), and to consider the media's duty to be a watchdog on society. In 2000, I designed and taught investigative journalism subjects at Masters level at the University of Tasmania where students learned how to use Freedom of Information (FOI) tools. They focused on one particular topic for an entire year. I later introduced similar subjects at James Cook University (JCU). The subject ran for two semesters at the University of Tasmania to counteract how long government departments took, back then, to respond to FOI requests.

In the early years of the twenty-first century, investigative journalism began to flounder following the decline of the traditional media industry and the rise of the blogosphere, which was wrestling 'news' from traditional mainstream sources. 9/11 in 2001 was seen as a pivotal turning point as bloggers were said to be the first purveyors of news of the burning towers in New York while the US mainstream media struggled to deal with the enormity of the event on its home turf. No one back then had heard of 'fake news' – never mind considered that it might be something that sells on social media and would become a hot commodity.

This evolution in news gathering became a focus of my research as an academic.

Julia Bartrim,[53] one of my Masters students at JCU who had enrolled in the investigative journalism subject, had researched the coal gasification debacle at Chinchilla about 300 kms west of Brisbane, the same area as the Linc Energy project. She canvassed the issues of the other major coal seam gas extraction projects and their effect on the Great Artesian Basin citing Dr Brian Smerdon, a Great Artesian Basin research scientist at the CSIRO, who told her: "The basin is also responding to geological timeframe changes ... it is still responding to changes [from] 50–100 million years ago, it is constantly evolving, it is undergoing changes now that are not even related to us."

She noted that, at the time, more than 30,000 gas wells were planned for the Surat Basin alone and also, that not enough research had been done on the effects of the CSG extraction. Bartrim wrote that much of the extraction had been approved by the Queensland Government "prior to the completion of rigorous scientific analysis of baseline levels of water quality and pressure within potentially affected areas."

Julia Bartrim's story described how one of these coal gasification companies wooed the locals promising the world. "It's a dirty business," one local had told her. "They start out sponsoring the local footy BBQ. On the surface they seem to be doing a lot of good." It was the kind of tactic I witnessed Adani employing following its government approvals to build the Carmichael mine, as the company infiltrated local communities in Townsville, Bowen and Collinsville. Sponsoring the odd community event is the cheapest way to garner support for their dirty missions and pretend the company cares.

There is no doubt that investigative journalism is now harder to fund. At least encouraging students like Bartrim, who had the time to investigate major topics under the auspices of their university research, helped focus on issues often too time consuming to investigate for the mainstream media.

My books too, six of which were written in the true crime genre, have always followed my mantra to expose the truth. The most recent focused on tracking down those responsible for the murder of Daniel Morcombe, a 13-year-old boy who had been missing for almost a decade. The book was written with Daniel's parents, Bruce and Denise Morcombe.

Only two weeks earlier in March 2017, on a whim, I had agreed to take part in this journey to India, organised and funded by the Australian Marine Conservation Foundation (AMCF) whose patron is the illustrious writer, Tim Winton. Imogen Zethoven is the Great Barrier Reef Campaign Director for the AMCF, a powerful, environmental campaigner who has fronted many an environmental baddie over the years. She has saved sharks in the Coral Sea and worked for the World Wildlife Fund (WWF) in Berlin. With startling blue eyes, she has an uncanny ability to ask just the right candid but well-informed questions demanding answers from some of the heavyweights in this global debate on climate change. Zethoven has been working on the Great Barrier Reef for more than 25 years.

In that time, she says she has seen its dramatic decline. "I first dived in 1980 when it was a beautiful ecosystem full of abundant coral," she tells me, adding: "It's become an entirely different ecosystem. I've now dedicated my life to trying to stop its destruction ... Over 12 months the one thing that's risen to the top is the Adani mine. We have to stop it."

Having heard of the Queensland Premier's trip to India, the idea was to find individuals whose occupations would be affected by the proposed Adani mine so that they could offer a different take on the facts and figures presented to the Australian public. The occupations included a 'farmer', a 'tourism operator' and a 'businessman' as well as an Indigenous person to fly to India to counteract the government rhetoric and provide an alternative viewpoint to the proposed Adani coal mine. Unfortunately, in the short two-week preparation for the trip, it had proved too difficult to find an Indigenous representative.

Tourism operators are difficult to find for obvious reasons. To proclaim the Great Barrier Reef is under threat of extinction is commercial suicide. Make hay while the sun shines – that is as long as the sun's rays are not trapped for too long in the ocean, which will permanently bleach the coral. Denial means life can continue. Truth can be ignored in much the same way a patient refuses to visit their doctor to find out whether a darkening mole is a melanoma.

Will my view make a difference? I like the absurdity of this trip. To mimic the alacrity of the politicians, jump on board a flight and head to India. This story is unfolding in an almost comic strip narrative. Truth, after all, is stranger than fiction. More than that, though, this journey is one fuelled by desperation – to try to get the world – especially those making these irrevocable catastrophic decisions in a vacuum – namely our politicians – to notice.

But I have personal reasons, too. For almost 13 years, I have owned, along with my husband, Grant Lewis, a 62-foot Gloucester schooner, a bluenose replica once commonly used as Grand Banks fishing boats that take tourists, primarily from Europe, the USA and Australia, to snorkel on the fringing reef off the Whitsundays, and to stroll on one of the most photographed beaches in the world: the silicate sands of Whitehaven Beach.

Our introduction to what was to become our family heirloom, *Providence V*, began in March 2003 on our honeymoon. Back then, a Tasmanian neighbour had described his recent holiday in the Whitsundays in North Queensland as "one of the best weeks of my life." Honeymoons should be about superlatives, surely. Ours was as spectacular as the neighbour had predicted. Diving off the deck of a 38-ft bareboat yacht, I was stunned at the magical world below revealed through my facemask: a hidden parallel universe waiting to be discovered. Each bay offered its own magnificence as though to upstage the one we'd just snorkelled. We saw stingrays and the comical Maori Wrasse with its humpy head and thick lips. More than once we saw dolphins and, of course, the ubiquitous green turtle that would ponderously flap past, rotating eyes beckoning me to follow. Fifteen years later, the photograph of us beaming from the back deck of the chartered yacht is on my bedside table. My love affair with the Great Barrier Reef, the only living organism to be seen from outer space, began the year we got married.

In May 2005, we embraced a sea change. We drove the family with two dogs (we have five kids between us) in our old Land Rover Discovery from Tasmania to North Queensland. Our luggage perilously perched on the roof, I exchanged my icy 40-degrees south homeland, after a decade in Tasmania, for the tropical temperatures of North Queensland. We watched the soil turn red as we drove north and the buildings drop away. Gazing at the land that fell to our west, we marvelled that we could travel for days without seeing the ocean. The vastness of this country swallowed us up.

Over the next decade, we established a tourism business: day and sunset sails from Magnetic Island. Our brochures proclaimed snorkelling on "magnificent fringing reef." Back then we couldn't have been accused of false advertising. But in 2015, ten years later, just before we left the island, I snorkelled in Florence Bay on the southern side of the island for the first time in several years. After corrective eye surgery I could finally snorkel without glasses. I was devastated by the difference I saw.

The colour in the coral had been drained from years of dredging. Cleveland Bay lies between Magnetic Island and the city of Townsville and the port stretches out from the city towards the island. Townsville, the largest urban centre in North Queensland and the unofficial capital, was founded in 1864 as a port for the fledgling pastoral industry in North Queensland and is the country's largest sugar, zinc, lead, copper and fertiliser port.

I learned later that the *zooxanthellae*, the algae that produces the colours in the coral, are susceptible to increased sediment as they rely on light to survive. Unable to withstand the onslaught of humans and the expansion of the Port of Townsville, the coral, and its dependent creatures, seemed to have given up dazzling. What was once a palette of vibrant colours appeared to be a drab muddy green. Before corals bleach, they are often a deep brown or khaki-green colour. We had tried to explain to our guests what was happening as they returned from snorkelling below: global warming, port expansions, dredging, pesticide run off ... all man-made disasters. They would look back at us in horror. How was this happening, they asked? Australia, after all, pedalled images of pristine wilderness like the Daintree and deserts with icons like Uluru. That's why they were here. The Great Barrier Reef had pride of place in their hearts. Surely Australia felt the same and always put the environment first?

In June 2012, a report by UNESCO[54] delivered startling news. A joint World Heritage Centre/International Union for Conservation of Nature (IUCN) reactive monitoring mission had undertaken a tour of the reef between 6 and 14 March 2012. The Report stated that the Committee was concerned about proposed coastal and port development up and down the eastern Australian seabed and how much impact it would have on the Outstanding Universal Value of the Great Barrier Reef. It said the reef was "one of the richest and most complex natural ecosystems on earth, and one of the most significant for biodiversity conservation." The Great Barrier Reef, listed in 1981, is one of 19 World Heritage sites in Australia and has the world's largest collection of coral reefs. The Report stated all of this development might place the reef's World Heritage listing in danger.

I was strangely relieved that our reputation as custodians of the world's largest living organism was in doubt. Finally, someone had caught us in the act. Now something might be done about it.

Industrial port construction, along the eastern seaboard, has been, and continues to play, a major role in the demise of the Great Barrier Reef. It was a similar story, we were to find, in India and with a similar timeframe. Perhaps the worst example in Australia is the Port of Gladstone, the largest bulk commodity port in Queensland and the sixth largest in Australia which services a range of industries including agriculture, coal, bauxite and liquefied natural gas (LNG).

The UNESCO mission's Report strongly recommended an independent review of all environmental concerns of approved developments in Gladstone Harbour and Curtis Island. The area below the low water mark is within the Great Barrier Reef World Heritage Area (GBRWHA). In 2010 and 2011, the approval of three multi-billion dollar LNG processing facilities on Curtis Island attracted international news with the World Heritage Committee expressing "extreme concern" that permission had been granted for the construction of the processing and port facilities.

One of the mission's recommendations was to "adopt the highest level of precaution in decision-making regarding development proposals with potential to impact the [reef] and to prevent any approval of major projects that may compromise its long-term sustainable development." Interestingly, Julia Bartrim's article, written in 2012, had discussed how the gas from the Surat Basin, which overlaps the Bowen Basin, would connect to the LNG export facilities at Gladstone. She had emphasised the experimental nature of these industries commenting that the three CSG projects in the Surat Basin "are the first of their kind in the world as never before have onshore gas resources been used as the primary supplier for LNG shipments."

The three Curtis Island LNG plants, as it transpired, were the trigger for UNESCO to sharpen their scrutiny of how the Great Barrier Reef was being managed. Its Report stated that the LNG processing plant was approved by the Federal Government but "no opportunity was offered to the World Heritage Committee to consider its results" in view of the potential impact the plant would have on the outstanding value of the reef.

The Committee also noted that while the LNG plant granted to Santos Limited and PETRONAS Australia Pty Ltd was subject to a number of environmental conditions, there were contradictory statements which stated the LNG plant was "not expected to have significant negative effects on the area's heritage value" but concluded there would be direct impacts on a range of issues such as seagrass, mangrove and "potential direct and indirect impacts on whales, dolphins, turtles, dugong and migratory birds." What followed – a Category-5 cyclone, Cyclone Yasi in 2011 causing destruction of corals and seagrass meadow – could not have happened at a worse time. This caused, according to the Committee's report, "15% of the total reef being damaged and 6% being severely damaged."

The World Heritage Committee had requested Australia to report regularly on monitoring the situation. When they visited the Great Barrier Reef in March 2012, the mission heard, among other things, strong concerns expressed by some groups about the environmental management and governance of the Port of Gladstone. In calling for an independent review, the mission suggested it be carried out by internationally recognised and widely respected scientific experts. The World Heritage Committee (WHC) supported the mission's recommendation in June 2012. However, the approvals for the aggressive industrial expansion were already in place. The environmental fallout was well and truly underway.

The dredging for this port in 2011 caused a 35 km plume of industrial sediment to flow into the World Heritage area stirred up from the harbour floor according to a study by James Cook University scientists. A Senate report into the port development dubbed it 'an environmental disaster'. Mangrove and seagrass beds were threatened as well as dugong and dolphin populations. Diseased fishlife included an increase in lesions in fish and 39% of mud crabs collected around the harbour were found to have rust spots indicating shell disease from ingesting metals such as copper and aluminum as well as high levels of arsenic.

A report by the University of Queensland, 'Investigation of contaminant levels in green turtles from Gladstone' led by Professor Caroline Gaus[55] noted that the large scale dredging and the dumping of dredged spoil occurring in Port Curtis/Gladstone Harbour during late 2010 through to 2012, was likely to have been the cause of the elevated metal levels found in stranded turtles. Clinical examination of 56 green turtles revealed infections.

The blood of captured turtles was found to contain a high level of contaminants including arsenic, cadmium, cobalt, mercury, nickel, selenium, and vanadium according to the report.

The fishing industry, worth $40 million, was under threat with 65 businesses at risk that fished in the area according to multiple media reports, with a three-week fishing ban being imposed by the Queensland Government on Gladstone Harbour in September 2011.

The usual fanfare in the media focused on the 52 conditions and 102 sub-conditions relating to the development including the dumping of 11 million cubic metres of spoil in the outer harbour and where it was to be dumped. One solution presented by the Gladstone Ports Corporation then Chairman Ian Brusasco was to excise the port from the World Heritage Area. Senator Larissa Walters, the then Federal Greens Party environment spokesperson's response was to the point when she said that such a suggestion proved the project had been an environmental disaster.

"It's the mass dredging that should be stopped, not the World Heritage listing," she was quoted as saying in *The Australian* in December 2011.

The question of monitoring compliance and what was to be done in the event of the breaching of these conditions was predictably left hanging. As is evident with Queensland Nickel's Yabulu refinery and Linc Energy's coal gasification project, the environment is sacrificed leaving an enormous clean-up bill to be funded by taxpayers following these industrial failed experiments. 'Environmental conditions', the catchcry used by ministers like Greg Hunt to justify approvals when approving the Adani mine, are not in any way sufficient insurance against environmental wrongdoing.

Ports, meanwhile, continue to be part of a developing Queensland.

The UNESCO mission, when visiting Gladstone in 2012, discovered that there were no less than 45 proposals for coastal development pending, including 11 for port facilities. Thirty-five of these proposals were to be decided before 2013. Four of the priority ports, under the program Queensland Sustainable Port Development are earmarked for expansion and are positioned along the 2600 km Great Barrier Reef coastline, home to 2900 individual reefs and 1500 different species of fish.

In 2013–14, according to the Queensland Government's Department of State Development,[56] the priority ports represented trade worth $32 billion, or 77% of the total throughput of all Queensland's ports. 131.8 million tonnes of coal were exported in 2016/17 from Queensland ports. The ports' redevelopments fall within a wider state program with the Queensland State Government looking to invest approximately $33.7 billion in transport infrastructure over the next ten years.

While the Port of Gladstone filled the headlines, there was little attention paid to one of these proposals with the potential for perhaps the most catastrophic consequences.

In 2011, the Adani Group had paid $1.83 billion for a 99-year lease for the Abbot Point coal terminal, north of the Queensland coastal town of Bowen, designated as one of the state's priority ports and a major port for 30 years. The then Premier Anna Bligh promised in a media statement that proceeds "would be set aside to fund Queensland's share of the recovery from the summer of floods and cyclones."

Abbot Point was Adani's first home in Australia. It was also the proposed site of the new coal terminal earmarked to ship the coal from the Carmichael mine. The sale went largely unnoticed until January 2014, when the Great Barrier Reef Marine Park Authority (GBRMPA) announced it had approved an application from the North Queensland Bulk Ports Corporation, responsible for strategic planning for ports, for the dumping of more than 3 million cubic metres of dredge spoil *inside* the Great Barrier Reef Marine Park so as to expand the coal terminal capacity. Under the proposal, the seabed would be dredged to create berths for six coal ships.

WWF Australia spokesman, Richard Leck, estimated that the material dredged during the port expansion would be "enough to fill 150,000 dump trucks that lined up bumper-to-bumper from Brisbane to Melbourne."

This decision made by the GBRMPA, a statutory appointed body whose charter is purportedly to protect the region's eco-system, was horrifying to me.

A senior researcher from JCU, Jon Brodie, warned that this would set a precedent for other ports up and down the coastline. He also warned of the effects of the dumping of dredging on seagrass meadows and coral reefs.

Dr Russell Reichelt, was – and still is – the Chairperson and Chief Executive of the GBRMPA when the decision to dump the dredge on the reef was made. He was also head of the Authority when it reviewed its position on the priority ports. Reichelt is a research scientist who worked at the Australian Institute of Marine Science in the 1980s.

As founding Chair of TOBMI (Tourism Operators and Businesses Magnetic Island) I had to reread the GBRMPA decision to dump spoil on the reef a few times in disbelief thinking it read more like a skit from an ABC comedy program *Chaser*.

In April 2014, with TOBMI committee approval, I wrote a letter condemning the dumping of the three million cubic metres of dredge on the reef. Shortly afterwards, I received a phone call from someone higher up in the tourism industry than our small grassroots group. Didn't I understand, he asked, quietly, that we would be compensated for the dumping? We wouldn't *lose* money. It was better that the regional and local tourism organisations provided a united front.

The message was clear: Don't bite the hand that feeds you. This has been the common catchcry I've confronted when talking about the truth in a business that promotes tourism.

In the end, after much public outcry, in December 2015, the Federal Department of Environment approved the dredging of 1.1 million cubic metres of seabed *to be placed on vacant industrial land at the port,* next to the existing coal terminal. The dredging still comes at a cost with the Greens and WWF noting that even that amount of dredging will endanger the internationally significant Caley Wetlands nearby. At the time of writing (2017–2018), plans to increase the number of new coal export terminals have suffered setbacks as many of the major mining companies that had sought to establish terminals at the port, including Rio Tinto and BHP Billiton, have withdrawn from their projects. A number of banks also reportedly withdrew support, leaving Adani and GVK and Hancock Prospecting at that time the only companies still interested.

In June 2015, GBRMPA had finally introduced a new regulation at the direction of the Federal Government to prohibit the disposal of capital dredge spoil within the Marine Park boundaries.[57] In November 2017, a review was ordered by then Environment Minister, Greg Hunt, and was headed by Dr Wendy Craik, a specialist in fish biology and Chair of the Climate Change Authority. Craik found, among other things, that there was a perception from some stakeholders of meddling by the Federal Government in the management of the Authority.[58]

One stakeholder, Dr Leanne Fernandes, commented that "political imperatives were perverting the course of management decisions" governing the reef and that GBRMPA had lost its voice over issues affecting the reef.

Dr Craik identified three high profile issues which had made major contributions to the reef's demise which included the Government's approval of three liquefied natural gas processing plants at Curtis Island near Gladstone in 2010 and 2011; the leaking of dredge spoil from a bund wall at the Port of Gladstone in 2011 and 2012, and further approvals for expansion of the Abbot Point Coal Terminal which included the proposed dumping of capital dredge material in the Marine Park in 2013 and 2014.

Dr Craik said the Abbot Point decision had focused national and international attention on the reef and "raised concern about management of the Marine Park and the independence of the Authority's decision making."

Significantly, Craik also noted that after the 2016 bleachings, there was a coordinated response involving in-water surveys, multiple briefings, public forums and media interviews. A similar response was not made after the 2017 bleachings "due to a lack of resources."

Is the Authority prepared for continued bleaching and how well resourced is it for these catastrophes?

In April 2018, Turnbull announced $500 million to save the Great Barrier Reef. This included a $444 million agreement with the Great Barrier Reef Foundation to tackle crown-of-thorns starfish "and mitigate the impacts of climate change" as though this was some containable issue. A Fairfax article[59] revealed figures showing that Commonwealth funding to arrest declining water quality on the reef had dropped by $11 million a year. The Government's funding announcement included a $56 million boost for GBRMPA. However, both the Australian Conservation Foundation (ACF) and the WWF Australia estimated that $475 million was needed to be spent on water quality alone.

As the Queensland Government commits to expanding more and more ports, the relentless assault on the reef and its marine creatures are often out of sight and out of mind. Even as far back as 2014, before the back-to-back bleaching of 2016/17, GBRMPA rated the long-term outlook for the reef's ecosystem as 'poor and deteriorating'. Crown-of-Thorns starfish (COTS) is one culprit in the destruction of the reef, as is poor water quality with pesticide run off. All of these features were playing out before the back-to-back bleaching.

Shipping is also a major threat to the future of the Great Barrier Reef. In 2012, around 3947 ships called into reef ports according to *The Conversation*. The Report written by Adam Smith, a former member of GBRMPA, said that the projected number of ships was expected to exceed 10,000 by 2032, and that the average size of ships visiting the reef has grown by 85% over the past 15 years. When the

Chinese bulk coal carrier *MV Shen Neng* ran aground on Douglas Shoal northeast of Gladstone in 2010, it left a 400,000 square metre scar, the largest ever recorded in the Great Barrier Reef.

Abbot Point, estimated to have 500 ships offshore waiting to load coal if the Carmichael mine goes ahead, already hosts 311 bulk carriers. In 2016–17, 25.4 million tonnes of coal left Abbot Point on these carriers according to the North Queensland Bulks Ports Corporation 2016/17 Annual Report. Green and Flatback turtles nest on the beach right next to the Terminal 0 site earmarked for expansion by Adani should the Carmichael mine go ahead. Turtles are a visible indicator of the reef being under stress.

In June and July 2012, 102 adult female turtles were stranded on Upstart Bay, south of Townsville around 39 kms from Abbot Point, where ships were offloading coal and transiting through the reef. Marine turtles are protected under state, federal and international legislation. Six of the seven species of turtle live in the Great Barrier Reef. Eighteen of the turtles were stranded alive. The bodies of those who had been given a post mortem showed neurological symptoms. I asked two of my senior students to investigate. Megan Stafford, a third year student, found that turtle strandings had increased.[60]

The confirmed turtle deaths on beaches bordering Upstart Bay, however, were deemed an 'unusual cluster' with most of them being female adult green turtles. Strandings are linked to devastation of seagrass caused by cyclones as well as pollution according to scientific literature. Dr Jon Brodie's paper specifically links water quality and marine turtle health. Brodie had also discovered that there were links in the Gladstone strandings and deaths of turtles from elevated metals in their blood, which came from dredging.

However, then Department of Environment and Heritage Protection Senior Conservation Officer, Dr Ian Bell, told Megan Stafford that the baseline data is important. He described marine turtles as "kind of like the canary in the coal mine ... People look at marine turtles and they look like a hard, boxy thing. But, the reality is they are really quite sensitive to the minor perturbations in the environment." Dr Bell said, "If you have turtles swimming around in your area of water, things will be doing pretty well in there. They are a very good proxy indicator for how healthy marine ecosystems are functioning."[61]

In 2011 and 2012, I came across many dead turtles washed ashore on Magnetic Island while walking on some of the island's 23 beaches. Official figures of turtles stranded off Townsville from 1 January to 30 June 2012 were 168 compared to only 14 in 2016 and 12 in 2017 for the same time period.[62] While the focus was on the rehabilitation of the surviving turtles, there did not appear to be much focus on the cause of their death except local opinions that it was because of Cyclone Yasi and a loss of seagrass habitat. Official reports state that 316 turtles were stranded in the Townsville District in 2012, accounting for almost a third of all the reported turtle strandings on the entire east coast of Queensland. 308 were stranded in the Townsville District in 2011 compared with 44 in 2009 and 96 in 2010.

Fresh tissue samples from the liver, kidney, muscle, lung and shell collected from a dozen of the turtles washed up in Upstart Bay were analysed initially at JCU's Vet School before being sent to toxicology laboratories in Brisbane and Amsterdam.

GBRMPA Manager of Species Conservation, Dr Mark Read, told Megan Stafford that although these were preliminary toxicology findings, the interpretation was ongoing due to the sensitivity of machines analysing the samples. "What we weren't expecting was that some of the material in the samples was at a concentration the machines couldn't handle," Dr Read said, adding, "In this situation, it occurred because a particular metal was at high concentrations."

Although the source of the metals was never found, the magnitude of the numbers of the deaths of turtles in one stranding is sobering. The story was hardly reported in the mainstream media with virtually no follow up even after the release of a Report by JCU, which included Read's findings.

A major river, the Burdekin, near the township of Ayr, south of Townsville, flows into Upstart Bay. There has been an approximate five to tenfold increase in sediment loads from the Burdekin catchment to the Great Barrier Reef lagoon since European settlement. Runoff from agriculture contains toxic metals, pesticides and elevated levels of nutrients. Mercury also occurs often in fungicides, the JCU Report determined, from sugarcane cropping near the bay. High rainfalls washed contaminants into the ocean. Although pesticides, like DDT, have not been used in Queensland agriculture since at least the 1990s, the report concluded this type of chemical was still found in the soil residue and river discharges during runoff events. The Report also noted that "a local source of marine chemical pollution" although undefined, was a *possible* (my emphasis) factor in the turtle deaths at Upstart Bay. It was an irrefutable sign of "undocumented environmental decline." [63]

With so many potential causes because of pollution, the cause is still not absolutely known. Dr Caroline Gaus who also conducted research in The River to Reef Research project [64] on the cause of the turtles' deaths for the National Research Centre for Environmental Toxicology said she found "chemicals associated with industry and agriculture" in the blood of the turtles from Upstart and Cleveland Bay closer to Townsville. The major issue, as is so often the case in this story, is that there are more than 30,000 chemicals in wide commercial use, according to Dr Gaus, and many of these have never been measured in the environment

A 2017 study by the Queensland Alliance for Environmental Health Services (QAEHS), a partnership between the University of Queensland and Queensland Health, investigated green turtles in Upstart Bay, the same location where more than 100 died in 2012. The study found that there were four to 25 times higher levels of cobalt than the baseline established in the Howick group of islands in far north Great Barrier Reef. [65]

* * *

As for UNESCO, which carries responsibility for World Heritage sites, as previously mentioned, it has cast doubt on Australia's reputation as steward of the Great Barrier Reef. But unfortunately, UNESCO and the World Heritage Committee have little political clout. Australia's response to the World Heritage Committee's concerns was the Federal and Queensland Governments developing 'The Reef 2050 Long Term Sustainability Plan' (Reef 2050)[66] in March 2015, ostensibly to counteract UNESCO's concerns. But this 'Plan' has few realistic targets and does not focus on the impact from Queensland's coal mines on greenhouse emissions.

The World Heritage Centre and Advisory bodies in 2017 concluded that while there had "undoubtedly been an unprecedented level of increased effort to reduce pressures on the reef," there was a need to accelerate attention to issues such as water quality, focusing on legislation to regulate land clearing, but above all addressing "the most significant overall threat'" to the future of the reef, climate change, and how this influences the effectiveness of the 2050 Plan.[67]

According to notes from the Reef Advisory Committee (RAC) meetings in May 2017, obtained by the ABC, the Queensland Resources Council (QRC) the mining industry's lobby group, urged key advisors on the Great Barrier Reef not to consider climate change in the Reef 2050 Plan. The QRC argued that there was no direct scientific link between coal mining and climate change although QRC Chief Executive, Ian MacFarlane, later told the ABC in a follow up article, in August 2017, that the notes were inaccurate and that dealing with climate change was important.[68] Mr MacFarlane stated then: "QRC agrees the Reef 2050 Plan should include Great Barrier Reef specific climate change actions if it is consistent with a broader national climate change policy and action plan."

He also said he supported recent findings that climate change caused coral bleaching, but stood by comments, attributed to QRC, about the proposed Adani mine. "There is a difference between coal burning and coal mining and QRC's position on the latter is mining itself is not a large contributor to climate change."

Clearly, as long as it's not in your own backyard, what happens to the coal after it is mined does not appear to be of concern.

Meanwhile, the Reef 2050 Plan is evidence of the continuing battle between economic growth on the one hand, and environmental concerns on the other. How much money will be provided to protect the reef remains to be seen. Alas, the World Heritage Committee does not have the authority to force Australia to refuse further port developments. Its only 'big stick' is to relegate the Great Barrier Reef to being listed as 'endangered', which it declined to do. Declaring a World Heritage site in danger, allows the World Heritage Committee (WHC) to allocate immediate assistance from the World Heritage Fund and can thus incite rapid conservation action. The Committee did, however, register its concern about water quality targets and land clearing. But it did not remove the reef from the World Heritage list altogether. During its 2017 meeting, the WHC expressed its concern about the effects of climate change and bleaching on the Great Barrier Reef as well as other reefs around the world.

The Reef 2050 plan *did* contain a commitment to not permitting industrial port developments outside of the four existing priority ports: Townsville, Abbott Point, Hay Point and Gladstone. The Queensland Government passed legislation – the Sustainable Ports Development Act – to enforce this in late 2015. However, the expansion of the existing ports, is still a threat to the environment.

Dredging is still continuing in the name of progress. In September 2017, Annastacia Palaszczuk's Government announced funding for a $193 million channel-widening project for the Port of Townsville, and in February 2018, the Federal Government approved the Environmental Impact Statement for the expansion. According to a media statement, the Palaszczuk Government committed $75 million in 2017–18 seeking a matched $75 million in funds from the Federal Government and $43 million from the Port of Townsville. The project will involve dredging 11.48 million cubic metres of sediment to widen and deepen the Sea and Platypus channels and an expanded harbour basin. This was in spite of her government passing the Sustainable Ports Development Act in November 2015 to restrict new port development in, and adjoining, the Great Barrier Reef World Heritage Area (GBRWHA). Dredging is a known issue affecting the reef. Dredging releases sediment in the water creating turbid plumes which migrate on to nearby sensitive habitats reducing light.[69]

In our first few years on Magnetic Island, Grant had regularly spotted dugongs in those channels. Towards the end of our time there in 2015, their numbers had diminished. One of the Committee members, whom I had encouraged to join back in the early days of TOBMI in 2009, had been outspoken about the dredging for the port in 2017. After I left, she was quietly moved off the Committee.

Confronted with the warning from UNESCO, and after signing the Paris agreement committing to fighting our contribution to greenhouse gases, the Federal Government went ahead to approve Adani's $16 billion open-cut coal mine. In April 2016, the Queensland Government approved the company's mining leases.

Chapter 4
The Midas Touch – Gujarat Open for Business – At What Cost?

Bruce Currie is the closest you can get to the quintessential farmer. His Akubra hat is welded to his head. He wears open-necked checked shirts, has a bristly moustache, a broad smile, large farmer's hands and a voice as deep as a well. He and his wife, Annette, own 1700 head of cattle in a good season but in a drought perhaps 400 head of cattle on a 25,000-hectare property called 'Speculation' north of Jericho, about 100 kms from where Adani is proposing to build the Carmichael mine. The property, which Currie describes as "the driest inhabited country on earth" spans the Great Dividing Range in the Galilee Basin.

The Curries moved from the Bowen Basin where Currie had inherited the family property about 50 kms north of Emerald, farming half cattle and half dry crops like sunflower, wheat, oats and chickpeas, to get away from coal mining and to devote their farming efforts to cattle which Currie felt was more sustainable.

But as Currie is fond of saying, after they bought the property near Jericho in 2005 they found: "We were out of the frying pan and into the fire." He was to find that the Galilee Basin was being eyed off by a number of mining companies including GVK Hancock, then a joint venture between GVK and Gina Rinehart's Hancock Prospecting, with several major coal mines proposed including Alpha, Alpha West and Kevin's Corner.

In 2014, the Newman Queensland Government declared the Galilee Basin State Development Area which includes two rail corridors for rail lines to Abbot Point - one from the central area where the proposed Carmichael mine is to be built and another from a southern section where GVK Hancock has its three proposed mines.[70] According to the ABC around 74 landholders are impacted.

Currie did not know it at the time but the owner of the proposed mining ventures, GVK, had connections in high places. On the eve of clinching a $1.3 billion deal with G.V. Krishna Reddy, back in June 2011, *The Age* and *Crikey.com* published stories revealing that Rinehart invited none other than Barnaby Joyce and Julie Bishop and a former Liberal Brisbane politician Teresa Gambaro to attend Reddy's granddaughter's wedding in Hyderabad in India.[71]

The Sydney Morning Herald in October 2013,[72] detailed the politicians' collective claims of more than $12,000 in allowances, some of which covered airfares, which was reportedly partly paid back. The article claimed half of the meetings Bishop listed occurred on the day of the wedding, June 11, and involved meetings with members of the wedding party including the bride's grandfather and Rinehart's business partner Dr G.V. Krishna Reddy.

In 2008, the Queensland Coordinator General declared the Alpha and adjacent Kevin's Corner proposed coal and rail line "a significant project" and the mines were recommended for approval by the Queensland Coordinator General in 2012 and the Federal Environment Minister the same year.[73] Like the Adani mine, the proposed mines are intended to transport the coal from the Galilee Basin to Abbot Point for export.

In Queensland, major approvals for large mines under State and Federal legislation are given a mining lease under the Mineral Resources Act MRA (1989) Qld, an environmental authority under the Environmental Protection Act (1994) Qld EPA, and under the Federal Government's Environmental Protection and Biodiversity Conservation Act 1999 (EPBC). Following the Coordinator General's Report, the mine was publicly advertised for objections under the MRA and EPA.

Currie discovered that GVK Hancock's own research reportedly showed that the draining of the groundwater for one of its proposed mines would run as close as four kilometres to his farm – but the company had failed to contact the Curries. The mine itself is around 15 kms from his eastern boundary. GVK Hancock, meanwhile, had stated it would be releasing a 'make good agreement' with landowners to protect their groundwater supplies.

One of Currie's main criticisms is that these mining ventures, which stand to appropriate farmers' land, do not widely advertise their intentions, so often the approval process is rushed through. He is also critical of the 'make good agreement' process, which essentially means farmers sign over their rights to the mining companies without guidance and later find they have no legal rights to rely upon.

Currie admits that back then, he was naïve.

"No one had spoken to us at the time," Currie recalls. "We thought if there was an issue, we would lodge an objection, that we'll make whoever is responsible to come and talk to us and we'll go through a 'make good agreement' and everything would be fine."

In September 2013, Currie represented himself in the Queensland Land Court, and lodged an objection to the company's plans along with other graziers and community groups. Initially, the Curries engaged a solicitor, but after several rewritten agreements with GVK Hancock in which the ground rules, he said, appeared to constantly change, as well as facing burgeoning legal costs, they decided to represent themselves.

"We got to about version three and every time the legal bill would go up and I had about enough," Currie told me. Legal bills conceivably could have been between $150,000 and $200,000. "For what? For a recommendation which the Government minister can ignore?" Currie asks. He is convinced that justice in Australia is only for the wealthy and that during the protracted legal proceedings, he just wanted to get back to running his business but was concerned that he had to stand up to this major threat to the family's livelihood.

Once the Curries made the decision to fight the project, many other landowners contacted them. There have been several challenges by landowners and graziers to the proposed mines especially tackling its environmental approval. After a three-month hearing, in 2013 the Land Court recommended that the impacts on groundwater supplies could be potentially "so severe and so uncertain" that the mining lease and environmental authority should be refused or further assessment be undertaken of the groundwater impacts. It was a victory, although a partial one, as the Land Court is only able to make a recommendation, not a ruling.

The Coast and Country Association of Queensland (CCAQ) fought several court battles over the Galilee mines. They challenged the granting of mining leases and environmental authority granted to several of the projects including Adani's Carmichael mine and the Alpha and Kevin's Corner mines. CCAQ's objections to the Adani mine were lodged in the Land Court of Queensland in March–May 2015,[74] focusing on the environmental damage which would be caused to the ancient springs at Doongmabulla Springs; the endangered Black-throated finch as well as the damage to the Great Barrier Reef through causing ocean acidification when the coal was burnt. The Land Court, however, recommended the Carmichael mine be approved subject to protecting the Black-throated finch.

CCAQ then appealed to the Supreme Court in August 2016 for a judicial review of the Queensland Government's decision to grant the Adani mine environmental authority as it had not complied with the Environmental Protection Act (1994) to safeguard the environment. However, this Review Application was dismissed in November 2016.

CCAQ had already objected in the Land Court in September and October 2013 to the mining lease and environmental authority being approved for the Alpha Mine[75] on three bases: groundwater, climate change and economics and objected to the Kevin's Corner Mine[76] in October 2015 for the similar reasons. The Curries were among a number of unrepresented objectors who also took part in the case against both mines mostly because of the effects of the groundwater being used by the proposed mines on their properties. After the Land Court recommended that the Alpha mine be either refused, or approved with additional groundwater conditions in April 2014, CCAQ then lodged a judicial review in the Supreme Court challenging the validity of the Land Court decision. CCAQ lawyers also argued that environmental harm through greenhouse gas emissions should have been acknowledged. Upon dismissing the judicial review, the Supreme Court noted that the argument about greenhouse emissions could not be considered as the coal would be substituted by another project should the Alpha mine not go ahead. On 2 September 2015, the judicial review was dismissed. An appeal by CCAQ to the Queensland Court of Appeal was similarly dismissed.

The CCAQ went further seeking special leave to appeal to the High Court in October 2016 on grounds relating to the Land Court's failure to consider greenhouse gas emissions when approving coal mines in Queensland. The application to appeal to the High Court was dismissed in April 2017[77] as the application was deemed to be "not a suitable vehicle" for addressing the questions raised in the application. On July 4, 2017, the Land Court recommended that the mining lease be granted and environmental authority be issued for the Kevin's Corner mine.[78]

Nevertheless, the initial win against a mining giant in the Land Court catapulted Currie on to the Australian political stage, convincing him to fight for his land and the groundwater he relied upon to survive. He was the perfect candidate as 'the farmer and grazier' for our trip to India.

* * *

After arriving at Indira Gandhi International Airport in New Delhi, Bruce Currie confesses that he has not eaten any of the plane food. This is his first trip to an Asian country. A pastor friend of the family had advised him to stock up on muesli bars and to avoid all other food, especially meat. His friend, he admits, had visited India more than 20 years ago, but nonetheless ... For the duration of our visit, he only strayed from the never-ending supply of muesli bars to indulge in vegetarian food, a first for his normal diet that consists, unsurprisingly, of steaks.

Imogen Zethoven and I are vegetarians. We delight in the boundless variety of vegetarian cuisine that only India can produce with such aplomb.

The fourth member of our party is Geoff Cousins, then President of the Australian Conservation Foundation (ACF). The ACF, according to its website, boasts more than 450,000 people who care about and act for a world where "forests, rivers, people and wildlife thrive." It was Cousins who came up with the idea of the letter to be presented to Gautam Adani, and who had personally approached Australian cricket legends Ian and Greg Chappell (knowing how much Indians loved cricket) and then went on to collect an impressive collection of signatures from other celebrities and businesspeople calling on Adani to abandon the mine.

Billed as 'a millionaire businessman', he was government adviser to former Prime Minister, John Howard, as well as CEO of the phone network Optus and has served on ten other boards ranging from PBL to Telstra. I had first heard Cousins' resounding baritone on the ABC's Radio National some months earlier defending the Great Barrier Reef and attacking Adani. His voice rang with confidence and truth, commanding respect. I remember making a mental note to find out who this man was. His voice was that of a businessman accustomed to being heard – not the expected soft dulcet tones of a Green politician.

Cousins is a man of paradoxes. Amongst his professional corporate careers, he's had some impressive wins environmentally. He is passionate about campaigning, he tells me later. He managed to provoke Malcolm Turnbull, then Federal Environment Minister, calling him the Minister Against the Environment and later campaigned against Turnbull during the 2007 election. Along with Booker prize-winning novelist, Richard Flanagan, he turned the tide against the Gunn's pulp mill in Tasmania, which included drawing on a star-studded list of celebrities to speak out against the pulp mill. He also presented 20,000 signatures from ANZ customers to persuade the bank not to fund the mill.

His approach to offer his help to Flanagan, who had written a stirring piece in *The Monthly* Magazine against the mill, was by describing himself in an email, according to an article by Greg Bearup in *The Sydney Morning Herald* in March 2012, as "the Devil arrived in a silken cloak." He had after all worked for Howard known for his lacklustre achievements on climate change.

Although on the same plane as us from Australia, Cousins travelled separately. He, too, had decided to make the journey to India to intercept the Premier and to present the letter from a host of celebrities and influential business people. He is funding his own trip. I am yet to meet him. A tantalising welcome card at the Indira Gandhi International Airport in New Delhi proclaims his imminent arrival.

Cousins' genius, as becomes clear when we get down to the serious business of disrupting the Queensland Government's message, is to draw on his former career as one of the most successful advertising men of the 1980s when he was chairman of the George Patterson advertising agency. In this business, brevity is all. Avoid any issue that the enemy (whoever they may be) wants to raise. Keep on message. Confidence is everything.

Both Cousins and Zethoven are clearly veteran travellers, travelling with small pull-along cases filled with mix and match navy jackets and pants and tops, thus managing to always look unruffled and professional. Cousins informs us later that he will be standing down as President of the ACF. But he is clearly committed to this journey and to defeating Adani.

We are a disparate band thrown together over the issue of the proposed Adani coal mine in Australia but, as the trip unfolds, each of us, as it turns out, contributes a unique perspective.

* * *

Our first destination, after reaching Gujarat is Hazira, a few kilometres from the Arabian Sea and about half an hour's drive from Surat. It will be the first time we are to witness the legacy of Adani's aggressive industrial expansion. Gujarat, unsurprisingly, given its location at the furthermost tip of the northwestern coast of India, was once home to India's first port. As far back as 1000 to 750 BCE, the state traded with Egypt, Bahrain and Sumer (in modern-day southern Iraq). Gujarat is home to the Indus Valley civilisation, one of the three earliest northern hemisphere civilisations along with Egypt and Mesopotamia).

Narendra Modi, India's sixteenth Prime Minister of India, comes from Gujarat. In May 2014, he glided on to the world stage in that role with a demeanour more like a Messiah than a politician with a beatific smile and warm handshake. Modi has humble beginnings. His family originates from what the Government of India classifies as 'Other Backward Class', a class considered socially and educationally disadvantaged in India. At the tender age of eight, he helped his father run a tea stall and from that early age joined the *Rashtriya Swayamsevak Sangh*, a right-wing Hindu nationalist, paramilitary volunteer organisation, and reportedly the parent organisation of Modi's ruling political party the *Bharatiya Janata Party* (BJP).

Gujarat is dear to Modi's heart. In 2001, he was appointed Chief Minister of the state, a position he held until becoming Prime Minister. His political party, the BJP, has ruled the state uninterruptedly for more than two decades. Aligned with strong Hindu nationalistic beliefs, Modi leads an exclusionary social agenda and this has reportedly led to global condemnation for persecuting Muslims particularly through his alleged incitement of anti-Muslim feelings in the Gujarat riots of 2002 which left 1000 people dead. The BBC[79] cited a senior police officer's sworn statement to India's Supreme Court that Modi had deliberately allowed anti-Muslim riots in the state. Modi has denied any wrongdoing when he was questioned in an inquiry into the riots.

Narendra Modi carved out a future lined with gold for the state projecting all of the right signs for investors. It was Modi who, as Chief Minister, set up Gujarat as 'open for business'. He reportedly abolished labour laws making it harder for workers to form unions, and easier for employers to hire and fire them. He also reportedly reduced the amount of money spent by the government on healthcare.

One Indian newspaper, *The Economic Times*, in December 2017, criticised him for a lack of policy innovation during his time as Chief Minister commenting, "he mainly did well at inviting large companies to set up shop in the state." One method was making the pathway to profitable business easier under the slogan 'Vibrant Gujarat'. His new ministry swiftly got on with the job of making the state attractive to investors, diluting many environmental laws which included companies no longer requiring clearance from the National Board for Wildlife for projects close to protected areas. One article accused Modi of approving a 'toothless' board without mandatory non-government individual wildlife and ecology experts.[80]

Modi also relaxed or abolished a number of other environmental regulations, often at the expense of the environment. According to the Indian online newspaper *The Wire* in June 2017, "the Modi Government have seen the transformation of the environment from being a field of relative stability and inactivity, to functioning as an active instrument of capital accumulation."[81] The article noted: "The sharp polarisation between extremely positive initiatives (like India's assertive global position on climate change, ambitious forays into renewables and bills institutionalising water for life) and negative anti-people actions (especially decisions regulating natural ecosystems like coasts, forests and wetlands, and the eroding of people's rights), is based on the government rationale to endorse everything that augurs well for business, new technology and international acclaim, even if this is achieved at the expense of the protection of ecosystems, conservation, people's livelihood and well being."

In October 2017, Narendra Modi was voted the third most followed leader in the world (with over 34.6 million followers on Twitter as of September 2017), behind Donald Trump (38.8 million followers) and Pope Francis according to Twiplomacy, a Burson Marsteller research project that tracks the use of Twitter by governments and international organisations.

Enter Gautam Adani. India has 121 billionaires placing the country as the home of the third largest group of the ultra-rich behind the United States and China. Adani group founder, Gautam Adani, is one of them. He was placed 154 on the *Forbes Magazine* Rich List and in 2017, the tenth richest in India. For the 2017 calendar year, according to the Bloomberg Millionaire Index, Gautam Adani was recorded as the biggest gainer in India with his wealth rising by 124.6%. As of 31 December 2017, his net worth soared to US$10.4 billion (AU$13.48 billion) from US$4.63 billion in January 2016.[82]

The Adani Group was established in 1988 and only began publicly trading in 1994. Gautam Adani has listed interests in mining, ports, power plants, real estate, renewable energy, food, and even defence. Until a few years ago, Adani was India's single biggest aggregator of cut and polished diamonds and gold jewellery.

Amongst the hype, however, there is another side to the glowing headlines about Gautam Adani. According to the 2018 Report for IEEFA by Tim Buckley, Adani Enterprise's net debt as at March 2018 was $US2.4 billion. Its market capitalisation is currently just over US$2 billion. Writing in the *Good Weekend* back in November 2017, Tim Elliott commented that some analysts "question Adani's ability to service its borrowings. Others have referred to his empire as 'a house of cards'. Not that this has curbed his appetite for risk."[83]

* * *

Gautam Adani's remarkable ascension to power parallels Narendra Modi's own rise. Their views and opinions seem to match. Earlier on, according to an article in the Indian newspaper *The Economic Times*, Gautam Adani is the man who built Rs 47,000 crore infrastructure empire.[84] It also reported that in March 2013, Adani withdrew his support as the major sponsor from the Wharton India Economic Forum after it cancelled its invitation to Modi to deliver the keynote address. When Modi was declared BJP's best prospect for prime minister in September 2013, according to *The Economic Times* in March 2014, his newfound status had an unmistakable effect on the Adani Group. The newspaper noted that shares in Adani companies quickly changed gears: "Adani Enterprise surged 124% ... Adani Port SEZ has rallied 48%, and Adani Power has gained 18% during the same period."

Adani and Modi have been friends for a decade dating back to when Modi was Chief Minister of Gujarat; they have leveraged all kinds of benefits from each other. During Modi's China visit, the year after he was elected Prime Minister, Adani and Bharti, a company whose services include telecommunications networks, got the bulk of deals with China Inc. worth US$22 billion according to an article published in the *Hindustan Times* in March 2015. It was Bharti Airtel Ltd back in 2006 that announced it was developing a telecommunications network for the Special Economic Zones in Adani's Mundra port, which included video surveillance.

Charting the relationship between Modi and Adani, *PagalParrot* (billed as the online news service which "gives you everything you want to know about India on the internet") alleged that the "net worth of Gautam Adani multiplied four times in just one year of the Modi Government."

One key reason for Gautam Adani's success was that Gujarat was the first Indian state to pass legislation to create Special Economic Zones (SEZ). Passed in 2004 when Narendra Modi was Chief Minister, even before the Indian SEZ Act in 2005, the SEZ was designed as 'an engine for economic growth' to streamline controls authorising foreign companies to acquire land for industry. It proved critical for the Adani Group to build the company's power plant and port in Mundra, which later developed over a 100 square kilometre area and became the largest port-led SEZ in India as a privately operated multi-project SEZ. According to

The Adani Brief,[85] citing Indian news articles, the Mundra Port and Special Economic Zone Limited is the previous name of Adani Ports and Special Economic Zone Limited, which Australian Securities and Investment Commission (ASIC) filings indicate is "the ultimate owner of Terminal 1 at Abbot Point Port in Australia."

Land inside an SEZ is exempt from all taxes, levies and trade duties for a decade of operation. An SEZ is also subject to different legal rules. The idea behind an SEZ is to attract foreign investment offering tax incentives (including customs duties) to international companies. SEZs are a law unto themselves. Rapid industrialisation, which followed the proclamation of SEZs, was to have a disastrous effect on the ecologically sensitive Gujarat coastline, just as the priority port expansion had on the Queensland coast abutting the Great Barrier Reef during a similar timeframe.

* * *

Hazira, our first port of call, boasts the entirely contradictory offerings of being a Centre for Health Tourism due to its natural springs, as well as being a deep water liquefied natural gas terminal and multi-cargo port. It is home to major polluting companies including Shell and Reliance. Its shipments include petroleum and bulk liquid chemicals.

In May 2013, Adani was granted Environmental Clearance by the Indian Ministry of Environment and Forests to build 12 berths including two coal berths to further develop its facility at Hazira port. The port was supposed to be developed in stages to include a liquefied natural gas (LNG) terminal and included a condition of compensatory afforestation of mangroves that was later reduced to 200 hectares.

In January 2016, the National Green Tribunal (NGT) which has the powers of a civil court and can order compensation for damages to person or property, found that the environmental clearance issued to Adani by the Ministry of Environment and Forest was "illegal and must be set aside." This followed a petition filed by the Hazira Fishermen Committee that challenged the project on the grounds of damaging the environment as well as displacing more than 300 fishing families.

According to *The Hindu* newspaper in January 2016,[86] the NGT imposed a heavy penalty of Rs. 25 crore (AU$4.8m) on Adani Hazira Port P/L (AHPPL) and its associate Hazira Infrastructure P/L for restoration of degraded environment: "What we find from the record is that instead of expanding port work in phase-out manner, expansion was already practically done almost without obtaining environmental clearance and coastal regulation zone (CEZ) clearance."

The article continued that the NGT also claimed: "It is evident from the affidavit of the forest department that this area, which once had abundance of mangrove stretches, presently don't [sic] have any mangrove vegetation."

India's Supreme Court refused to put a stay on the revocation of Hazira's environmental clearance noting that "cancellation of environmental clearance does not affect the shipping and port operations," according to The Centre of Media and Democracy (CMD) site Source Watch.[87] They noted that the Supreme Court directed Adani to deposit the AU$4.8 million penalty it had received. Adani Hazira Port Pvt Ltd (AHPPL) appealed the decision to the Supreme Court of India but was unsuccessful.

* * *

We are visiting the fishermen who took on the multi-millionaire's company and won against its expansion. Beside a dusty road bordering the port, we stop the car at one of a number of shanty villages that sprawl along the roadside housing around 80 families. They claim Adani's SEZ has effectively cut off their fishing grounds in the inter-tidal zone and narrowed the creek that they used to access the ocean. The environmental clearance granted earlier by the Environment Minister was declared illegal. This included 25 hectares around the creek being reclaimed.

The fishermen had alleged that AHPPL developed two additional container jetties and three multipurpose jetties in the non-LNG port area, even before receiving the environmental and coastal zone regulation clearance. They also alleged that clearing the area to build port berths and two container jetties as well as three multi-purpose jetties had led to large-scale destruction of mangroves. The NGT had also found that Adani's Environmental Impact Assessment overlooked the presence of two vulture species and did not consider their conservation. They were identified as White-backed and Long-billed vultures and were critically endangered.

Adani, in its defence, denied it had damaged the environment, nor had it restricted the fishermen's fishing grounds, and denied there were any vultures recorded as living in the area. It stated that the clearing would not destroy flora or fauna or mudflats. It argued, instead, that the changes were 'minor' and did not constitute illegal activities.

In finding against Adani, the NGT was scathing in its judgment noting that the expansion was "already practically done almost without obtaining environmental clearance and coastal regulation zone (CEZ) clearance." Even more damning was that the company had been "undaunted by the absence of Environmental Clearance" and proceeded with expansion after 2006 without any regard for the impact on the environment. What was once an "abundance of mangrove stretches" now had no mangrove vegetation.

* * *

Geoff Cousins is dressed in a green cap and shirt and his ubiquitous beige slacks. Bruce Currie has a blue pinstriped shirt on and his Akubra hat. He is fussing a little, wanting to know if it's time to bring out his heritage green cotton long-sleeved shirt which he has had especially made for the journey. On the back is emblazoned a white map of Australia with the silhouettes of a kangaroo, a boomerang and a koala. Currie has stepped into the role as our Ambassador from Down Under, the kind of Aussie the world expects. He is determined the Indians will embrace this.

As we enter the village, Cousins is introduced to a middle-aged man who heads the Hazira Fishermen's Committee called Dhansukhbhai Rathod. He has become the hero of the village because he is one of the petitioners who won the court action.

We are ushered to an unofficial stage on the deck of a pink painted house with green shutters at the beginning of the village. A number of plastic chairs have been assembled. M.S.H. Sheikh, a Surat-based environmentalist who is supporting the fishermen in their legal dispute, is a youthful bespectacled man who is prematurely thinning on top. He is to be our interpreter. We are each issued with a red rose and a can of Coke. The seats are quickly filled with attentive faces. A man in a red cap and striped blue t-shirt is clearly going to be one of the most outspoken.

After Cousins introduces himself and our delegation, telling the villagers that Adani is proposing to build the world's largest coal mine in Australia, he gets down to business: "It doesn't matter if you have the government licence. You must still have the social licence. The Australian people," he tells them, "don't want it."

Imogen Zethoven explains how the Carmichael mine will have an enormous impact on the Great Barrier Reef, air pollution and global warming, and Currie talks about the issue of the proposed coal mines in the Galilee depleting groundwater on his farm. I briefly outline the effect on tourism.

We are, therefore, interested, Zethoven says, to hear the locals' experience with Adani. Redcap describes the coal dusting and cancer-like diseases affecting some villagers. Later, we hear that an older female doctor is concerned about the level of respiratory diseases she has found in villages near the power plant, particularly among children. Roads have been built around the village with trucks continually roaring through the community bringing further hazards to the villagers.

"The fishing," one villager tells us, "has now only 10% remaining from the original stocks. What's more," he adds, "the taste of the fish is not good ... Hydro carbon kerosene-like smell."

Sheikh interprets, waving his palms upwards in a gesture of helplessness.

"Not only are the fish contaminated, but they can't get to their fishing grounds due to the SEZ and the narrowing of the creek that leads to the ocean," he adds.

The faces before us have an inured sense of resignation. They have lived in this area for centuries. No one can ever remember their ancestors living anywhere else. There is no option to relocate. Their livelihoods are the same as their fathers! The sea provides. Sheikh says there are 200 people in the village who depend on the fishing and they are 'traditionally poor!

At some distance from the men, dressed in purple and orange saris, the women congregate. Children peek out shyly. A few tiles on the roofs of the shanty houses are perilously close to falling down.

"Do they get any compensation? Any money for what's happened?" asks Cousins.

"There is NO compensation for the restrictions from creeks to the sea or the intertidal zones," Sheikh tells us.

"Have they been offered jobs?" Cousins asks. "In the port?"

Sheikh questions the group. "They only hire outsiders," he interprets. "They don't hire local people. At first they said they would employ the locals and the villagers were happy. But that was only a promise that never happened."

This is an ominous message for us considering Adani's promises of jobs back in Australia which has won the politicians and many regional townspeople over.

In 2016, Adani proposed an outer port expansion at Hazira which would add 19 new multi-purpose berths to the 12 already approved in 2013, bringing the total number of berths to 31.

"They want to expand the port even further through the forest – 183 hectares of protected forest ... The people are dependent on the forest land for the grazing of the goats and they are harvesting foods from this big forest and they are dependent on the fishing – they put small nets across the creek. The whole entire protected forest has been given to Adani. Adani will make an expansion of the port at this side and they will lose the entire resources of the village."

"Did they consult with the Indigenous people?" asks Cousins. Sheikh shakes his head.

As the meeting winds up, Cousins asks Sheikh if he has told the villagers we are to present a letter signed by cricketers Ian and Greg Chappell to Adani. Sheikh nods that he has.

"Is India going to beat Australia in the cricket?" asks Cousins. There is lots of predictable laughter.

"We think about our children," the village chief pulls a little girl towards him. "And our grandchildren." Sheikh relays this to us.

"That's why we've come," says Cousins adding, "I am a very old man. A father and grandfather and I'm very concerned."

The villagers are planning to cook us a feast that we gently decline, touched that they would offer this when they have so little and are facing such a grim future.

Leaving the village, we pass by the Adani port. It is our first encounter with enemy territory. Barbed wire fences surround the perimeter of the SEZ. Small seedlings growing just behind the perimeter fence forecast future privacy.

As we near the edge of the port, we stop the car. A number of small trail bikes with Indian youths are grouped to the left of a small track.

To our left lies an enormous mountain of slag from the industrial development of the port.

We jump on the back of a trail bike and travel pillion style. Zethoven's hands are clasped firmly at the rear baggage rack. Currie's Oz heritage green shirt disappears up front. I wonder what will happen if we encounter security even though we are on a public road. We pass a truck with a wooden back. But no one stops. The track gets narrower and sandier and the earth blackens. There is no turning back now. Shanties line the road and the mudbanks. The track opens out to the beach. Beside us to our right the Adani port sprawls, all turbines and high floodlights.

When I arrive, Cousins and Sheikh are rubbing their fingers on the mangroves growing in a ditch near the track. Their fingers come away covered in coal dust. "You cannot cut this," Sheikh says, disapprovingly pointing to the mangroves. "What is going on is the port is expanding that way and this whole area will be gone."

The mudbanks ooze mud. My sandals, the only ones I have packed, are covered in black coal dust. A man on a scooter is out along the horizon scavenging for steel instead of fish. A heron flaps behind him and heads skyward. Stagnant waterways are crossed by dirt roads protected by large concrete pipes. A lone hermit crab with one claw scuttles down a hole in the mud. There is something desolate about this area that was once a thriving local habitat.

Adani had been restrained from carrying out any construction activity back on 18 January 2016. It was a victory of sorts. But, since our visit, the future of the fisherfolk seems to have changed for the worse. Under Modi's reign, Adani's future seems ever brighter. In August 2017, five months after our visit, India's Ministry of Environment, Forest and Climate Change approved Terms of Reference (ToR) for the outer port expansion, giving Adani three years to prepare an environmental impact assessment.

The Gujarat Government has since allowed Adani to expand its Hazira Port. In February 2018, Adani won against another industrial Indian company, Essar, who had challenged Adani's expansion. In February 2018, the Center for Media and Democracy's Sourcewatch reported that Adani's website shows six berths in operation at Hazira Port: two for dry cargo, two for liquid cargo, and two for containers.[88] The port handles all types and grades of coal, including steam coal and coking coal, both imported and domestic. By 2020, should Adani successfully pass the environmental impact assessment, the company will be able to build 31 berths.

After the jubilation of the win through the National Green Tribunal, however, the future for this fishing community is even less certain now. More than a year after our visit to India, on 2 May 2018, according to *The Economic Times* and various other Indian media outlets, the Supreme Court set aside the National Green Tribunal order quashing the environmental clearance (EC) granted in 2013 to Adani-Hazira Port Pvt Ltd (AHPPL) for development of port activities at Surat. The court also directed that Rs 25 crore, which the AHPPL had deposited following the NGT's January 2016 order, be refunded to Adani. The order stated that the matter was settled between the parties and the fishermen had been paid adequate compensation.

Chapter 5
Confronting the God Adani

Ahmedabad is the obvious choice for Adani's HQ. Adani House is positioned almost halfway between Mundra, the home of Adani's coal-fired power plant we are yet to visit, and its port at Hazira. It is 16 March 2017. Tensions are high. There has been discussion in the car about how we will approach this climax to our visit. What kind of reception will we receive? Will we all take part? What if there are arrests? Are they expecting us? We've been told that almost as soon as we entered the country, God Adani would know of our presence and we would almost certainly be followed.

Six months after our visit, a *Four Corners* crew is detained and questioned by police in their hotel room. Our local crew on the ground who have set up interviews have been particularly discrete to make sure they are never photographed, and we have to be aware of this even when we do an occasional selfie and they are inadvertently in the background. The videographer has told us he cannot cover our arrival at Adani HQ as the company has already got into trouble filming elsewhere. We can fly back to our country. They live here.

Suddenly, as we are still discussing strategies, we drive past a building with white steel gates. The driver pulls over half a block away and we are all getting out. At the last moment, my concerns evaporate. It seems churlish to have been considering not participating. I am overwhelmed by the importance of what we are here to do.

Geoff Cousins, whose single-mindedness has helped focus us all, leads the delegation. With racing hearts, we squeeze behind him in single file past cars, motorbikes and scooters parked erratically on the side of the road walking back to Adani HQ on what should have been a footpath. In typical Indian style, hardly any footpath exists. Then we see the Indian media contingent: about 30-strong, some with large TV cameras at the ready focusing on the entrance to Adani HQ. Noticing our arrival, the media train their cameras on us as we go through the gate, past a security guard in khaki suit. We climb the dozen concrete steps at the entrance to the building. A siren eerily echoes off the many other skyscrapers crowding the street. Several other officials stand by. Cousins counsels that at all costs, we *must* stay inside the building to achieve our purpose. Unbelievably, no one stops us.

Inside the darkened interior, the receptionist at the large, polished desk is dwarfed by the vastness of the lobby. "No," she says politely. No one is expecting us. Cousins flourishes the Open Letter with around 90 signatories, signed, apart from the Chappells, by many other Australian luminaries including former Archibald prize winner artist Ben Quilty; Professor Terry Hughes; Pulitzer prize winner author Geraldine Brooks; Booker prize winner Richard Flanagan; twice Miles Franklin-winning author Tim Winton and former Greens Senator, Bob Brown. The letter urges Adani to abandon the Carmichael project.

"True," the letter reads, "the Queensland and Federal Governments are bending over backwards to fast-track this mine. True, they have changed water laws, stripped farmers of appeal rights, are attempting to change Native Title laws and have earmarked $1 billion of public money to build the rail line. But we urge you to think about global warming and public health and listen to the wishes of the people. It would be a great shame if this one project were to damage the image of India in Australia."

Cousins tells the receptionist, "We need someone – a company representative – to accept it."

Within a minute or two, as though by magic, a congenial businessman with an ample girth appears, all smiles. I duck to use the Adani toilet also off the lobby, stalling to see what will happen next. When I emerge, the same man is shaking everyone's hand

and introducing himself as Roy Paul, General Manager, Corporate Communications for Adani. He puts out his hand and accepts Cousin's offering to everyone's relief. He hands out his business card. Displaying years of perfecting confident handshakes, Cousins manages to find just the right blend of compliments and routine pleasantries. He receives an assurance from a still smiling Mr Paul that he will deliver the petition and letter to Gautam Adani. Then there is more grinning and chit-chat before we depart. We have been inside for perhaps ten minutes. Outside, the camera flashes pop. Cousins holds an impromptu media conference. The audacity of our move as we gather around him is beginning to sink in. Cousins is at his bristling best.

"We have just presented a letter to the Director of Corporate Communications for the Adani company which explains that nearly 100 very prominent Australians, including two former Australian cricket captains and many famous businessmen oppose the Adani coal mine in Australia, but it would very much support investment in renewable energy and clean energy."

"What is the basic problem you are facing in Australia?" asks a bemused Indian journalist.

"This will be the biggest coal mine ever built in Australia right next to the Great Barrier Reef ..." Cousins answers. "*The Lancet* published an article saying that they regarded the Adani coal mine as a serious risk to public health. India doesn't need more pollution. It needs less."

We all trot out our by now well-rehearsed takes on our purpose. I speak as a tourism operator and talk about the mind-blowing prospect that we will have no jobs and no reef if we continue mining fossil fuels and we are forced to confront more coral bleaching from global warming.

The Indian media contingent seem faintly incredulous as though they can't quite believe we have fronted up to God Adani Headquarters to have our say. A man cycling past, in a dark blue shirt and black pants, plastic bags swinging off his bike handles, gazes at us. He is in no hurry. Clearly captured by the street chaos, he exhibits the kind of Indian curiosity where time stands still. We are all still on edge. It is surreal; anti-climactic even. Where is the reaction we expected? The handcuffs? A prison cell?

A bare electric light bulb and interrogation followed by the expected official response to our incarceration from the Australian Government: "We cannot interfere with the laws of another country."

Windows from Adani's HQ hierarchy of floors look down on the street. Perhaps someone is using a long lens to identify us later when we will be pursued? After five long minutes of conducting media conferences outside the HQ, a man in a white shirt finally appears at the door waving angrily.

"You must not stand here. You must go."

Cousins briskly tugs at the lapels of his light-blue flecked jacket as though he has been awaiting this signal and heads off down the street. He is followed by a few of the TV cameramen. He looks, for all the world, like a character on set in a TV drama doing a major shoot.

Later, Cousins writing of the incident in a chapter in *The Coal Truth* by Greenpeace's CEO David Ritter (2018),[89] reveals that our ground crew had told us not to enter Adani HQ and especially not to convene a media conference outside. He had been told it was illegal to hold a media conference in the street and we could be arrested, or worse. One of the ground crew, Cousins wrote, when questioned if the security people were police or Adani security, had replied they are "one and the same."

And then, it is over. As we scramble into the car, an Indian man appears at the driver's window.

"Where is your hotel?" he asks.

Cousins tells him.

"Why did you tell him that?" Zethoven and I ask both panicked. "He's one of us, isn't he?"

"No," we chorus.

We drive swiftly to the hotel and begin packing even though we have booked for one more night. Now, though, moving hotels seems to be a good idea for other reasons. Cousins receives an update in the car. He has done a quick bit of research and deduced that Annastacia Palaszczuk and her entourage are arriving at Bhuj airport the following day for her visit to the Mundra power plant.

For days, we had been trying to work out the Premier's itinerary. After all, one of the objectives of our mission is to "create turbulence for politicians supporting the Adani coal mine" and to "disrupt the all-systems-go Adani mine's narrative of the Palaszczuk Government." But no one, even the most friendly of journalistic colleagues, is letting on where she might be. I am struck by how much the media's sense of duty nowadays seems to lie in protecting rather than interrogating the Government.

In 2008, I conducted a research project measuring the number and type of sources of news in two North Queensland newspapers: both Murdoch owned – *The Townsville Bulletin* and *The Cairns Post*. Almost half of the sources in news articles, randomly selected from that year's coverage in both newspapers, came from one level of government. Massaging the message is critical for every politician's wellbeing. Courting the journalists is part of that mission.

* * *

We leave Ahmedabad. By early evening, we are passing near the Rann of Kutch, about 270 kms west of Ahmedabad. Adani's port and power plant at Mundra is about 141 kms away on the coast. The darkening sky promises an impending storm. Wherever we look, massive pylons populate the landscape like alien beings. In between there are salt pans which lie like decimated white rice paddies. It is an arid land devoid of population reaching out to the Arabian Sea although ecologically important for local and migratory birds and home to the unique Indian Wild Ass. During the monsoon months this entire area is under water, which, in October, begins to recede. In between the salt pans are Hindu temples erected to honour one or another of the Gods.

The Little Rann of Kutch has been a traditional source of salt production for 600 years. Back in the days of British rule, it was used to partly fund the military expenses of the British Government. Around 75% of India's salt is generated in this area.[90] Children begin working there as young as ten years old. Like the camel owners and fish workers, they live in temporary shacks, using the traditional methods of their ancestors: raking the salt, sorting out the crystals which are worth more money and leaving them in piles to be collected later. Coal dust, however, contaminates the salt with toxins from the fly ash, we are later told, including mercury and arsenic. There are around 3000 salt panners who have continued the same ancestral tradition through the ages. They lease around three to five acres to dry out the salt for sale. Hearteningly, these salt panners have been helped by a partnership between a US based renewable energy company and the World Bank which has replaced 232 diesel pumps[91] with hybrid pumps that run on solar during the day and on diesel for four hours at night. This has halved the expenditure on diesel and increased the salt production by 15%. The solar panels have also greatly reduced the cost of electricity bills and there are plans afoot to increase the number of hybrid pumps.

Surprisingly, among the salt pans are multiple wind turbines. India only entered the wind power market in the 1990s. By the end of 2015, however, India had the fourth largest installed wind power capacity in the world, a tagline it continued through to 2017. That same year, renewable energy accounted for 18.37% of the country's total installed power capacity. Much of the country does not have an electrical grid, which is a perennial issue. One of the first applications of solar power has been for water pumping to begin replacing India's four to five million diesel powered water pumps.

By the end of October 2017, the total installed wind power capacity was 32.72 GW (Gigawatts). Wind power accounts for nearly 9.87% of India's total installed power generation capacity and generated 46,011 million KWh (Kilowatt hours) in the fiscal year 2016–17 which is nearly 3% of total electricity generation.

Even Adani has jumped on the solar bandwagon. Six months after our Indian visit, it opened what the company claims is the world's largest solar power plant in the southern Indian state of Tamil Nadu producing 648 MW (Megawatts) at a single location. Typically, again, however there has been criticism over the project reported in the Indian media[92] dating back to 2015 involving unfair land deals and media reports stating that Adani had assured it would provide jobs for locals, free water and electricity. The promises have reportedly not been kept. Instead, locals claimed the solar power plant was a 'water guzzler'[93] which was allegedly sourced from bore wells only five kilometres from the village without permission from district authorities who were also angry that Adani had allegedly signed a deal with the State Government to sell the power at a higher rate than could be found elsewhere. The taking of resources and upheaval of communities seem eerily familiar.

Back in Australia, Adani has declared it will build a solar plant in the heart of the Australian coal country – a 100–200 MW plant at Moranbah in Queensland's Bowen Basin. In its first phase, 65 MW of solar at this plant is said to be due for commissioning in October 2018, according to a tweet from Adani Australia.

* * *

Ironically, it was a Labor State Government aided by the Federal Liberal/National Party Coalition Government that helped pave the pathway for Adani to access Australian coal.

Annastacia Palaszczuk was a junior minister to Premier Anna Bligh in 2009 in the early days of Adani's courtship. Her father had been Minister for Primary Industries in Queensland. She was also adviser to the Minister for Resources, David Beddall, from 1991 to 1995 and worked on Tony Blair's 1996 campaign after receiving an academic scholarship. She is the thirty-ninth Premier of Queensland. Between 1998 and 2006, she was Senior

Ministerial Advisor to former Premier Peter Beattie when the then Premier's portfolio included Mines and Energy as well as the Environment. In 2006, Palaszczuk entered parliament and from 2009 held various portfolios under Bligh. In 2012, when Bligh was overwhelmingly defeated by Campbell Newman's LNP (Liberal National Party), Palaszczuk was one of only three surviving members of Bligh's cabinet. She announced she would stand as a candidate for the head of Queensland Labor and thereby as Leader of the Opposition. After that defeat in 2012, no one had expected Labor to win the next election. But win they did. In 2015, Palaszczuk was thrust into the role of Premier following the resounding defeat of her opponent, then Premier Campbell Newman. She became the first woman in Australia to take a party from opposition into government.

Politics is in her blood. Her father Henry Palaszczuk, who was born in Germany to Polish parents, was a veteran State MP. Her father's announcement that he would be retiring at the 2006 election prompted her to join the ranks of politicians. She had been studying to become a solicitor. Instead, she stood and won her father's former seat in Inala, a suburb in south-west Brisbane, then considered to be the safest Labor seat in Queensland. In 2015, one of her first commitments as Premier was to return to "core Labor principles," which included "worker's rights, *protecting the environment* and investment in education" (my emphasis).

I had met Annastacia Palaszczuk once before back in October 2016. Her chosen venue for the launch of the Whitsunday Community Cabinet meeting was the Cruise Whitsunday's arrival hall at Port of Airlie in the Whitsundays. Turquoise and pastel giant-sized photographs of turtles and white sands in aqua-blues flank the walls offering the kind of welcome you might expect from a gateway to the Great Barrier Reef. I'd spent the afternoon at Proserpine State School in a lacklustre hall where state politicians shuffled papers, tried not to look bored while feigning concern about their role as one of the caretakers of the world's largest living organism.

At the launch that evening, Palaszczuk told the enthusiastic crowd of tourism operators and businesses that the reef was her passion. To prove it, she pointed out that she had, in 2015, even appointed a Great Barrier Reef Minister, Steven Miles, adding this title to Minister for National Parks. Her government, she claimed, had done more to protect the reef than any other government. It was, and still is, one of her favourite phrases. Behind her, a dazzling photograph of the reef lit up like the super imposed screen behind a nightly television newsreader lending her a *faux* authority to speak for the reef itself. The mostly local crowd nodded as she spun the rhetoric. "In fact, tourism is worth more than $3 billion to the Mackay and Whitsunday region and supports more than 13,000 jobs," she cooed.

I wanted to shout out loud: "And you are doing your utmost to wreck those jobs by soliciting the building of Australia's largest coal mine with an ultimate 4.6 billion tonne carbon footprint!"

As I scanned the crowd that evening, no one else appeared to mirror my angst.

During the canapés of prawns and calamari, I had spied Steven Miles, a fresh-faced, amiable youngish punter, then still in his 30s, entrusted with the care of the reef itself. Miles' PhD thesis was on union renewal but he had listed, on the parliamentary website, the Australian Conservation Foundation as one of his community group memberships. I also discovered that in 2007, he had joined Al Gore's Climate Leadership Program.

I began by asking him what his job as the Great Barrier Reef Minister entailed.

Part of the art of the journalist is, of course, to open with what in the trade is described as 'icebreakers' to encourage interviewees to reveal information. No one blurts out the truth without some prompting. Steven Miles has an undergraduate degree in Political Science and Journalism. I began to relay my personal story, telling him of witnessing at first hand the corals beginning to disappear on Magnetic Island, albeit through dredging, but nevertheless man-made, and the effect it had on our business.

"... it is evidence you see every day that the coral may never come back," I finished.

Miles shifted uneasily. Statistics are the province of politicians. Anecdotal talk backed by personal experience is harder to combat. It has the potential to make politicians uncomfortable. Perhaps as a former journalism graduate he sympathised or maybe he had been exposed to some good sources on climate change?

I came in for the kill.

"Why then is this Government pursuing this coal mine that has the capacity to kill the Great Barrier Reef? How could your Government consciously do this?"

"The only person who can answer that," he said looking swiftly around to ensure no one is eavesdropping, "is ... "

His head gestures towards the podium where Palaszczuk is standing with her trademark red lipstick smiling in that lopsided, amiable way of hers for a crowd of admiring locals. According to Madonna King writing in *The Sydney Morning Herald*'s *Good Weekend* in April 2015 shortly after Palaszczuk's appointment as Premier, she had been told by her offsiders to smile because when she forgot, her brow furrowed and her voice lacked authority making her sound "unsure, nervous even."

King quoted Palaszczuk: "There were a few people saying, 'Just keep smiling ... everything lights up when you smile'."[94]

I headed for the podium.

Relaying the same story, she displayed the attentive look cultivated by politicians, lots of eye contact and that same smile, brown eyes warm and inviting.

"What I can't understand ... have been really trying to understand," I said, "is how you can give such overwhelming support for a mine that, according to an Adani representative in the Land and Environment Court, is only going to provide 1454 jobs. The 10,000 jobs is a lie that came from Tony Abbott when he was Prime Minister and has been repeated by many other politicians including the current Prime Minister, Malcolm Turnbull. There's never been anything to back that up."

The look that crossed Palaszczuk's face truly surprised me. Her jaw literally dropped. Her eyes widened. In keeping with the poker face of a journalist, I quickly hid my astonishment. She didn't know? Surely, she can't act that well?

"What do you mean?" she blurted.

"The mine isn't going to save regional Queenslanders by providing jobs. That number is on the record from the Adani company itself. It's going to destroy 69,000 jobs in Queensland tourism largely created because of the Great Barrier Reef."

Half an hour later Palaszczuk's entourage was leaving. A woman who had been standing nearby when I was talking to Palaszczuk approached me. I had presumed she was with the Premier's entourage.

"You don't understand," she said hurriedly. "What these media people tell her – they give her figures ... and she has to rely on these ..."

I found out that six months earlier, upon announcing her Government approving the three Adani mining leases, Palaszczuk had told the *Brisbane Times* that the leases had undergone "extensive government and community scrutiny" and were a step towards creating jobs in the region outlining that Adani had estimated more than 5000 jobs during construction and a further 4000 during the operation of the project.[95] And this from a Government that had invoked a critical infrastructure status to fast track the mine (this status had never before been bestowed on a Queensland mining project) which involved less public scrutiny. According to the ABC, in an article published in December 2017, out of ten personal meetings with the Premier, six of these meetings were with lobbyists pushing the Adani cause.[96]

* * *

Early the following morning, on 17 March we leave our accommodation in Bhuj. Cousins and Zethoven have bought plane tickets. The plan is for them to enter the airport at the same time as the Premier's arrival, ostensibly to board a plane they will never fly in. Currie and I (the backup team) are to wait outside in the airport car park just in case. The project reminds me of my police reporting days from two decades ago. Back then, I would crouch behind a hedge during a police siege having been tipped off on the old police radio. Or, in those highly charged days at the beginning of my career when writing my first book, *Brothers in Arms*, I would slip into jails dressed as a bikie moll with my co-author and best friend, the late Sandra Harvey, to meet with the Bandidos. Once, heavily pregnant with twins, I sat with a photographer outside a funeral parlour for five hours having been told the business transported bodies through the adjoining restaurant. Here I was back on the beat.

In the airport car park, a few souls loiter. Most of the business, however, is happening inside the terminal itself. There is a buzz of expectancy as they await the arrival of such a senior politician from Australia. Cousins and Zethoven, pushing small carry-on bags, have already entered the airport.

Typically, as this is a breaking story, as I have learned over the years, things do not go according to plan. For a start, the arrival lounge is segregated from the departures hall. Zethoven and Cousins are physically cut off from the Premier. Outside, musicians in maroon waistcoats and orange turbans are beginning to assemble. Trumpets and the steady beat of a drum pick up in tempo heralding her arrival. A pull up banner proclaiming the Adani logo is on display.

I text Zethoven. Within minutes she and Cousins are outside the terminal. The videographer then takes my phone. We have long ago decided that his SLR camera will not be useful for sending immediate footage. He can easily be anonymous among the crowd. Currie has had issues with his phone ever since we arrived in India. We now have no communication.

Palaszczuk, it is clear, is to receive a welcome fit for royalty.

The automatic doors of the arrivals hall open. A number of dark-suited men emerge first past the musicians. Leading them is a smooth-looking western man – model material – wearing Maui

Jim sunglasses, a light blue shirt and what looks like Moleskins. He scans the crowd expertly. Photographer and journalists mill around waiting. Another Indian man, who looks like an Adani PR representative, also strolls out. Imogen Zethoven later identifies him as an Adani official in public relations. The Premier is immediately behind this man. The Australian entourage has been stamped with a dark red spot in the third eye. Palaszczuk, dressed in a white jacket and black slacks, looks relaxed. The television cameras begin dutifully rolling. Flanked by Jenny Hill, Mayor of Townsville, on one side and Andrew Wilcox, Mayor of the Whitsundays, on the other, Palaszczuk's smile lengthens. The drummers' beat quickens. Like the soundscape from an E.M. Forster movie about India, the drums become wilder and wilder until the drummer is in a frenzy. Mr PR Adani permits himself a small smile. The trumpet whines like a petulant child to a crescendo. Then abruptly it is all over. The Premier walks in that long-strided way of hers to a waiting black minivan. 'Adani 1' on an A4 page is posted on the back. The media gather around the van expectantly.

What a wonderful welcome it has been, says Palaszczuk now looking a little less prepared, and a little less confident. How proud she is, she tells the crowd, that her regional mayors have travelled so far to be here. She is here, she adds, to look at the port and focus on solar and agriculture. There is no mention of coal or the Mundra power plant.

In a Government statement released on 18 March 2017, she says that the purpose of her visit is all about going to the Mundra port, inspecting Adani's solar panel plant and "much of the 40 km coastline of the port which still has the capacity to increase its current dock facility tenfold in an effort to meet the growing needs of India's middle class." No mention of a marine sanctuary and the coral reefs just offshore and the effect of this expansion. Oh, and chickpeas. Apparently the Premier and her Mayors had flown a quarter of the way around the world to "help Queensland famers to identify the right locations to grow the right crops to feed this enormous population."[97]

Why the media release did not once mention the lucrative Adani coal deal with the mining leases already signed by the Queensland Government begs to be answered. Perhaps it was because the headlines about our visit to Adani HQ have already done the global media circuit.

"What are you hoping to achieve?" one of the media contingent probes her uncertainty.

"Well ..." Palaszczuk begins, "from my point of view I want to see the port operations. I want to see exactly how the results ... of agriculture and solar can benefit Queensland, but fundamentally this is purely about jobs for Queenslanders. There is nothing more important. I am not going to shy away from my commitment and my determination to do whatever it takes to get the jobs that regional Queensland wants."

Cousins and I have meanwhile positioned ourselves at the minivan door.

"Good morning Premier," Cousins quickly introduces himself. "I think you know why we are here ... I hope you saw the letter that we sent." Palaszczuk acknowledges this and Cousins adds in a quiet voice "that's good ..."

"Good morning Premier ..." I introduce myself, "... you mentioned jobs ... there are 69,000 jobs in tourism and you are single-handedly, along with the Federal Government, wrecking the reef and those jobs."

She arcs, slightly smiling whether she recognises me or not. The smile harbours annoyance.

"There's no greater supporter of the Great Barrier Reef than me and my Government," she responds.

"The Adani coal mine puts the reef at risk ... that's the problem," adds Cousins smiling wryly.

"And you are single-handedly, along with other levels of Government, destroying the Great Barrier Reef," I add.

Zethoven has appeared by our side. "And the Adani mine does put the reef at risk which has already suffered two back-to-back bleaching events ..."

"All of you have jobs ... and there are regional Queenslanders that are fighting for jobs," Palaszczuk raises her arm and clenches her fist dramatically for emphasis.

"I'm a regional Queenslander but I don't know how long I'll have my job," I say. "How many jobs will be offered by Adani?"

"Ten thousand regional jobs," she begins turning to the waiting car.

"Rubbish ..." I say.

"Absolute rubbish," we chorus. A packet of potato crisps is wedged in the back between the two seats. A snack for the Premier on her way to the power plant. Then she is off.

We begin to walk back to our car. Moments later Imogen Zethoven calls out. Her mobile phone is missing from her handbag. I immediately call her phone. It rings out. Then Cousins calls it. This time the phone is switched off.

Everything is on her phone. Her entire life. She is aghast. A crack has shattered the promise of the morning. For several days after this, Zethoven is unable to regularly contact her office, without any of her contacts in a country far away from home. The last time she had seen the phone was inside the airport terminal when she was with Cousins. The last text she received was from me suggesting they move outside. She uses my phone to inform her office of the missing phone.

But we have footage. Back at the hotel in Bhuj, Zethoven and I scan the footage from the videographer as soon as we are able. Zethoven identifies the 'PR man' I had noticed and reveals that his name is 'Raj'. She says she had an encounter with him shortly before the trip to India after a public debate on Adani organised by *The Courier Mail*, a Queensland Murdoch-owned daily Brisbane newspaper, at the Brisbane Powerhouse. Raj, she said, had been quite hostile to her after she had mistaken him for Adani's CEO Jeyakumar Janakaraj and had accused her of being racist, claiming she believed all Indians looked the same. She had seen him for the first time since that incident at the airport when she was with Cousins. He had been charming, welcoming her and Cousins, whom she introduced, to India.

The videographer had begun filming from the moment Palaszczuk left the arrival hall. We watch the Indian band assemble and play. There are several people in the entourage including Blue Shirt. The crowd begins to move toward the black minivan and the impending media conference once the band finishes. Cousins and I move slightly off to the left towards the door of the minivan. Zethoven is standing far over to our right. As is her custom from years of travelling, her right hand protectively cradles her small black handbag slung over her left shoulder, which contains her phone. Then she looks behind her, presumably for us. Two western men are close to her. Raj is standing away from the crowd watching what is going on from the sidelines. One of the men is Blue Shirt who is behind her and the other a nondescript, grey-haired man with a slight middle-aged spread, old-fashioned glasses and the kind of finely-checked shirt you would find at a cheap department store. There is ample time to slow down the action. Checked Shirt appears to have arrived with the Premier and another woman in her early forties with pale shoulder length grey/blonde hair. Both look like archetypal public servants.

The action unfolds in less than a minute as Cousins and I wait at the minivan to begin firing questions at the Premier. Zethoven is still at the other end of the minivan when Checked Shirt turns a full 360 degrees around to face her, a strange manoeuvre given that he is looking straight at the crowd and everyone else is looking at the Premier about to give her media conference. Checked Shirt then turns back full circle to face the Premier before bending down and fumbling with his bag on the ground. Blue Shirt is behind off to her left. Behind Zethoven is John McCarthy, a journalist with *The Courier Mail*. Zethoven had met McCarthy when she took part in the same panel hosted by his newspaper where she had met Raj. As Zethoven realises that Cousins and I are closing in for the kill, she squeezes quite close past Blue Shirt to head for the other end of the minivan to get closer to us. Checked Shirt then abruptly leaves the crowd passing behind the Premier's vehicle to the other side of the van where the sliding door is open. Then we have the exchange with the Premier. There had been a space of around 15 minutes between when Zethoven last used her phone and discovered it was missing. No one has been captured on the video footage (the critical time between her last using it and finding it missing) taking her phone. Zethoven filed a Police Report at the Bhuj police station that afternoon and bought another phone.

On 21 March 2017, after arriving back in Australia, John McCarthy emailed Imogen Zethoven to request an interview about the Indian trip. She replied a few days later saying she has been delayed in getting back to him as her phone had been stolen. His response was completely unexpected. McCarthy tells her that her phone was found in the Hyatt Hotel in Mumbai, 859 kms away from Bhuj, where the Queensland delegation had been staying as well as John McCarthy himself. He had thought Zethoven was also staying there. There was no SIM card inside the phone. The reason he knew this, he explained to Zethoven, is that he had been the last one to text her after the arrival at Bhuj airport, as he wanted to interview her about the Indian trip. When someone from the hotel staff opened the phone he presumed that his name had appeared on the last text. The hotel staff had then contacted him thinking he might know the owner. McCarthy also told Zethoven that Blue Shirt was a police officer.

While it is not unexpected for a head of state to spend money on security, the cost of protective security for Palaszczuk's 11-day Indian trip from Queensland police which included visiting Singapore and the UK is on the record as AU$38,168 with three Senior Constables and one Sergeant from the Counter-Terrorism and Major Events Command.

* * *

We made the ABC news that night on 16 March 2017. Our confrontation made the front page of *The Times of India, The Economic Times, Hindustan Times* and a multitude of smaller newspapers throughout India as well as the ABC, *The Australian,* the regional Queensland Dailies, *The Townsville Bulletin* and *The Guardian.* My local newspaper, *The Whitsunday Times,* recently taken over by Murdoch, ignored the story. The video footage of the ambush of Annastacia Palaszczuk at the beginning of her Indian tour was shown through most of the coverage. Even my cousin in Singapore saw us on the news. The world was watching. Why are Australian Governments threatening the existence of the Great Barrier Reef? And why are they so keen on coal?

Chapter 6
The Coal King of the World

Mundra Port is the largest private port in India and is built on the northern shore of the Gulf of Kutch. Mundra is where Gautam Adani "really made his money," Tim Buckley, Sydney-based Director of Institute for Energy Economics and Financial Analysis (IEEFA) told the *Good Weekend* Magazine in November 2017.[98] It was Adani's foothold in Mundra, "the lynchpin of his empire" that transformed him into a billionaire "off the back of enormous social inequality," Buckley had said.

Back in August 1995, Adani had been granted clearance to handle general cargo, including LPG, and a chemical storage terminal when the Gujarat Maritime Board approved setting up a jetty at the Port of Mundra. By 1997–98, Adani, who had been importing plastic granules for his brother's plastic-film manufacturing business, decided to move beyond trading into infrastructure. Mundra Port was his first project. The 3000 acres of coastal land had been given to agribusiness group Cargill and Adani for salt production with a jetty at Mundra.

However, according to an article about Gautam Adani in the Indian magazine *Outlook Business* in 2013 entitled 'The Alchemist',[99] the deal fell through and Cargill backed out. But at the beginning it provided motivation for Adani to get into ports. Liberalisation had started and the Gujarat Government was privatising the ports as a joint venture with the state. Mundra, according to *The Economic Times of India*, was Adani's "heart and soul ... When he was nothing, this is where he started from." The article went on to say that by 2016, Adani had "a string of ten ports on the Indian eastern and western coastlines."[100]

Back in 1998, the first small tanker had been anchored in the Mundra port. In 1999, the Gujarat Government had released its manifesto on the industrialisation of Gujarat, focusing on building port infrastructure in 1995. Adani ventured into coal trading. The coal would land at Mundra. At this stage, he had no experience at "building anything, not even a simple building, let alone a port," Adani revealed to *Outlook Business* Magazine in 2013. In 2000, the Government granted clearance for a port expansion project including a railway line. Adani had focused on this critical part of the development encouraging private-public partnerships, which allowed ports to connect to the national railway grid.

But Mundra was destined to be far more than a port. As I noted earlier, in 2003, it became India's first multi-product port-based special economic zone (SEZ). In 2001, Narendra Modi had been made Chief Minister of Gujarat. Adani had the ability to import coal at his doorstep and it was then that he began his dream of thermal power generation.

In January 2012, the Mundra Port SEZ became known as Adani Ports and Special Economic Zone Limited (APSEZ). By the following year, the APSEZ averaged an operating margin of 71%. Three different components, the SEZ, the Port and the Power project took up approximately 6300 hectares of land according to then PhD Candidate with the Centre for Studies in Science Policy in New Delhi, Manju Menon.

In 2006, Adani entered the power generation business. At this time, the company was already the largest trader and importer of coal in India, as well as operating the country's largest private port, Adani told *Outlook Magazine* in 2013. In 2009, in keeping with 'Gujarat being open for business', the entire area was declared an SEZ, exempting it from all taxes, levies and trade duties. Adani's proposed waterfront development seemed to have a life of its own expanding the whole idea of just a port. In 2013, Adani put in an application for a ship-recycling facility on land dredged near its port at Mundra. At a public meeting, Adani was accused of supplying false information in its Environment Impact Assessment

(EIA) by stating there were no schools within a five-kilometre radius of the project.[101] Adani denied the shipyard had anything to do with the Mundra SEZ, but said it was "part of a waterfront development plan" which had been cleared in 2009.[102]

Alarmingly, the proposed ship recycling unit, at that time, was to dismantle and break up ships weighing 4000 to 16,000 tonnes – across the road from one of India's largest marine sanctuaries – and the facility included a beaching and storage area for steel, machinery and electrical items. Concern was raised about the dangerous substances coming from older ships such as asbestos. In October 2016, according to *Scroll* Magazine,[103] senior ministry officials began asking questions about Adani's requested environmental clearance for the shipbreaking yard with an investment of Rs 146.8 crore. By May 2017, the ministry was processing environmental clearance for the shipbreaking yard after an expert panel allegedly 'gave a nod' to the project according to *Scroll*. In June 2017, APSEZ was given approval, according to *LiveMint* which confirmed this with APSEZ.[104]

It further added: "The beaching method of breaking ships practised along a 12-km stretch of Alang-Sosiya – hundreds of nautical miles away from Mundra Port – is often criticized for its lax safety and health aspects. Under the beaching method, which has been heavily criticized, ships are first grounded during high tide and then dismantled, posing hazards to workers and the environment."

One recent *Reuters/gCaptain* News Report in May 2018 stated that 543 of the 835 large oceangoing ships were intentionally run ashore and dismantled by hand at shipbreaking yards in Bangladesh, India and Pakistan which has resulted in many deaths and created environmental hazards.[105]

It was not just the SEZ that helped Adani. In 2005, the Indian Government had pushed through a slogan: 'Power for All by 2012' launching an initiative to build coal-based Ultra Mega Power Plants (UMPPs), each of minimum 4000 MW capacity. These UMPPs were to rely on imported coal, mostly from Indonesia, to fire them. Adani lost out to Tata Power when the UMPP (the first in India) was built next door in Mundra, but Adani shrewdly offered his neighbour his dedicated coal handling import terminal to feed Tata's UMPP.[106]

The Adani company had in the meantime built a 4620 MW coal-fired power plant in 2013, according to the *Business Standard*, which sold coal-fired electricity to Gujarat and another Indian state, Haryana.[107] Tata Power had a 4000 MW power plant in 2013 and sells coal to Gujarat, Rajasthan, Punjab, Haryana and Maharashtra. Tata bragged on its website that it had "the most energy efficient coal based-thermal power plant in the country with lower greenhouse gas emissions stating the power plant would fill 2% of India's power needs."

Indonesian coal primarily fires their power plants from a mine in Bunyu Island under a 15-year fuel supply agreement followed by a final phase, which imports coal from the Mahanadi coalfields in Odisha, India. Adani's journey to capture one of the world's coal resources dates back to 2010. At the same time as Adani signed up to acquire Linc Energy's coal assets in Australia, the company also signed a US$1.65 billion deal with the Indonesian Government and its mining company PT Bukit Asam to set up rail and port infrastructure in Bukit Asam in south Sumatra to access coal to be exported to India, according to an article in the Indian online magazine *LiveMint*.[108] In return, according to the article, Adani had exclusive rights to more than 60% of the coal from the province. At the time, the coal reserves in Indonesia were said to be ramped up to 60 million tonnes in the next few years, around the same output as Adani had initially forecast for the Carmichael mine per year.

More than 66% of India's electricity is from thermal power plants and about 57% is from coal-based power plants. The majority of the coal from the Carmichael mine in Australia, should it go ahead, is supposedly destined to come to Mundra as these two Indian power plants predominantly rely on imported coal.

Mundra is the largest of four thermal coal-fired power plants owned by Adani Power.

When interviewed by *Outlook Magazine* in 2013, it became clear, however, that Gautam Adani understood the perilous position private power stations might find themselves in because of their reliance on imported coal. Adani was clearly frustrated by the then Indian Government. At a time before Modi was Prime Minister, Gautam Adani told the Magazine that the government should have "cohesive policies" as it relied on private organisations to provide the coal. "That is also the reason why we acquired mines in Indonesia and Australia," he confided.

The question of accessing the coal and dealing with 'environment issues' was risky, he said: "What no one realises is that we are heading into a scenario where beyond four or five quarters, equity component of most private power projects will be wiped out. Are we saying that banks, which have a chunk of loans on their books, will run the show? Ultimately, is the consumer benefitting?"

As to who is funding many of these projects, a 2016 Report entitled 'Coal Currency Mapping Coal Project Finances in India' by the Centre for Financial Accountability, contends that international financial institutions contribute around 11% of the funds. Most of these institutions came from Asia, the Report stated, with the China Development Bank the largest investor in the sector.

In 2017, Adani's prescient comment in 2013 forecasting the precarious fate of Indian power plants when he granted the interview to *Outlook Magazine* came to fruition. In April 2017, only a month after our visit to India, a decision by the Supreme Court reversed the fate of the coal-fired power plants touted as the biggest not only in India but the world. The cost of Indonesian coal had soared. The court quashed Adani and Tata's plea to increase their agreed electricity tariff to compensate for escalations in Indonesian coal costs, which according to some newspaper reports, Adani relied upon for 60% of its fuel requirements. However, according to the *Business Standard*, the court did allow hikes in coal prices arising out of changes from Indian law.[109]

During the writing of this book both Tata and Adani offered to sell majority stakeholdings in each of their Mundra power plants to the state of India for one rupee citing that the power plants were unviable given the price of the imported coal. This sale never gained traction with the financial markets speculating each plant had a negative value of as much as $US1 billion according to Tim Buckley. One newspaper stated that Adani was transferring the 4620 MW plant to its newly created subsidiary for an equity value of Rs 406 crore compared to the Rs 6000 crore the company had invested in the project.

Adani, in the meantime, has other plans for Mundra. In April 2017, *The Economic Times of India* reported that the Adani Group was working on an LNG terminal that will have an initial annual capacity of 5 million tonnes a year. It is also working on a 1.6 million tonne LPG import terminal. The project cost of the LNG import terminal is estimated to be about Rs 4500 crore. And according to a *Business Standard* in December 2017, Tata had recently bought a coal mining licence in Far East Russia.

* * *

We arrive in Mundra deep in the heart of enemy territory. Our ground crew point out the barbed wire fences of the Adani SEZ delineating the Adani empire. After the trip to Adani HQ and the disappearance of Imogen Zethoven's phone, everyone is a little on edge. On the horizon, the stark chimneys that outline the power plant reach boldly to the sky.

According to the environmental activists we later interview in New Delhi who have spent time in Mundra: "You will not usually see smoke – it's more like invisible smoke from Tata's power plant. Where the Adani stacks are, though, you always find brown smoke which means that the particle emission is much higher in Adani's power plant." In spite of them being allowed entry to Tata's power plant, they told us that Adani had reportedly refused them access.

In a drab hotel lounge room heavily screened by thick brown curtains in Mundra, we watch as a group of dedicated Indian environmentalists project satellite images of the drastically changed Mundra coastline following the building of the Adani coal-fired thermal power plant[110] and later Tata's. Bharat Patel is the moustached Senior Program Manager for Environmental Justice who has lived in this area for 16 years. He has been an active campaigner against the environmental issues at Mundra and is general-secretary of MASS (Machimar Adhikar Sangharsh Sangathan), the trade union affiliated with the National Fish-worker Forum.

In 2009, the Ministry of Environment and Forests' Expert Appraisal Committee (EAC) for Infrastructure Development, Coastal Regulation Zone which reviews applications for environmental clearances of SEZs, granted Adani an exemption from holding public hearings for the development of Mundra SEZ according to Manju Menon, PhD Candidate at the Centre for Studies in Science Policy in New Delhi. Similarly, the Queensland Government, by invoking critical infrastructure capabilities to the Adani project, the first to be granted to a private project,[111] was also able to fast track without sufficient public scrutiny decisions made about the mine.

Menon writes that in 2008 Adani had been seeking environment clearance for a Waterfront Development Project (WDP) which, according to a Centre for Environment Education Report (CEE)[112] would be part of the SEZ and include 55 berths including the existing 12; four port clusters: West, South, North and East; a Liquefied Natural Gas terminal, two shipyards, three desalination plants, and a road and rail network. The associated ship traffic from these ports in 2013 was forecast to total 1520 per year. The capacity of the desalination plant is 300 million litres per day and almost 1.5 times this capacity is discharged into the sea as saline water. "It was ironic," writes Menon, "and very obvious to the people who had gathered for the public hearing held for the WDP in November 2008, that the company would have its way, legally or otherwise." The public meeting was only the second meeting, Menon writes, that Adani had had in the decade it had been involved in expansion at Mundra.[113] Menon notes that the formation of MASS was "a milestone in the trajectory of local action against the corporatisation of this coast."

As general secretary of MASS, Bharat Patel has devoted much of his time to this project. He shows us a 2013 report into the Adani Port and SEZ commissioned by the Ministry of Environment and Forests from the Centre for Science and Environment. Patel is a researcher canvassing different people's views: fishermen, pastoralists, salt panners, and farmers. We drink hot, sweet chai out of a pot. The images he shows clearly tell the story of the Adani expansion in Mundra and how a group of committed environmentalists helped the fisherworkers with their rights: forming a co-op to deal with the issue of the quality of the fish being reduced from companies like Tata and Adani polluting the oceans. We are also introduced to Gajendrasinh Bhimaji Jadeja. He is a Sarpanch at the young age of 30: an elected chief of the village. Jadeja wears the well-earned badge of honour of being the only individual to successfully take on three court actions against Adani. We are invited to his nearby village to find out more.

The group has obtained satellite images from Google Earth and the National Remote Sensing Centre. In 2000, giant sand dunes fill the image before us. Creeks flow into the Arabian Sea. One of the most prominent features of this part of the Mundra Coast, the CEE Report states, is the vast intertidal zone comprising a network of creeks, estuaries and mudflats. It is the intertidal zone that has supported the fishing families for centuries – the area between the low and high tide – that used to occupy an area of 8–20 kms and used to be "an immense area to fish in." The Gulf of Kutch, it notes, is one of the few coastal zones in the world to have such rich biodiversity. But by the new millennium, the natural beauty of the area was in grave danger. After 2001, when an agreement was signed with the Gujarat Maritime Board (GMB) to develop the port and then, in 2002, another company signed up to handle crude oil out of the port, the Mundra SEZ was incorporated. Eventually, the port and its associated development would end up consuming 60 kms of coastland.

Gujarat has the longest coastline in India – approximately 1914 kms – a similar length to Australia's Great Barrier Reef Marine Park. The Gulf of Kutch is India's first Indian Marine Wildlife Sanctuary and one of the few places in India with live coral. Since 1991, coral reefs and mangroves in the region have been afforded the highest protection according to a case study[114] into the park. It was officially declared a Marine National Park in 1982. Covering an area of 458 square kilometres, it has 42 tropical islands offshore. It is home to around 1500 marine and coastal species with 49 species of hard corals, 23 species of soft corals, 70 species of sponges, 421 species of fish, 27 species of prawns, 30 species of crabs, 199 species of molluscs, 16 species of echinoderms, 172 species of bird, three species of sea mammals, six species of mangroves, and three species of sea turtles, 108 species of brown, green and red algae, and about 136 different creeks. There is a plethora of marine life including sea horses and dugongs and four types of large whales.

Two weeks before our visit to Gujarat, *LiveMint*, an Indian online newspaper, detailed the decay of the coral pointing out that the dead coral now "outnumbered the live ones."[115] These corals were given the highest degree of protection under the 1991 Coastal Regulation Zone legislation. The journalist noted that the intrusions of the SEZs (ports, oil pipelines, and industrial expansion) were "corroding the vast seabed, affecting the lives of millions of tiny creatures and microorganisms." The Adani and Tata Mundra Ports lie directly across the Gulf of Kutch from the marine park. The case study into the park notes: "The rampant industrialisation threatens the sensitive marine ecology" blaming the lack of political opposition to the "single-minded drive towards industrialisation in Gujarat" as well as overlapping accountability in various government regulatory bodies. The coastline is now the site of giant petroleum- and petrochemical-based industry. According to one report, 70% of

India's crude import from this industry is expected to take place through the Gulf of Kutch.

"Now look at this," Patel says, putting up slide after slide showing the port, a darkened area on the satellite image, reaching out into the ocean. By 2008, the coastline had irrevocably changed. The last slide in 2013 is of an industrial wasteland. The sand dunes have merged into vast cleared areas of land.

"Slowly it's destroyed," he says, his words hang in the air. There is silence in the motel room.

Patel confirms that 65–75% of all of the ships that import crude oil into India come into the Gulf of Kutch. "There are now so many ports and so many power projects in the gulf. Turbidity is very high and the acidity fluctuates and slowly the coral is dying."

Untreated effluents from industries along the coast have directly challenged the reef-building corals. In 2015, an Ecosystem Health Report Card for the Marine Park by the Gujarat Ecology Commission identified pollution as one of the leading factors in the degradation of the marine habitat.

When the *LiveMint* journalist visited the islands off the Gulf of Kutch he saw "heavy sediment deposits choking the coral reefs across the shoreline of all three islands." He saw green turtles stranded on a sediment-coated reef – the Gujarat beaches are breeding grounds – and a baby reef shark was struggling to stay alive. Meanwhile if you google the official Gujarat tourism website, you will see flashes of colourful pictures of coral and anemones across its home page promoting weekend getaways and homestays. Nothing about the decay.

Since arriving in Mundra, all we have seen is dusty roads and industrialisation similar to other landscapes we have passed on this journey. I had no idea that just offshore was the same kind of magical underwater world we have back home spilling with coral and fish and creatures of the sea. How could our politicians be so gullible as to actively court one of the main polluters who has already, along with other industries, destroyed a marine environment that will more than likely never recover? I have a sinking feeling that we are watching our own future. The Adani Group has first hand experience of what exactly it means to destroy a coastline and its unique marine habitat. Like the east coast of Australia, particularly across the length of the Great Barrier Reef, Gujarat too battles with the number of ports bringing with it a corresponding increase in pollution. Gujarat has the highest number of ports in India and is estimated to be handling 39% of the country's total national cargo.

Why did our politicians not know of this before courting disaster?

* * *

And it has not been for the want of trying. The APSEZ was legally challenged soon after it began construction at Mundra. Following a tour of the site by the then Minister for Environment and Forests in 2010 and after complaints from environmentalists, a Committee was set up. The chair was Sunita Narain, an Indian activist and environmentalist who is Director General of the India-based Research Institute the Centre for Science and Environment, a non-profit public interest and advocacy group, and editor of *Down to Earth*. In 2016, she was named as *Time Magazine's* 100 Most Influential People. Narain also appeared with Leonardo DiCaprio in the documentary *Before the Flood* that explored the impact of climate change on the monsoon in India.

The Report, which Patel shows us in detail, outlines the many examples of the Adani company's alleged violations as well as its non-compliance with environmental conditions. The Committee found that after the port was built, there were "massive ecological changes in the landscape of the Adani Port and SEZ area including changes to the many creeks which fed into the area." It showed how the company allegedly bypassed "the statutory procedures, by using different agencies, at the Centre and State, for obtaining clearances for the same project." The company also bypassed public hearing procedures allowing little say over how it expanded its operations. There had been no environmental clearance, for example, for the construction of the Adani airstrip and aerodrome. The report claimed there had been mass destruction of mangroves and levelling of sand dunes with mangroves destroyed during the laying of pipelines for the oil terminal. Nor, the report suggested, was the distribution of fly ash sufficiently monitored to counteract local air pollution and land degradation. Salinity was another issue, with the Report noting that the environmental conditions imposed on Adani included that there was to be "no withdrawal of water during and after construction." No monitors had been installed to monitor groundwater. Adani has denied it had violated any clearances.

The Committee recommended that an Environment Restoration Fund (about 1% of the total cost of the project) be imposed on Adani which was to be used for the protection of marine ecology; mangroves, restoration of creeks as well as funding independent studies and, importantly, monitoring the Adani expansion and providing social infrastructure and support for fisher communities as well as assisting them to access their fishing grounds. Any funds should also be used for a voluntary return of grazing land to improve the productivity of the land. It also recommended cancelling an application from Adani to extend the northern port due to the massive culling of mangroves. Fly ash should also be properly monitored, it noted.

"Does the marine park still exist?" Imogen Zethoven asks.

"Yes, it still exists," comes the response.

Four years later, after Modi came to power, one of the group tells us, the Report documenting the environmental degradation was effectively shelved. "Modi said the Committee doesn't have powers to put a fine on Adani," Patel explains.

Following the airing of these allegations on ABC's *Four Corners* program in October 2017, the Adani Group stated that the Gujarat High Court had dismissed the public interest litigation in April 2015. Later, I learn that in 2014, Sunita Narain was dropped by Modi from his high level panel on climate change.

In September 2015, final orders from the Environment Ministry under the BJP-led National Democratic Alliance allowed the project to proceed with an approval process for the northern port stating that satellite images did not prove the changes to the land had been made *before* 2007. Online Magazine *Scroll* claimed that internal documents found the decision had been made before the results of the damage were known. The Magazine stated that Adani had spent Rs 3.16 crore defending its alleged culpability. Adani has consistently claimed it did not violate any regulations, nor had it broken any laws. The ministry orders questioned the legal basis to force Adani to pay anything for a restoration fund and ordered further scrutiny of the alleged damage to determine cost. However, according to *Scroll* Magazine,[116] the Ministry relied on Adani's own evidence that it had not breached environmental conditions rather than an independent verification. *Scroll* published extracts that it claimed came from the Ministry of Environment's Regional Office Report in January 2017 which found Adani had complied with all environmental obligations. By August 2017, the Magazine stated the ministry's file dropped all references to taking legal action against Adani.

In November 2017, nine months after our visit to India, the Supreme Court appointed a Committee to enquire into the allegations that Adani had violated environmental norms including levelling sand dunes. Adani had proposed to divert 2400 hectares of forest land which had been considered, because of its mangroves, to be ecologically fragile. Economic progress, as usual won at the cost of the environment.

The Indian Express reported in March 2018[117] that the Forest Advisory Committee which met in January 2018, had noted in its minutes that "the establishment of port based SEZ is necessary for development of the country." Diversion of land is essential to Adani's prosperity. Adani was permitted to divert 1552.81 of forest land (other than 24 hectares of reserved forests in Dhrab village). The land had some conditions – it was stipulated to remain as a green area and was prohibited from being used as a golf course, beach resort, park, a private aerodrome or residential dwelling but it was allowed to be used for the Adani Mundra SEZ.

Adani was also told to ensure Coastal Regulation Zone rules were followed and find land for compensatory afforestation at its own cost. It was a win for Adani. The extension of his SEZ at Mundra, at that time meant a significant extension of the company's power base.

Imogen Zethoven asks whether we can enter an SEZ.

"It's foreign territory," is the answer.

"They can make their own laws? Shoot someone?" Zethoven persists.

"Yes armed security. But there has been no violence per se. But you never know ..."

* * *

Jadeja's village is Navinal; a small community of 3000 people in the centre of Adani territory. Navinal is one of 14 villages that lie within the Adani Port and SEZ. Jadeja's village is more like a continued sprawl of a larger township. Apart from taking on Adani and winning, the 30-year-old village chief has also taken on the Tata power plant. In 2008, the IFC (International Finance Corporation), the private lending arm of the World Bank, lent US$450 million to build Tata's power plant in Mundra.

Jadeja is a disarming 'human missile' in the fight against these industrial giants' encroachment. He helped US-based environmental lawyers document the Tata plant's impacts on his community, and won approval from his village council to sign the village on as a plaintiff in a lawsuit that accuses the World Bank Group of violating its commitment to 'do no harm' to people and the environment. By lending Tata money, Bharat Patel was one of the petitioners in the case. The suit, filed in April 2016 in the US District Court in Washington DC, claimed the development bank financed the project even though it knew pollution and habitat destruction caused by the plant would harm fisherfolk, farmers and others living nearby.

They argued the Indonesian coal used by Tata was high in sulphur and that Tata had not installed flue gas desulphurisers and that the IFC should not be above the law in its role in funding the ensuing disaster. In September 2016, however, the villagers and fisherfolk heard that the IFC had immunity from lawsuits in the US and the case was discharged. However, on 21 May 2018, the US Supreme Court announced it would hear the case for challenging the World Bank Group's immunity.

Richard Herz, Senior Litigation Attorney at EarthRights International (ERI), the lawyer representing the fishermen who were disputing the rights of the World Bank to be immune, released a statement: "International organisations like the IFC are not above the law and must be held accountable when their projects harm communities. The notion of 'absolute immunity' is inconsistent with Supreme Court precedent, and it is contrary to the IFC's own mission as an anti-poverty institution. We are glad the Supreme Court has agreed to hear this case and hope it will correct this error."[118]

It is not the first time that the World Bank has been under scrutiny for acting against the interest of the environment in Kutch. In 1996, it gave the Gujarat Government loans for projects on the integrated coastal zone management and one of the loans of US$1.05 million was made available for the creation of a State Environmental Action Program (SEAP) for Gujarat. Nilanjana Biswas in an earlier quoted Report entitled 'The Gulf of Kutch Marine National Park and Sanctuary: A Case Study', commented that the Report "revealed a strong pro-market bias including the modernisation of harbours."

* * *

It is a mark of determination that the villagers and fishing communities will not back down. Jadeja, like Bharat Patel, will not give up no matter how many times he might lose. He is not scared of taking on big opponents including Adani. We sit inside a single storey concrete building with cool tiles and green walls and a pink concrete railing on the verandah. We are accompanied by one of the Muslim fishermen in an Izar, a wide band of cloth wrapped around his waist like a sarong. Outside, a group of Indians shoot the breeze in the usual unhurried way of their people. We are not introduced but gather they are also fishermen.

Jadeja tells us, through our videographer, that in September 2014 he had been directed, as village chief, to grant 967.5 acres of grazing land from the village to the Navinal Gram Panchayat, similar to our local government of which Jadeja was head. Megha Bahree reports in *Forbes Magazine* that under Indian law, land meant for grazing cattle can be used for something else if there is excess land but the village chief has to give permission to take the land.[119] Multiple cases have been filed by village chiefs in villages affected by the Adani expansion at the Gujarat High Court contesting the government's actions going back to 2005 and earlier.

"On that land," the Magazine article commented, "Adani has built his cash cow – the country's largest private port by volume – as well as a 4620-megawatt coal-fired power plant. The victims of this are the villagers. Between 2005 and 2007 at least 1200 hectares of grazing land was taken away from villagers in the name of progress," Bahree reported.

Jadeja is one of these village chiefs who strongly objected to giving up important grazing land for the village. He is a quiet shy man, dressed in a white shirt. A large black mobile phone sticks out of his shirt pocket. He has a youthful, round face with a moustache and sparse beard. He smiles hesitatingly; his eyes cast downwards as though he is bearing the weight of the community.

In April 2015, according to his lawyer's petition presented to the Gujarat High Court, he was locked up in Surat jail 700 kms away from his young family (Jadeja explains he has two children, now aged four and six), after being charged with being a dangerous person under the Gujarat Prevention of Anti-Social Activities Act after his time spent documenting a case against Adani. Jadeja had been involved in village protests against the cutting down of mangroves and creating artificial sand dunes as well as the levelling of one of the creeks near the Navinal village according to his lawyer's petition who stated that these actions, in part, led to the entire SEZ minus the Adani port being closed down between 10 January 2014 and 16 July 2014 until conditional environmental clearance was given to Adani to re-open the SEZ.

This action, Jadeja's lawyer estimated, was worth "hundreds of crores." His lawyer maintained that all three court actions petitioned by Jadeja had been decided in favour of the village and against Adani. In court, his lawyer described Adani's actions, as "a classic case of corporate arrogance." His lawyer noted in the petition that if anyone wanted to leave the village, they had to get permission from Adani as the village was part of the SEZ which is "deemed foreign territory." He added: "Those who support Adani will get contracts and life with full money but with all environmental hazards. Those who oppose Adani have to suffer at the hands of political executives, police and bureaucracy which work for the Adani Port and SEZ Limited ..."

Jadeja had, his lawyer petitioned, many times "been lured with offers and contracts for not opposing the activity of the Adani Port and SEZ" and to stop legal action against the company. "Many times the detained [Jadeja] was threatened with dire consequences if he did not toe the line as a part of carrot and stick policy. However the detained did not budge and therefore he is in detention now," his lawyer stated.

He went further in the petition alleging: "It is at the insistence of Adani Group. It is a punishment for being involved in three litigations ... It is only to teach a lesson that whosoever will fight for constitutional right, for right to life and dignity, for the legitimate right of the villagers and for sustainable development. The individual liberty is curtailed by the State ... at the instance of the Corporate House [Adani] which is close to the power in the State of Gujarat."

Jadeja had also objected to the use of the village grazing land by Adani and had refused to sign over the 967.5 acres, as there was only 17 acres available to be assigned. His lawyer said that he had accompanied Jadeja to meet with two District Magistrates from Kutch and Bhuj to protest about the discrepancy over the land and Jadeja had been told he would face "dire consequences" if he did not sign a petition for the larger amount of land. He was later, in the presence of his lawyer, threated with being charged as a dangerous person and that even if the court refused to detain him, Jadeja would remain in jail.

According to one Indian newspaper reporting on the court case, Jadeja was perceived as a "thorn" in Adani's side and "an impediment to the company's growth."

Jadeja struggles with his English, but he manages to say three words succinctly: "Don't trust Adani."

We walk through the main street of the village: the Australian farmer Bruce Currie in his green shirt, Imogen Zethoven in her tennis cap and me with a grey scarf around my head against the dust that swirls through the streets. A herd of cows walk past. Jadeja used to grow cotton, millet and castor in some fields near the village until patches of white salt appeared in the fields and the soil became useless, a legacy of eradicating the mangroves.

He talks haltingly in English competing with tooting trucks and mooing cows.

"If Adani is staying in Australia, it will be the same situation as here. They will destroy any environment, water sources ... any livelihood. Do not listen to the Government who says they won't do this. If they come to Australia, they won't listen to anything."

As we part, I ask him one last question: "What advice do you have for Australia?"

"If you give them a little space, they will take more and more ..." he says firmly. He has the weariness of a man who, although he has had some wins, knows that he has a long way to go.

* * *

Jadeja's lawyer, Anand Yagnik, has an unassuming office up several flights of stairs overlooking a busy thoroughfare in Ahmedabad. Yagnik, who practices in the Gujarat High Court, is sitting behind a large wooden desk. He tells us that he has single-handedly "filed the maximum of matters against Adani." Behind him is a massive calendar. He is dressed in the ubiquitous white shirt of Indian officialdom, clasping his hands in front of him. With a handlebar moustache, stern expression and glasses, he is a serious man with a deadpan humour laced with irony.

When I ask quickly whether I can record our conversation he replies dismissively: "I am always on the record." Not waiting for questions, he proceeds to give us an impromptu lecture. The topic is on the way Indians do business.

"There are two types of lawyers," he says, "ones who fight for 'the cause' and those who fight 'for industry.'" A retainership from the industry is "a key source of money" for the legal fraternity. "With God's grace," he tells us, "I am one of only two advocates here who refuse to accept such a retainership."

His warning is blunt and similar to Jadeja's. Adani will continue with the same way of operating in Australia as the company had done in India. The key to the company's success is relationship building, he says. They will establish good relations with both political parties: conservative and labour. But in India, he ponders, the path for Adani is easier than it might be in Australia.

"One must understand three things," he said. "In India, liberalisation means to liberate industries from all laws and impose laws on the people – this is the meaning of a *laissez faire* economy... Second principle is that violation in India is far cheaper than compliance ... therefore the message to industry is to keep violating. At the most you'll have to pay a fine. Prosecution in India is almost impossible. Third one is that exploitation is a source of profit – whether you exploit resources, exploit politics, exploit the people. You have resolve to commit exploitation, otherwise there's no source of profit."

Yagnik talks in the typical Indian way in riddles drawing on Middle Eastern fairytales and portrays the Adani Group as the "Thief of Gujarat."

"And in Australia?" I ask.

"Yes," he answers swiftly. "Do not allow these people to do business in Australia."

To continue good relations with the Indian Government, he says, Adani handpicks employees from the ranks of some of the highest retired public servants in the land: Finance Secretaries; Cabinet Secretaries and Defence Secretaries ensuring a continuing company link with Indian bureaucracy.

"It is not the parliament of India that has the power. It is the stock exchange and the relationship behind the curtain among those bureaucrats through whom the industrial houses operate ... the Prime Minister of India, Mr Narendra Modi, won the 2014 election flying in the plane of Adani. He left Gujarat to become the PM after they won the election – in the plane of Adani. You can understand the kind of clout that he enjoys. And that is not an incident in isolation. This has been happening for some time ... "

As to India's concern about the environment, he says the law in India needs changing, citing three obsolete environmental laws which were framed as long ago as 1920 or 1925 with low penalties: a 200 rupee fine or three to four months in jail. "We were not paying attention to those laws and therefore we were not paying attention to the environment," he said, adding that India is happy to accept the excuse that a developing country cannot be asked to maintain pollution standards because it is antithetic to development.

"Development deals with human beings. Growth deals with profit and losses. Even now the judges in India – who substantially belong to upper middle class and elite middle class – sincerely believe that the environment is a concept of developed countries. It is a conspiracy on the judges' part to keep countries like India underdeveloped, and impose their expectations of having exploited the world for hundreds of years. This dogmatic theory runs deep in our blood ... So your country is very different to my country."

Adani, he warns, flourishes in this landscape and that is obvious by their environmental destruction in Mundra, which, he said, included building a wall of sand, after dredging for the port, which was 15–25 feet high running across an area of 40–47 kms. After reclaiming the land for the port, he said, the Mundra lighthouse ended up 3.7 kms inland. This reshaping of the coastline resulted in massive destruction of mangroves.

"You know the mangroves are a barrier between the sea and the land. They create a balance. They do not allow salinity to make further ingress. Mangroves are God's gift ..."

Zethoven asks about the state of the energy industry in India reminding him that the then Energy Minister, Goyal, had been steadfastly on the record as saying that fossil fuels will be phased out. This seems contradictory, she says, with India's expansion in coal. Yagnik asserts that Modi's relationship with power manufacturers is an important one and that Modi's victory as Prime Minister was substantially *because* of his relationship with the power sector in India.

He then proceeds with a history lesson on the development of coal in India. Power manufacturing between 1950 and 1995, he says, was a monopoly of the state, which had been using coal-based thermal power plants since the 1960s. By 1991, the technology used in these power plants became obsolete and they had become a liability. A drastic change in the technology was recommended. However, between 1995 and 2015, the price of providing electricity had become so expensive that the government reached a crisis point: it had failed to provide cheap power.

In 2003, the Electricity Act became legislation, which, significantly, allowed private companies to enter the power game and to become involved in coal production with companies such as Adani, Essar and Tata. From around 2008, these private companies began importing coal from places like Indonesia, Africa and Malaysia. At this time, the Indian states had entered into a non-negotiable agreement with the government called Power Purchase Agreements to be in place for 25 years, which would guarantee a fixed price for electricity.

Coal, after all, remains India's major source of electricity and supplies three quarters of the country's electricity use. So after private companies became involved in coal production, India gradually changed from a country with a power deficit to a power surplus and even began providing electricity to countries like Pakistan and Nepal. But there was an imbalance in the different Indian states, he said. Gujarat was in surplus of power (10,000 MW), compared to other states. However, in 2009/10 the price of coal across the world increased, resulting in an increased cost of producing electricity and led to many companies with thermal power plants defaulting on their loans because they had promised to provide electricity at a fixed price.

In 2016, the Central Electricity Regulatory Commission (CERC) ruled that Adani and Tata, who had filed cases before it, could pass on these extra costs to their customers. Both Adani and Tata had filed power purchase agreements (PPAs), which stated that the only way they could revise the tariff was if a government body or court imposed a cost or *force majeure*. Both companies argued that the increased cost of Indonesian coal was a *force majeure*. A Committee was set up to evaluate how much the compensation might be. In April 2017, the Indian newspaper, *The Wire*[120] reported that the decision was made without public process. However, the article noted that in April 2016, the Appellate Tribunal for Electricity (ATE) reversed the CERC decision but said it accepted the Indonesian coal situation could constitute a *force majeure* and agreed a compensatory relief should be offered to the companies but it failed to state the amount of the relief.

Coal in India was increasingly becoming an expensive source of power. As a power source, it relied on imported coal as well. It was at this time, Yagnik explained, that Adani became the largest supplier of coal in India.

"They were not extracting coal in India. They were *importing* coal and providing coal in India at a cheaper rate ..." he said.

This is Adani's masterplan – to provide coal to African countries and eastern countries as well as India. Every state in India, he points out, is like a country of the world in terms of the number of people. "They wanted to have control as far as the coal is concerned. Adani wants to become 'the coal king of the world' – that is a source of power for the 60% of the world which is underdeveloped and developing and which requires power. Nuclear energy," he adds, "is only available in five or six countries in the world."

The private companies involved in coal importation had applied for a compensatory tariff stating they could not produce the electricity for what had been agreed in the non-negotiable agreement. The price of coal escalated to 4.50 rupees. As this debate was going on, Adani started exploring possibilities to extract coal itself.

On the one hand, Yagnik said, there are 40–50 crore (400–500 million) people living in places where electricity hasn't reached as 40% of Indians continue to live below the poverty line. "They do not have two meals a day," he explains, adding: "Unless you can extract coal at a much cheaper price, the deficit will continue because the coal extraction will never be able to match the ever-increasing requirement of coal in India. The deficit will require the *importation* of coal ... we will continuously be in deficit production."

Chillingly, Yagnik's take on all of this is that Adani wants control of coal so they can determine the price – not only in India or Southeast Asia – but the world at large.

"It's not only related to their own manufacture of power. They have a multi-strategy. First of all, they want to control access to the coal. Then they provide coal to their own companies and provide coal to the Government of India. They are also providing coal to Pakistan and private partners." He pointed out that the Mundra power plant is only 800 kms from Pakistan.

As our meeting concludes, Geoff Cousins assures Yagnik that we will stop the Adani Carmichael mine going ahead. Yagnik smiles wryly describing himself as "a champion of cynicism."

Cousins appears ruffled.

"I have to tell you, Sir, we will beat them," he tells Yagnik. "And we have already beaten several other multinational companies.

You can tell anyone from Adani that you talk to that you have met a group of people from Australia who will finally defeat them."

Only weeks after our visit, a landmark judgment was handed down by the Indian Supreme Court. Appeals were filed to the Supreme Court by all of the parties. The Supreme Court set aside the agreement to allow Adani and Tata to benefit from a tariff ruling that no compensatory tariffs were allowed. It rejected the proposition that the rise in Indonesian coal constituted a *force majeure* and instead stated it was a known risk taken by the companies. It also ruled that the Power Purchasing Agreement could not be overridden by the CERC.

According to an article in April 2017 in *The Wire*, this decision put an end to the ethos 'bid low today, raise price later' by players like Tata and Adani. Shares in Adani Power fell by 18% according to *The Business Standard*, the largest drop in nearly eight years. Tata's fell by 6.7%. This decision by the Supreme Court was to challenge the whole viability of the Mundra power plants and sour the Adani success story.

* * *

The local fishermen of Mundra are down on the beach on the mudflats in front of some toilet blocks emblazoned with Adani's logo. For eight months of the year while they fish they occupy the shanty huts up from the beach, before the area is closed for the breeding season. Wooden boats in cherry red and emerald green lie like stranded whales along the beach at low tide. A Muslim fisherman in a Taqiyah, a white skullcap, takes us to his boat. He leans, a proprietorial arm up against his brightly coloured boat. Others are painting their wooden boats in scarlet reds and deep blues and hammering and banging in repair mode.

"What has changed, since the power plants appeared?" I ask through our ground crew.

"The water from the outflow channel has increased the temperature of the water and the mangroves getting cut has significantly reduced our catch. Before, at three kilometres into the ocean, we used to find fish. Now the port has been built, the fishermen have to go out as far as 12 kms further into the sea to find fish."

A couple of boys scamper around the beach, the tide at its lowest ebb. Anchors stick up out of the sand with ropes coiled around them. Two dogs playfully bound up from the ocean.

The fisherman continues: "But ten kilometres from the land is the route the ship has to come into the port. We don't take this route when we fish because we know the ships are coming. But the ships change their routes and there are more ships coming. Three different nets have already been destroyed and that's put more cost on us."

As we leave the beach, Bruce Currie drops on one knee next to a drying rack of small fish for a photograph. The fish are Bombay Duck, a staple diet of the locals, the fish workers. The fish are out for drying and hang like a row of washing – albeit in air polluted with coal ash and fly ash – Bombay Duck is the locals' bread and butter. It is the women who do the sorting, drying and selling.

Across the sand dunes, the power plant chimneys are stark against the sky. Wide spreading thorn trees offer shade. The austere military style toilet blocks are a paltry offering to these fishermen whose livelihood has been displaced.

And what does Gautam Adani think about all of this?

When quizzed about the controversy over his many developments at the expense of social and environmental issues, in one of his rare interviews he revealed his thinking to the Indian business magazine *Outlook* in 2013: "Let's face facts," he is quoted as saying. "Wherever there is development, there is bound to be some amount of damage. But it's important that you balance that out ... while there are some genuine concerns, that is not the case with all ... we are taking every possible step to create self-employment or jobs for the affected. But, beyond a point, it is also the responsibility of the Government to ensure that its welfare schemes reach the populace."

Chapter 7
Digging up the Dirt on Adani

The Kutch district is the largest district in India and a rare ecological zone due to its rich biodiversity as it contains coral reefs, mudflats and mangroves with a vast intertidal zone and network of creeks and estuaries. It was once rich agricultural land, especially the strip along the coastal belt that has sweet groundwater. Groundwater monitoring is carried out four times a year by the Ministry of Water Resources.

As early as 2013, five years after the Adani power plant was constructed, the groundwater status was listed as semi-critical. The Tata power plant opened in March 2012. The water below 150 metres was deteriorating due to increased salinity and over exploitation and was causing kidney and gastric problems for the villagers. The Groundwater Kachchh Report[121] conducted by the Ministry of Water Resources stated there was "an urgent need for management of the limited resources available." It also noted that the Gujarat Government was, at that time, pushing to industrialise the coastline and there were many "new industries in queue."

According to a PhD thesis written by Sazina Bhimani,[122] Mundra had experienced rapid industrialisation including 31 large to small-scale industries comprising the power plants, steel plant and oil refineries, and noted that the Adani SEZ, in particular, had "paved the way for further industrial development." The 2010 Kutch Coast – People, Environment and Livelihoods Report[123] released in 2010 from the Centre of Environment and Education (CEE) noted that in spite of mandatory environmental impact assessment studies, including one by the National Institute of Oceanography, the biodiversity and marine ecology of the areas was critical. They all concluded, however, that "the overall impact would be insignificant." Governments, whether in India or Australia, seem to believe that by acknowledging there is a major concern, they are doing their duty. It lets them off the hook. Indeed, the ultimate penalty for their decisions may not be witnessed in their lifetime.

When construction of the Mundra power plant began, Adani not only extracted groundwater but, according to a book chapter published by the CEE,[124] Adani was also sourcing water from the Narmada Canal. The largest lined canal in the world it is a contour canal (artificially dug and following the contours of the land) that brings water from the Sardar Sarovar Dam through 460 kms of Gujarat and into the arid state of Rajasthan. It is the largest water resources development project in India. The canal is a joint venture between four different states including Gujarat. According to the People, Environment and Livelihood Reports, 47.5 million litres of water per day from the Narmada was allotted to various industries including the Adani group. Adani and its subcontractors, we are told during our visit to India by a group of environmentalists in New Delhi, were drawing on the groundwater during the construction of the power plant. This exploitation of the groundwater by industry including Adani had a significant negative impact on the area's groundwater and increased its salinity, according to Sazina Bhimani's 2014 thesis.[125]

Groundwater contamination was listed as one of the major issues in the Ministry of Environment and Forests (MoEF) Report[126] released in April 2013 from the Committee headed by Sunita Narain. The Report noted that the environmental conditions imposed on Adani included the requirement to monitor the groundwater to check against salinity ingress but the report noted the company had failed to do this.

The Report contends that thousands of gallons of water are sucked in from the sea through a pipeline. Once sucked in, the water is kept in a reservoir from where it is pumped into the turbines to generate electricity and then it is eventually pumped out. The Committee found that the reservoir did not have any lining to protect the groundwater. It found the soil was permeable and could easily be contaminated. The Committee recommended Adani create an Environment Restoration Fund that was either 1% of the project cost (including the thermal power plant) or US$37 million, whichever was higher as a substantial deterrent for non-compliance of environmental conditions. That fund should be under the stewardship of the Ministry of Environment and Forests and used to repair environmental damage and to put more stringent monitoring in place to ensure compliance. It also recommended the company should reconstruct the channels taking in and sending back the water as well as repair or construct a new reservoir with impervious lining. And an independent study should monitor saline ingression every five years.

Megha Bahree, writing in *Forbes Magazine* in March 2014,[127] noted the groundwater issue. She wrote that the Adani Group, in response to her questions, had said salinity ingress was a local phenomenon and that its power plant used technology to ensure there was no stray fly ash. In April 2011, the Gujarat Pollution Control Board conducted a site inspection and issued directions to Adani to carry out a detailed assessment of underground water quality including salinity ingress. Adani Power Ltd commissioned a company to conduct the study and it reported that except for two samples, all other samples were found to be unfit for drinking water. One condition for clearances required that the proposed power plant should not carry out any activity that would lead to saline water ingress. The company was also asked to monitor groundwater levels. However, the MoEF Report[128] found that no groundwater monitors had been installed.

Adani's alleged environmental breaches were well known at the time when Gautam Adani engaged in his courtship of Australian politicians. On 9 August 2013, *The Australian* newspaper noted that the Australian Government was going to decide the next day whether to allow the dumping of up to three million cubic metres of dredged sediment on the Great Barrier Reef to allow the expansion of the port at Abbot Point. This article quoted India's Toxic Watch Alliance spokesman Gopal Krishna who commented that "Adani are habitual violators of environmental law. Even before environmental clearance is given they begin projects."

As Tim Elliott from *The Good Weekend* surmised in his profile piece on Adani in 2017, "... he [Adani] has been afforded extraordinary concessions, from cheap land to enormous tax breaks. Despite our vastly different heritage, the approach seems to be working equally well in Australia, where support for the mine from the major parties is based largely on the promise of jobs ... The Federal Government, for its part, apparently regards the mine as something akin to a humanitarian obligation, claiming Australian coal will help lift hundreds of millions of Indians out of poverty."

* * *

Threats to Australia's groundwater are Bruce Currie's main focus as a grazier. During our trip to India, he never tires of explaining the importance of groundwater for Australia and the farming community in particular. If the Carmichael mine goes ahead in Australia, Adani plans to extract an average of up to 4.5 billion litres of water per year. Currie is candid and admits that, in the past, a lot of harm was caused by graziers and farmers extracting water from the Great Artesian Basin, which covers an area of more than 1.7 million square kilometres.[129] Times, though, have changed, he says. Farmers now realise the importance of conservation.

But then came the threat of massive coal mines opening up in the Galilee Basin, and Queensland Government promises of free access to unlimited groundwater for mines like Adani's Carmichael mine. Since Adani received Commonwealth environmental approval for this mine in 2014, Federal Government studies have shown that the mine directly threatens the Doongmabulla Springs – a sequence of 160 separate wetlands stretching across a large area inland of Clermont, one of the world's last unspoiled desert oases as well as a spiritually significant place for Traditional Owners. Josh Robertson focused on this while reporting for the ABC in March 2018[130] pointing out that the Federal Government commissioned a Report several years ago to quantify the cumulative impacts and risks that multiple coal and gas projects were having on Queensland's water resources.

That should have been an important document to revise the swift approvals of mining leases and licences but this did not happen. According to documents sourced by the ABC, Adani ignored the information from a bioregional assessment that demonstrated that, while planning went ahead for the proposed Carmichael mine, the source of the ancient springs was still uncertain. Adani's groundwater plan ignored this scientific uncertainty and assumed that its proposed mine and the springs tapped different sources. Adani's plan did not determine *how* the company would deal with that risk, nor had Adani used any exploratory techniques such as seismic surveys or drilling deep bores to find out.

* * *

Kutch means an area that is both wet and dry. Once famous for its crops of sapodilla, a brown, fleshy fruit slightly smaller than a tennis ball, the district also produced dates, coconuts and castor oil.

Soumya Dutta, Convenor of Energy and Climate Group Beyond Copenhagen Collective, one of the environmentalists in New Delhi, explains the effects of extracting groundwater on the agricultural land in Kutch. "When you are levelling the coastal areas and constructing these big power plants with concrete you cannot use salty waters," he explained. "Companies like Adani are supposed to desalinate and do, but they also actually extracted groundwater. Agriculture disappeared ... with the sapodilla. Once the Adani and Tata power plants were built, black spots started to appear in the fruit. Within three years, the orchards were gone. The farmers have cut down their orchards because they could not sell them. The production is gone. Fly ash, coal dust and saline water from Adani Power and the nearby Tata plant are ruining the crops and making the soil less fertile."

Adani's website has stepped up its branding to profess that the company cares. A video on its website celebrates how much the company has transformed the region, offering thousands of jobs and bringing a 'magical' change including infrastructure and hope to 'a backward community'. The video derides its critics as 'self-motivated environmentalists' who bring their own agendas against Adani. The fact is, the company states, that thousands of jobs have been created in Mundra. People are able to sit around in air-conditioned offices feeling satisfied with life. The land clearing, devastation, alleged theft of groundwater and the continued destruction of rich agricultural land and the coral coastline through industrial pollution are not mentioned. The hijacking of the livelihoods of fishermen, agriculturists and pastoralists is also notably missing from the expensively shot, aesthetically beautiful video promoting Adani.

The company portrays itself as the saviour, not the grim reaper, of the community. Presumably Gautam Adani believes that Australian politicians and the public will notice this message. Adani has brought in family members aka Trump style to alter the corporate narrative, according to an one Indian newspaper article in *The Economic Times*[131] which reported that in January 2016, Adani's wife Priti, a dentist, and elder son, Karan, took charge of APSEZ along with Adani's nephew Rakshit Shah, Chairman of the Mundra port. Adani's wife and son, in particular, the newspaper reported had been "for quite some time, working quietly, sensitising the group even as litigation and accusations of past misdemeanours flew thick and fast."

Karan is ardently, without stepping on toes, trying to harmonise his new approaches with those of the elders in the group, including his father's. "The challenge is in merging of the thought processes," he says. However, there is little evidence to support the claims in the newspaper article that Adani had attempted to address the issues facing the fishing community, or Adani's claim to be 'greening' its ports which have 5000 trucks entering and exiting the Mundra port every day even with a rail link for cargo. And in outlining what changes his son Karan referred to in the newspaper article, there was no reference to any of the environmental degradation of the marine environment.

In March 2017, however, the majority of Australians still seem to live in ignorance about the Adani Group's past in India and who exactly is this group, Australian politicians have been soliciting to our shore for nearly a decade.

* * *

On a churned-up field about five kilometres from the Adani power plant, we meet Valji Gadvi, a 42-year-old date farmer dressed in a white dhoti who has agreed to talk to us. Standing next to his John Deere tractor, he tells us about his experience. Close behind him the chimneys of the Adani power plant are visible against the horizon. His young son, smartly dressed in a blue shirt, sits on the tractor and smiles at us uncertainly. Gadvi also has four daughters and a wife. He has lived here all his life and as far back through the generations of his family as he can remember. I ask questions through the videographer: "What happened to your farm after Adani came to the area?"

"Before Adani I had a good crop," he answers. "But now I don't get the same produce. I used to grow cotton and castor oil. Earlier I would get about 1600 kilograms of cotton. Now it's been reduced to half: 800 kilograms."

Around 2008, he first noticed the reduction in the crop from the time the power plant started construction. Back then, he had a further ten acres of land and used to farm dates. He would make 4–5 lakh in rupees (AU$8,000–$10,000) from the crop.

"Now this has been reduced to zero because of pollution," he says.

Fly ash and coal dust from the power plant meant he gave up on dates as a crop.

Soumya Dutta, one of the environmentalists from New Delhi, tells us that it is estimated that there has been a 50–60% reduction on the yield of dates since the power plants were built.

"So what does he do for income now?" I ask.

Gadvi says he has a few cows. He milks them and sells the milk. That is his main source of income. He tells us he visited the Adani company officials three or four times but nothing came of the meetings.

As he talks, he points to his son still sitting on the tractor telling us there has been a noticeable effect on his health. "My boy," he explains, "is having breathing problems."

The boy still smiles at us not reading our concern. Twenty minutes later as we leave the farm, Gadvi is already in the driver's seat of the tractor. His son still sits beside him. The tractor lurches over the barren land dragging the loader behind it. He is getting on with his life as best as he can.

On our way back to the fishing village, we pass a herd of camels clustering around a tall spiky bush. They arch their necks to reach the highest branches. Even from afar, we can see the leaves are blackened by coal. Behind them, the chimneys of the Adani power plant loom large. Kutch is home to the Kharai camel, one of the rare camel species in India. These camels have the ability to swim through deep-sea waters that they need to do to survive the monsoons and they live on mangrove islands for a period of two to three months so they can access rainwater. There are around 2200 who feed on mangroves and other saline plants. They are the main source of livelihood of mainly Jat and Rabari communities in several villages, including Mundra. They have traditionally a small carbon footprint as they rotate the camels' grazing and the pastoralists survive on camel milk and roti and live in temporary huts. But, increased salinity, due to the massive culling of mangroves, has greatly affected the camels' lifespan.

A recent article in *The Weather Channel* notes: "Industries in Kutch – salt, thermal power, cement and shipyards, among others – pose a huge threat to the dwindling mangroves. Most of these industries require constructing jetties in the sea, which results in the cutting down of mangroves that are fodder for the Kharai camels. The increase in salinity throughout the region and the growth of industrial activities has minimised the availability of camel food and water sources."[132]

As well as agriculturists and horticulturists, those dependent since time immemorial on animal husbandry have been badly affected by the industrial expansion. A total of 14 villages have already lost more than 1400 acres of grazing land to the SEZ according to the CEE report. In the early years after the Adani power plant was under construction and there were notices about their land being handed over to the SEZ, villagers threatened to bring 8000-odd cattle and buffalo into Mundra to block all of the roads unless the notices were withdrawn. The threats had no effect.

In one village I speak to a pastoralist sporting a red Kufi cap and a big white moustache who would rather not be named. The sad story is repeated. He too has lost grazing land. He talks about the amount of coal dust that has settled on plants, meaning the cattle go hungry. He tells me that he has uncovered a number of diseases in the cattle that he has not seen before.

The more time we spend in India, the more evidence we collect that Adani is a well-oiled machine: offering future jobs; allegedly seizing land and pedalling all sorts of promises to win the confidence of local people. What inevitably follows is sustained, irreparable environmental destruction without regard to the consequences. The main motive, it is abundantly clear, is to make a profit.

Adani's expansion into the Australian coal industry aided by the pleas from our politicians at the Federal, State and Local level, has made Gautam Adani even bolder. In Mundra, the company actually financed its own 40-mile railway line, linking the Mundra port to the national railway network, as well as building a 1.1-mile-long private airstrip that SEZ tenants can use for chartered flights. Two Queensland local governments, the Townsville City Council and the Rockhampton Regional Council were going to jointly fund a AU$30 million airstrip for Adani for the Carmichael mine using ratepayers' funds. The Councils would have never even owned the airstrip and it was hundreds of kilometres from both cities. The argument for funding the airstrip was that it would encourage fly-in fly-out (FIFO) workers, which is hardly delivering a result for those ratepayers who fund the project.

In January 2018, an ABC report noted that the Local Government Department had been asked to investigate the decision to fund the airstrip by the Crime and Corruption Commission (CCC) and whether or not the Council followed due process. In June 2018, in a surprise statement, Townsville Mayor Jenny Hill announced the $18.5 million earmarked for the airstrip would now go towards funding other projects in the city. She cited Adani's failure to meet the Council's June deadline to obtain financing and get on with the project. Rockhampton region's Mayor, Margaret Strelow has declared she will not follow Hill's lead.[133] Hill was publicly critical of Adani in February saying they had to make sure "milestones are met and that is an issue for the company."[134]

In 2018 it is now looking less likely, but only due to public outcry, that the Federal Government will provide a $1 billion taxpayer loan to build the rail line to link the Carmichael mine to the coast. What will happen with the airstrip remains unclear. But the fear, at the time of writing (June 2018), is that the Adani Company now has the funds to build the railway line themselves.

* * *

The group of concerned environmental activists, including scientists and journalists, meet up with us the day before we are due to leave New Delhi. They have been actively involved in the fight against coal mining in India. The meeting place is in an underground room in a suburban street. They have particularly targeted Adani and Tata. The Tata power plant, around two kilometres from the Adani power plant, was built after Adani's. Several of the group of around 15 people tell us that they are bemused at the proactive worship and red carpet treatment Australian politicians have shown Adani. It is clear these people are also deeply concerned about the catastrophic legacy, not only for Australia and the Great Barrier Reef, but for the rest of the world because of the huge carbon footprint which would be produced by the proposed Carmichael mine.

This group of environmental activists caution that they now have to be more careful 'fighting Adani' given his friendship with Prime Minister Modi. Around 2010 and 2011, they helped mobilise grassroot groups against the building of the Mundra power plant. They say they succeeded in the rejection of an application by Adani to expand its power plant in Mundra by arguing the application should be refused on environmental grounds. The group firstly identifies potential industrial polluters through environmental clearance applications as soon as companies apply through the Ministry of Environment, Forest and Climate Change.

"That is the earliest stage you can know that something is going on somewhere," Soumya Dutta explains.

In India, there is real danger when villagers and farmers confront coal mining projects that involve land seizures. *Source-Watch*[135] has compiled a list and map of people who have been killed, sometimes shot during protests by police, injured, arrested and one woman who set herself on fire after police had allegedly threated to bulldoze her home in November 2012 when she was protesting against the Katni power station in Madhya Pradesh. One of the protests listed involves the fishing community and salt pan workers protesting about Adani Power's proposed 3300 MW power plant in Bhadreshwar village, a small village near Mundra. There are no official reports of people killed or injured during a protest against Adani.

The environmentalists talk about the coal situation in India and the role Adani plays in that landscape. India has the world's fifth largest coal reserves, but the deposits are of very low quality relative to those found in other countries such as Australia (which has the fourth largest coal reserves)[136] or South Africa. They also

131

tell us imported coal is critical for anyone in the power game in India, as Adani has recognised. Adani, they say, has two or three different mines yet to open.

As of March 2017, they said Adani operated four power plants, with several more power plants planned in various states in India. Some were still at the application stage and others have been approved with land being cleared and ready to be built. The Adani Group has met with resistance, they say, as some of the mines are in forestry 'no go' areas. They have also experienced pressure from Indigenous groups.

Since we visited India, however, the times have certainly changed. With Adani Power in financial difficulty, reporting a US$227 million net loss for nine months to 31 December 2017,[137] India is turning away from long-term thermal power purchase agreements because of the cheaper alternatives offered by renewable energy. Tim Buckley from IEFFA writes, in April 2018, that around 60 GW of thermal power projects in India are now under financial stress.

The Adani Group, however, is a chameleon, adept at game changing. The company now acts as the contractor in state-owned mines to remove the coal, we are told, bringing in their technology to carry out the mining and then selling the coal back to the State Government. From the largest coal importer in India, as the Adani Group notes on its website, it has gone on to be one of the largest coal miners. "It might be particular States such as Rajasthan or the State Electricity Board who buy the coal back from Adani," Dutta explains.

However, all has not gone smoothly. We learn more about another reason, apart from a dependency on imported coal, as to why Adani is in such precarious financial circumstances. After a political decision in 2015 to double India's coal production by 2020, and with private companies already invited to mine the coal, Coal India reached its highest production under its rapid coal expansion plan. Then the demand for coal fell dramatically.

In August 2016, India exported coal for the first time to neighbouring Bangladesh.[138]

The demand for electricity and therefore coal is now growing at a much slower rate than anticipated, according to a report from India Energy Agency Coal 2017 Analysis and Forecasts to 2022.[139] Private companies who have been involved in mining are "walking away from their projects even if it is at a cost." The Coal Vision 2030 Study[140] found that overall coal demand in India was estimated to be 900–1000 million tonnes per annum by 2020, and 1300–1900 million tonnes per annum by 2030 and that no new coal mines needed to be allocated beyond those in already in the pipeline.

Dutta claims that in 2016, 44 million tonnes of coal was "lying in our stockyards." He said that India's Central Electricity Authority report in 2017 stated that no more power plants were needed until 2027. Various media reports I later consulted confirm Coal India, which produces 82% of India's coal and is the world's largest coal company, was preparing to close 37 coal mines to be decommissioned by March 2018.[141]

"Because today India has installed power capacity which can generate electricity 316,000 MW and our peak power demand for this year 2016/17 is projected by the ministry to be 166,000 MW. You can clearly see even if we generated 65% of the entire capacity for the next six to seven years, we don't need any more power plants," Dutta explains. The other factor leading to the demise of power plants is that the Indian Government, under Modi, has firmly targeted building up to 275,000 MW of renewables by 2027 as a cheaper, local source of electricity, providing a major diversification away from coal fired power generation. India has pledged to generate 40% of the nation's electricity from non-fossil sources by 2030.

This question has been puzzling me since we began our discussions.

Why is Adani forging ahead to pursue coal as a viable business if the government of India clearly prefers to facilitate a US$300–400 billion diversification into lower cost, more sustainable renewable energy? According to Dutta, Adani predicts that in the future coal power consumption may still rise. That, he says, is the gamble.

"Both the government and the industry are projecting a rise in demand for power. For power, the economy has to grow fast and that will generate more power demand. And the consumption of power has grown very, very fast. Now they are targeting 2030. Not today's demand."

On top of these issues, India will always need higher quality coal to blend with its own coal. Imported coal is used for blending with Indian coal. Coal is graded according to the carbon content.

"You can't just replace coal with Indian coal," the environmentalist said. "Now they are experimenting with blending – 20% of Indian thermal coal, 80% of imported coal."

India's Minister of Railways, Coal and Finance, Piyush Goyal admits that India will be forced to keep importing coal but they will only bring in as much coal as was needed. Goyal has stated many times that he wants coal imports to be phased out.[142] Modi has also promised to provide power to every Indian citizen by 2019.[143] Coal could power up to 100 million homes in India. Goyal himself is an advocate of renewable power although admitting coal will "be the bedrock for some time."

Adani has made much of being the saviour by importing Australian coal as a motive for alleviating poverty in India. As it states on its website, at various times, the company has promised to support electrification projects that will lift 100 million Indians out of poverty. But during our trip to India, the environmentalists we met in New Delhi and others told us that the Carmichael coal, which was to begin production in 2020–21, might be destined for the export market rather than providing electricity to India. In other words, the motive is profit not welfare. More than a year later, Adani's motivation for getting its hands on Australian coal has become clearer.

Coal prices, particularly from countries like Indonesia, went up from US$36 to $40 a tonne, then to US$90 and to well over $100 a tonne for Australian coal, says Dutta. The Mundra power plant relies on imported coal for the vast majority of its fuel requirement. Six months after our visit to India, in September 2017, the Adani group reportedly[144] transferred the Mundra power plant to Adani Power for Rs 106 crore after apparently investing Rs 600 crore in the project. By 2017, Adani's Mundra power plant is AU\$9.77 billion in debt – half of the debt of Adani Power.

This dramatic change in the fortunes of the Mundra power plant was triggered by the Indian Supreme Court rejecting the Adani and Tata bid for a compensatory tariff to counter the increased prices of imported coal. Since then, both companies have been actively looking for other markets who are willing to bear paying higher costs of expensive imported coal to create the electricity.

Back in March 2017, Dutta told us that the Adani Group had been planning to export the Carmichael coal to eastern India near the border of Bangladesh where a 1320 MW power plant was proposed to be built in the Indian state of Jharkhand. It was an Indian investment and Indian technology, Dutta said. Adani also, they told us, planned to export to Nepal. A power plant, Dutta explained, takes four years to build and is expensive and lasts around 40 years. Just as Dutta and his associates had forecast, before it was announced in Australia, in April 2018 Adani proposed the Godda Power Project in Bangladesh as a new market for the Carmichael coal following the challenges faced by the Mundra power plant due to increased imported coal prices.

Tim Buckley from IEFFA claims in a report entitled 'Adani Godda Power Project Too Expensive, Too Late, and Too Risky for Bangladesh'[145] that the project was "being promoted at least in part by Adani to justify its struggling Carmichael coal project in Australia." As mentioned earlier, Buckley has described the proposed Carmichael coal mine as a 'stranded asset', stating that the proposed mine has cost Adani Enterprises \$AU1.4 billion over the past eight years. Tim Buckley told me that there were several reasons for this including the isolated location with investment requiring roads, rail, airports, water and power infrastructure making it a high capital cost.

Additionally, he points out: "The quality of the coal is low, meaning the logistics of transporting the coal 400 kms to the port, then a quarter of the way around the world, makes it uneconomic relative to higher quality Australian coal that is much closer to the coast." And, lastly, Buckley states that the cheaper cost of renewables is undermining India's demand for thermal coal, as renewables are now one fifth of their cost in 2010 when the Adani Group acquired the coal deposit in the Galilee Basin.

As he comments, "So, Carmichael is a stranded asset, unable to provide an economic return on investment. The move by global banks to reduce funding thermal coal also means the project is 'unbankable' that is, unable to attract independent financial institutions' support in the absence of massive government subsidies."

In spite of Adani Australia's Chief Executive Jeyakumar Janakaraj promoting the new project as a way to "lift millions of Bangladeshis out of poverty," the power purchase agreement, notes Buckley, "is geared primarily toward assisting Adani companies at the expense of Bangladesh."

With India's growing reliance on imported coal up until 2016, Dutta said, India had also been caught in the grip of "a coal-importing racket." Coal is being imported at a higher price than what was being paid. These artificial costs were allegedly passed on to the supplier who then increases the cost of the electricity to consumers.

In April 2016, according to *The Adani Brief*, a number of Indian media outlets reported the investigation of five Adani Group companies accused of inflating the quality, and hence, the value of coal imported from Indonesia. The Directorate of Revenue Intelligence (DRI) found evidence to "suggest huge over-valuation to the extent of about 50% to 100%," according to *The Adani Brief*. It is understood that the DRI has since dropped all charges against the Adani Group over the overvaluation of coal imports.

The Adani Group has strongly denied all allegations. In August and October 2017, the DRI (adjudication) dropped all charges against the Adani Group relating to the inflation import of power plant equipment worth Rs 1600 crore. K.V.S. Singh, the Director General of DRI (adjudication) in his August order had said, "The contract price was arrived at independently through international competitive bidding process." He had also said that Adani Power Rajasthan Limited has adopted transparent and good corporate governance practices of procurement.

* * *

The talk around the table with the environmentalists turns to India's position on climate change. Imogen Zethoven asks the group about India's role in the Paris agreement and what its post-2020 climate change actions will be.

"Does India have an INDC? (Intended Nationally Determined Contribution)?" she asks.

"India," Dutta explains, "has used its status as a developing nation to not accept a limit on peak emissions. When the emissions do peak, India does not accept a deadline to stop or limit emissions."

So effectively, I am thinking, as one of the major polluting nations, India appears to pay little regard to the Paris agreement ... but then to be fair, nor does Australia.

The group is scathing about the social impact on the villages around Mundra from the aggressive expansion of the power plants.

"Both Adani and Tata brought in large number of migrant workers when the power plants were being constructed – a phase which goes on for four years. 90% of the workers were migrants."

The group estimates that there were as many as 8000 to 9000 migrant workers from Odisha and other states who flooded Mundra and its surrounding villages and a large number of them were semi-skilled. According to Sazina Bhimani's 2014 thesis, there was a 57.21% decadal growth in population in the Mundra town attributed directly to industrialisation of the area through the large number of immigrants attracted by employment prospects.

"As a result, alcohol consumption and other social ills – family violence against women and children – have gone up. The number of police raids and seizure of alcohol has gone up," Dutta said. (Gujarat is a 'dry' state.)

And, of course, there are the hidden costs of environmental pollution. They say that both the Tata Mundra and Adani Mundra power plants consume about 29 to 30 million tonnes of coal per year.

"If you have to wash 30 million tonnes of coal and put that water into the Gulf of Kutch – it's an enclosed gulf, it's not an open sea – what does it do with all that coal ash in that small area? Fishing has been devastated.

"Particulate emissions from power plants contain heavy metals, as well as all sorts of other pollutants including toxic volatile organic compounds and sulphur dioxide. Coal-fired power plants are a major source of particulate matter," says Dutta. "Tata's have better filters in place.

"Tata is trying to project a better image. Adani doesn't care much. Adani is far more ruthless."

Apart from the debate about the effects of the proposed Carmichael mine in India, there has also been plenty of discussion about the effects of the mine on existing Australian coal mines. An article in the ABC in July 2017[146] cited research from global resource analytics company, Wood Mackenzie, which pointed out that while both the Federal and Queensland Governments were stressing the economic benefits of new mines in the Surat and Galilee basins, it would come at "a severe cost to jobs and economies in other regions" including ten new mining projects in NSW being displaced; the Hunter Valley thermal coal output falling by some 86 million tonnes (37%) and the Bowen Basin declining by a third of its output with 17 million fewer tonnes mined. The general manager at The Infrastructure Fund said the impact of the Galilee basin mines on the Port of Newcastle would be "pretty devastating."

"I'm an investor, not a politician, but it seems a perverse outcome when you are taking jobs in one part of the country and promoting them there and displacing them or destroying them in other parts of the country," he told the ABC.

* * *

D. Thomas Franco Rajendra is a quiet unassuming man whom we meet in the hotel meeting room. He had been recently elected as General Secretary of the All India State Bank Officers' Federation which is an independent trade union representing more than 90,000 officers employed by the State Bank of India. He tells us that he has an interest in environmental issues particularly relating to climate change.

Rajendra found out about the Adani project after the Chairman of the State Bank of India became part of a delegation by Modi to Australia in 2015. Gautam Adani was also part of the delegation. Narendra Modi was the first Indian Prime Minister to visit Australia for 28 years. At the time, the State Bank of India had stopped short of sanctioning a loan for the Adani Carmichael mine after signing an MOU (Memorandum of Understanding) in November 2014. But the bank had ordered that Adani had to get all of the clearances from the Australian Government for the mine before they would lend any money for the project. "I understand Adani got all of these," Rajendra asks us over the top of his spectacles.

Zethoven is quick to reply. "Not quite." She outlines the problems that still existed, then, with the $1 billion NAIF loan and other legal challenges from the Australian Conservation Foundation as well as Indigenous challenges to appropriating land to build the Carmichael mine.

Zethoven asks whether the State Bank Officers' Federation was able to take an active role in convincing the State Bank of India not to finance Adani.

"The bank will not finance Adani unless the profitability of the project is ensured and all the clearances are given by the various agencies," Rajendra states firmly, adding that advising the bank is not the role of the Federation. He encourages us to write to the Board of Directors and the Chair of the State Bank of India, explaining that his organisation did not normally intervene in the lending practice of the bank unless it is obvious that it is 'wrong' lending, for example, if a company had a background of making constant losses.

He requests further information for his trade union about our environmental concerns adding that he does not think the Carmichael mine will be a big employment generator. Imogen Zethoven hands him a briefing paper from the Australian Marine Conservation Society on the effects on the Great Barrier Reef from Adani's proposed mine.

"But," I ask, "if Adani is investing in nineteenth-century technology when renewable energy is cheaper, wouldn't that make the banks scared?"

Rajendra does not immediately answer.

I continue, "We have been told as well any lending for Adani depends on the viability of the project and that Adani had to demonstrate that 75% of the coal production was locked into contracts."

"The bank," he finally answers my initial question, "is influenced by the Government, and the Adani group is close to the present Government."

Zethoven asks whether it would be useful to let the State Bank know about the refusal of Australian and international banks to lend money to Adani. He agrees.

"This Adani group itself has come into prominence only recently," he tells us. "It's not a traditional business house. It was during the present Prime Minister's period as Chief Minister of Gujarat that they got some small contracts – they got the port in Mundra; then they had some solar projects; gas projects; now they have got into many ports and terminals like Chennai. They have ports – in Andhra Pradesh they are also building a port. Now they are diversifying into many other activities. But the growth has happened only over 10 to 15 years and their level of debt is quite high."

Zethoven asks if the bank will consider the amount of carbon emissions the coal from the proposed Carmichael mine will contribute to India's carbon footprint. Rajendra shrugs. He has no answer for this. As the meeting draws to a close, he passes over the email address of the Chair of the State Bank.

To date, the State Bank of India has reportedly not committed to funding the Carmichael mine, or its associated offshoots. Following a spate of Stop Adani protests, Australia's big four banks all withdrew support for the Adani mine in 2017.

* * *

Back in my hotel room, the phone rings. It's my husband Grant.

"That spot, you know where we regularly go snorkelling. It's showing signs of bleaching."

"What?"

I am brought home abruptly as to why I am here. The coral on our home turf is also showing signs of stress. I had thought, for the time being, the southern part of the reef had escaped bleaching.

There had been hardly any signs as far as I knew reported further south in the back-to-back bleaching events of 2016 and 2017. But in this out-of-control world it was quite possible anything could happen.

* * *

The former Minister of Environment, Forest and Climate Change, Jairam Ramesh, has his offices in a leafy suburb of New Delhi. He is to be one of our last interviewees in India. Environmental debates were first introduced to the Indian national political agenda during Indira Gandhi's prime ministership in the late 1960s. Ramesh was minister from 2009 to 2011 – a significant time for Adani when the company was seeking environmental approval for their power plant at Mundra.

After being petitioned by the MASS (Machimar Adhikar Sangharsh Sangathan) – the group representing the fishing community from Mundra – Ramesh decided to make their complaints about Gautam Adani a test case: "To follow the laws of the land. I wanted to say to him: 'Go through the process and identify what needs to be done.'"

His office is spacious with deep leather armchairs. He sits opposite us across a large wooden coffee table, an unruffled handsome man with a quiet dignity wearing the same sense of resignation we've encountered with others who have tried to take on Adani.

"Mr Adani is a very influential businessman here," he says quietly. "Mr Adani has agreed to 30 or more conditions imposed by the State Government in Australia but he did not comply with conditions in his own country so he cannot be expected to comply with conditions in another country."

Even though, by now, we are well and truly acquainted with the wrongdoings of this company we are shocked by his words.

He watches our faces.

Ramesh tells us that he and Gautam Adani have been "having a running battle since 2009" ever since the construction of the port at Mundra and when Adani ended up "destroying hundreds of thousands of acres of mangroves.

"When I was minister, I issued a notice to him but before I could take action, I took up another ministerial position. That created some complications for him ... but when *this* government came to power," he sighs, adding: "He is very influential ... he is very well connected to the present government."

Ramesh seems ready to give his views. He suggests we make the Adani project an international cause. He describes how a bauxite mine in India was stopped by a powerful locally-backed group as well as an international action which involved Bianca Jagger.

His smile is ironic. Chuckling, he tells us we have been making news even in the 'interiors' (regional newspapers) in India. He was once a newspaper columnist and he applauds us for the Open

Letter to Adani signed, by among other celebrities, the Chappell brothers.

"I was out in the boondooks – the interior of India – with hardly any internet and the first thing I saw was this story about the Chappell brothers. Although you know Australian cricketers are not that well liked in India ... "

There is much laughter.

"India's biggest bank – the State Bank of India – when our Prime Minister went to Australia – he announced a billion loan for the project but then it was withdrawn. I'm told that due diligence was done by the bank and it was decided that they should not give the loan so they haven't signed that loan."

He said he knew of several people in the State Bank who had been concerned that Adani had yet to gain all of the clearances. "This was causing a lot of heartache."

"Ultimately," he adds, "it is the Australian people who will have to defeat this project. Your civil society and your media will have to fight a rearguard action."

When I tell him about our Australian politicians telling the public that Australian coal will help the impoverished Indians, he laughs incredulously.

"That's bullshit."

"Mr Adani plays this card very skillfully. Talking about coal and poor people. It's not the first time he's done it."

He adds later: "There are less environmentally disastrous ways of making India rich. There's also less disastrous ways of lifting people up from poverty."

"If India is putting in 100,000 MW of solar power that produces power at three rupees a unit,"[147] Ramesh says. "why would they invest in a coal plant that will cost three times that?"

He rises gracefully to his feet and walks towards his large mahogany desk across the room picking up a framed photograph and bringing it back to the coffee table where we are sitting. We look at the picture. Six tigers, majestic and strong, stare back at us.

"This is a very unusual photograph," Ramesh says. "Six tigers in one photograph. You never see six tigers ... tigers are very solitary animals. It is unique. The only photograph in the world perhaps with six tigers. But, there's a coal mine proposed here. These six tigers are in the area of a very big coal mine, which Mr Adani has been eyeing for the last 15 years and he almost got it. When I went there in 2010 I saw that it's not only a huge tiger reserve,[148] but also one of India's richest teak forests. In the centre of India. It's bang in the middle ... I cancelled the application when I was Minister for Environment and Forests. Unfortunately, one of his biggest supporters was one of my own party members – one of my ministerial colleagues – but so far Adani hasn't been able to get the allocation.[149] He could get it any day and if this happens this entire tiger habitat gets destroyed." Ramesh adds that Adani manages the media very well.

"Mr Adani thinks ... he's managed the Australian system as well."

* * *

Outside Ramesh's office, before stepping into a taxi and heading to the airport, Geoff Cousins announces he is flying from New Delhi straight to Canberra where, along with former Greens leader, Bob Brown, cajoled out of retirement, he will launch a campaign called Stop Adani at Parliament House in Canberra.

The launch will take place on the same day we are due to arrive back in Australia, 22 March 2017.

"It will be bigger than anything we've seen since the Franklin Dam was stopped," Cousins advises. "This mine will not go ahead. There are people training up now all over Australia to take on this fight."

I want to believe him. But as I land at Brisbane airport, we seem like a forlorn group. Even if we have achieved world headlines, to what end?

I have filed some paragraphs with the juiciest quotes to submit to the Chief of Staff of my local newspaper, *The Whitsunday Times*, recently taken over by Rupert Murdoch. The story is brutally culled and relegated to the Letters to the Editor. Andrew Wilcox, the Mayor of the region, however, is treated to an 800-word article on a prominent inside page beefing up his achievements presumably to justify his hefty bill for his trip to India.

Australia? A land of protest? Where are these people? More importantly, how will they be galvanised? I stop short of scoffing at Cousin's remarks. After all, he is a man of determination and he has invested so much already both personally and professionally on stopping this mine.

Chapter 8
The Swirling Dervish

The 29 March 2017, a week after I return from India, is our fourteenth wedding anniversary. We have booked a retreat halfway between our home in the Whitsundays and the coastal city of Mackay. Packing the car, Grant has already checked the weather. He's been down to our boat and secured it with extra lines. A few days earlier a tropical low started to develop over the Coral Sea off Papua New Guinea. High sea temperatures of 29–30°C mean the low has an opportunity to intensify. It is cyclone season after all. We stop taking bookings and begin to literally batten down the hatches.

Living in the tropics, we've done it all before. Satellite estimates greatly help to evaluate cyclonic activity nowadays although there is always the unknown – where will it hit the coast? How fast is it travelling? What is its trajectory?

Back in March 1911, a year before the Titanic sank, the *Yongala*, a 300-foot iron steamer, did not even have a radio onboard when 122 souls on board including a baby, a racehorse called Moonshine and a bull went to their watery graves south of Townsville. The vessel had steamed out of Mackay as the recently invented Marconi wireless had just been dispatched for the ship from England, but the radio was still in transit when the cyclone struck. The Captain never knew about the impending cyclone.

We had survived cyclones Yasi (2011) and Larry (2006). This one seemed destined further north. The chances of it hitting Airlie Beach and our beloved *Providence V* seemed unlikely. We drove to the retreat that was up a country road off the highway and parked the car for three days of peace and quiet. Our only visitor was a peacock that strutted across the verandah. Surprisingly, it settled rather ungracefully at our feet as though seeking comfort. The retreat was known for its bird life. Already then I sensed there was change in the air. Something in the hurried way the sulphur-crested cockatoos screeched across the skies.

Day two of the anniversary getaway and Grant is spending more time checking the Bureau of Meteorology than reading a novel. The cyclone has been upgraded. Winds of up to 100 km per hour have been recorded around Proserpine, which houses the local airport for the Whitsundays. The owner of the retreat, delivering a sumptuous breakfast, exudes calm.

"We should be right," he says emphatically.

I want to believe him.

"I think you're panicking unnecessarily," I murmur. Grant's furrowed brow signals my words will make no difference. He has brine in his veins, I've once told him, having made a living as a fisherman, a commercial diver, and, when we first met, he was diving for sea urchins along the chilly east Tasmanian coast in known spots for white pointers. (He has lived his life working around the weather.) I often tell our guests he is "the weather guru." Almost 100% of the time, he is spot on with every forecast.

Outside the morning light has changed to metallic grey. Light rain begins to fall. The wind has picked up. We are used to the wet season in the surly tropics: thunderous one night, sizzling the next. For some years now, increasingly like many other changing global weather patterns confronting climate change, the traditional wet – the usual February downpour that would last the whole month – has not eventuated.

On the computer screen, the map of the swirling dervish they are calling Cyclone Debbie dominates. Its dance swallows up the screens on the laptop computer and the mobile phone, taunting any attempt at peace. Debbie is 500 kms north east of Townsville in the Coral Sea. By the time we do pack the car and leave a day early, the winds have heightened. The owner of the retreat has stopped all optimistic chitchat making no attempt to convince us to stay. As we drive towards Airlie Beach, the winds buffet the car. It is not until later that I hear a 31-year-old tourist died in a two-car crash, reportedly killed because of wild winds near Airlie Beach.

We have booked into a hotel near the marina. The prediction is that Debbie is heading for the regional township of Ayr, about two hours drive further north. 3500 residents had also been evacuated from the area between Home Hill and Proserpine, with a further 2000 told to leave the coastal town of Bowen as well. Retired people are included in the evacuees. Our hearts go out to them, knowing the panic they must feel. Palaszczuk is on television urging people to go to cyclone shelters. But the shelters in Airlie Beach are in the high schools and are only to be used as an absolute last resort.

Queensland Police Deputy Commissioner, Steve Gollschewski, asks North Queenslanders to listen to advice from emergency services.

"If you are in a storm surge zone and are directed to move, you must move," he advises.

"You can shelter in your house from wind, but you can't shelter from a storm surge."

So many North Queensland homes are on the seafront. More than 100 schools have been closed across the North Queensland coast. Shop fronts in the small town centre of Ayr in North Queensland are being boarded up and filled with sandbags as locals make final preparations.

The media coverage has been focused on Townsville and Ayr. Then, the predictions change. Debbie is one of our slowest moving cyclones, moving at around six kilometres an hour. Global warming increases the intensity of cyclones. Although still a Category-3, Debbie's winds at the centre are already 260 kms per hour – strong enough, according to the Bureau of Meteorology (BOM), to cause "structural damage and dangerous debris." As we head back to Airlie Beach from the retreat, her trajectory is a curved line still heading for Townsville. Then, Debbie is supposed to be heading inland through the former gold rush town of Charters Towers.

The longer the cyclone stays over the warm waters of the Coral Sea, however, the greater the chance of intensification, is the latest pronouncement from the BOM which now plays like our favourite TV channel on all devices. South of the cyclone, however, is always where the most damage occurs and that means us. Daily rainfalls of up to 400 mm are being forecast.

By 3.15 pm on 27 March, Cyclone Debbie has been upgraded to Category-4. It has taken all of 12 hours to rocket from a Category-2 to Category-4. The dark red and paler pink circles on the computer screen, looking for all the world like a dart board, is aiming straight for us – the classic 'eye' of the cyclone is clearly visible. The 'core' of Cyclone Debbie is said to be 100 kms wide and is 'very destructive' according to the BOM. Premier Palaszczuk announces through the media: "The window of opportunity to leave is drastically closing."

We abandon the rental home at Shute Harbour (a 15-minute drive from Airlie Beach) hurriedly packing only essentials; taking in furniture from the verandah; tying down what we can. With only a pull-along suitcase, laptops and phones we head for Shingley Beach hotel, a place where we last stayed on our journey north from Tasmania. We know the manager, the late Nigel Pemberton who sadly died during the writing of this book. He often booked guests on *Providence V*.

It is no longer the Shingley Beach hotel that we know. Panic has set in. The reception area is buzzing as the central hub. Pemberton, it transpired, has a barbecue with gas so when the electricity goes, we can still cook. We bunker down in the upstairs room. 'Bertha', our 11-seater van can't quite fit into the cement car park. With some trepidation, we leave her in the street. Falling branches are the worst missiles. As I walk up to the hotel room, a tiny bush turkey scrabbles frantically in the dirt. I imagine what little resistance it will have to the oncoming winds. I think of the other wildlife bunkering down: the twittering rosellas, wallabies and the shorebirds – sooty and pied oystercatchers and the cockatoos who still seem to be clinging to the branches of the eucalypts. They are all silenced by the enormity of what is coming.

Our provisions only just fit into the bar fridge. My daughter, Phoebi calls. In professional mode as a Masters student in Psychology, she tells me she will update relatives, as we may have no phone connection. She confirms it's looking increasingly likely we *are* in the line of fire and Debbie should make landfall around 8 am. At least it will be light then, I think. Back in the hotel room we huddle over the laptop looking at old downloaded movies I never seem to have time to watch. The disconnection with the outside world is yet to occur. Everything seems surreal. How will we know what is happening? It hadn't occurred to us then how long it will be before we can reconnect with civilisation. That evening, around 10 pm, the television stops working abruptly. We didn't think about a radio ... such an anachronistic item in this digital age. Plunged into darkness as there are now no lights, Phoebi calls again, her voice strangely symbolic in the darkness. The mobile phone, at least still has battery.

"Mum, are you ok? It's *not* going to be over soon. They say it might be a couple of days."

They are the last words I hear before falling asleep. Her voice enters my dreams. When I awake in the early hours, the eerie sound of the wind is low and howling – a relentless sound that will plague us for days. As we look out of the window on to the small balcony, there is no way to open the sliding door. White starred lilies in the flowerboxes have somehow survived. The water lashes down. The balcony floor is slowly filling to become a pond. In the distance, yacht masts bob desolately like ghosts in the grey mist that cloaks the marina. There are no birds anywhere. No one is out there. It is as though the world has come to an end. I watch the poles holding the marina walkways. The water is still far below. At least the high tide didn't coincide with the arrival of Cyclone Debbie. Debbie had been forecast to arrive to coincide with high tides, with predictions of a 7-metre (23-foot) surge. But this hadn't happened.

When Yasi struck in 2011, the marina at Port Hinchinbrook broke free leaving boats beached along the main road through the small coastal town of Cardwell or lying on the bottom of the harbour. The damage was around $30 million. It was widely reported that the pylons holding the marina walkways had been cut too short by the developer – Gold Coast entrepreneur and developer of Sea World, the late Keith Williams, when it was built in the 1990s.

Paddling down the hotel walkway, wind gusts up the road in front of the hotel whipping the tops of the palm trees that line the beach. For hours the scene remains the same. There is no link to anyone or anything. No radio; no TV; no internet – nothing. It's as though we've fallen into another world, the world of nightmares. Hades has our pass and he is not letting us return. Downstairs Pemberton has fired up the barbecue. People are bringing supplies to cook. Pemberton is like a scoutmaster directing his charges.

Then relief. Around mid-morning, the moaning stops. It is replaced by a strange quiet. Still no one has appeared outside. It is the eye of the cyclone: the centre of the storm that can be anywhere from 30–65 kms wide surrounded by a ring of towering thunderstorms. The eye can be the most hazardous, especially at sea when wind-driven waves all travel in the same direction around the eye wall, but at the centre of the eye they converge from all directions and slowly build until they become rogue waves up to 40 metres high. No wonder the 300-foot steel and iron Yongala sank even with a greatly experienced Captain at the helm.

Outside, it is even eerier than before. Everything is still... waiting ... we feel like victims after an assault ... lying there wounded but knowing the worst is yet to come. Victims of cyclones are often lulled into a sense of calm by the eye. Venturing out to inspect the damage, they get caught on the eyewall on the other side of the cyclone with violent winds. Grant has been talking about going out to our berth to check on *Providence V*. I try to dissuade him, but he is adamant. Before we discuss it further, he begins to jog towards the marina. A couple of other shadowy figures join him on the same mission, dark shapes just visible in the thick grey mist scurrying along the wharf. When he returns about 15 minutes later, he looks crushed, as though he can't comprehend what has happened. It is an unfamiliar expression for me. He usually copes well in the worst situations.

"Two boats broke lose. One's a big white boat. It's been pounding into her ... gouging out her wood ... the marina is barely holding together."

Behind the reception desk is a large radio – our only contact to the world. We have a mobile telephone provider that has no signal. Pemberton has a different one that works. I call Phoebi.

"Where's it crossing the coast? Does anyone know?"

"It's right above you ... now."

Even though I know this is the case, this confirmation from the outside world is shattering. I find out later that Cyclone Debbie actually crossed the coast at 2.40 am.

"What's happened to *Providence*? Do you know?" Phoebi asks.

Our beautiful boat, part of our family for almost as long as we have all been together. I begin to cry. I had been hoping she wasn't going to ask.

I finish through tears: "There is nothing we can do ... for the moment."

The wind, when it returns much later, has shifted although I don't notice.

Grant sniffs the air. "Changed to the north from the south-east," he announces. It is the kind of pronouncement I know I should heed. Quietly uttered but full of meaning. My first introduction to the mystery of boats was reading *The Shipping News* by E. Annie Proulx where each chapter opened with an epigraph taken from *Ashley's Book of Knots*. I have almost mastered a bowline but it's taken a while. When we first met in Tasmania, I was reminded of this Newfoundland romance.

"And?"

"Those boats will now be crashing into someone else ..."

His face shows relief even though it seems wrong to be wishing misfortune on others.

The frustration he feels in not being able to protect our beloved *Providence* when he's spent 14 years caring for her must be unbearable. There is nothing much to say.

The evening is more of the same relenting greyness that gradually succumbs to black. All afternoon the rain has been driving in sheets up the street in front of us. Branches snap periodically but the trees hold. The shadecloth in front of the hotel is rent asunder. We can just make out the mast of *Providence V* and her Jolly Roger flag among the other spikes of masts sticking up into the gloom. There is no opportunity to check on her further.

Debbie's destructive slow-moving crossing is to pummel the region for 16 hours with 250 km per hour winds. But it is the ensuing relentless downpour straight after the destructive winds that rips apart buildings and proves the most damaging, rendering many homes and hotels unable to be rebuilt due to water damage.

The following morning Grant returns to our rental property in Shute Harbour from Airlie Beach. I follow in Bertha (who miraculously has survived). The promontory that we share with a few other houses faces south-east and directly on to the Coral Sea into the path of Cyclone Debbie as she crossed the coast. Shute Harbour, where the ferries once departed for Hamilton Island, fared worse than anywhere else in the Whitsundays.

Outside, the world looks like a set from the ABC's television series, *Cleverman*. Or, at the least, the aftermath of an apocalyptic event. Large trees lie across the road. Power poles are uprooted. Live wires lie exposed. By far the biggest impact, though, is the desolating silence and the inability to communicate with anyone. How much we depend on instant communication.

A stillness has replaced the howling wind. I feel a deep sense of abandonment. Everywhere is deserted as though the place had been evacuated. Even the birds have fled. Surely someone will scream in the streets at the horror of it all. But there is no one – the same dull grey skies as yesterday. It's as though the sun has never shone. Empty roads. No cars.

A trip to the local supermarket and I discover where everyone is. They are here in this darkened shop with no lights, waiting for up to an hour for provisions. Everything is added up using pen and paper. There is not enough power for the cash registers. No one wants to risk using their phone battery, which can't be charged if the electricity fails. I wait with two bags of ice. Twenty minutes later, in the steamy heat, they have almost melted. There are still 20 people in front of me. I put them back in the freezer. There are at least 100 people queuing speechlessly cowed by the enormity of the events of the last 24 hours unified by one desire: to survive. Most of them are from a generation that has never had to endure the horrors of abstinence. The tales from our parents and their parents who survived world wars are stories. We are not good at this. Being deprived.

After leaving the supermarket and, 15 minutes later, approaching Shute Harbour, mounds of leaves lie across the road and more fallen branches. The trees, stripped bare of their leaves, stand naked and vulnerable. Houses appear in the bush where I'd never known houses to be before, the occupants' lives bared for everyone to see.

Considering the majority of houses in Shute Harbour have sustained major damage, our rental property has fared okay. 'Structurally speaking,' it has survived. 'Cyclone speak' phrases that we learn to roll out in those early days and weeks – a short form appraisal of events while everyone is too preoccupied to need to know more.

This is how people communicate post-cyclone. There are survivors and those who struggle. In the ensuing weeks, and, for at least a year later, marriages collapse; buildings fall down or are abandoned; businesses fold. People pack up everything they own and leave town. Mercifully, compared to Darwin's Cyclone Tracy in 1974 when 71 people were killed, there was reportedly only one fatality in the Whitsundays – the tourist in the car accident.

As Debbie travelled south, however, mass flooding claimed 14 lives including a mother and her two children who drowned when their car plunged into a river.

The snail-paced recovery in Airlie Beach mirrors the sluggishness of the cyclone. A year later 'tradies' such as plumbers and carpenters still occupy a large share of the rental properties as they are also working on the badly damaged Hamilton Island. Shattered houses are still not back in the rental pool. Damage to the sugar industry was said to be $150 million. Around 60,000 homes were without power in the Bowen, Mackay and the Whitsunday regions. Electricity took far longer than anyone realised to be reconnected in Airlie Beach.

* * *

Our house in Shute Harbour is on the edge of the promontory looking straight out to sea. The views are the kind that evokes a sharp intake of breath from visitors. My parents had visited. We'd had a family reunion of the kids at Christmas all the while thinking this must be a dream. One winter, we had seen a cavorting humpback calf with its mother from the verandah. We kept our kayak down at the beach and would go for picnics to the islands half an hour's paddle away. But we can't really live here anymore. The dream vanished after the cyclone.

We had to leave our cars at the top of a driveway that was choked with fallen branches and leaves. The swimming pool is like an ominous dark lake. A fallen tree lurked at the bottom of it. Outdoor fences were wrenched off, lurching over my vegetable garden. Louvre windows were smashed. The south-easterlies with lashing rain had forced the sliding doors open. Water had seeped through into the wooden floorboard of the lounge room drenching the curtains in the bedroom, as well as the bed and furniture. A heavy glass outdoor table had been hurled upside down off the top verandah and shattered. Glass had fallen into the pool. Worse, the glass partitions in the verandah of the neighbour's house, which had just been sold for more than $1million, had also blown into our pool.

Food was beginning to rot in the fridge in the tropical heat. There was no water in the taps. Nowhere to wash. No washing machine – or computer – no phone. The mobile telephone tower had gone. Those items that our life revolved around had vanished.

It took six weeks to get the telephone landline back and several weeks before electricity returned. You could not ring the tradespeople whose businesses were booming in the ensuing days after the cyclone. Even to book the slipping yard to get *Providence V* out to be fixed was impossible. There was no one there to receive calls. Worse still, we couldn't track Debbie's movements. Or tell our loved ones we were okay.

Our daughter Jess came around that day after the cyclone with her boyfriend Steve. They brought a bottle of red and a mobile phone that had reception. Sitting on the dilapidated deck around the pool we drank a glass. Jess posted some photos on Facebook. It was the first sign anyone had seen that we were still alive. I found out later that my father had taken his mobile phone into his art class. He never carried it usually. My daughter had left hers switched on when she was attending a university class. Gradually in the ensuing months, our sons likewise confided that they thought we were gone. The Facebook shot of us drinking red wine trivialised the moment. It told nothing of our trauma or our plight.

I found out later an elderly man in an electric wheelchair had been stranded nearby with no way of getting to any food source. A neighbour had alerted everyone to his plight. The final number of boats that loosened from their moorings and broke free during the cyclone is hard to fathom. Unconfirmed reports estimated 47 yachts were missing from Shute Harbour. One of our casual skippers, Mal Priday's, yacht was pushed 18 metres into the mangroves. The insurance company took months before eventually writing it off.

I posted my rage on Facebook, heading my post:

THE FORGOTTEN TOWN

So five days post Cyclone Debbie and our neighbourhood is still without power and water and fuel only arrived in town yesterday. One of Australia's favourite holiday destinations with more than half a million visitors each year nationally and more than 200,000 international visitors. Shame on you – local state and federal governments ... Boil your drinking water – what with Premier? When there is no power and Bunnings have run out of generators? If you ever want to experience the end of the world as we know it – that's what it's been like in Airlie Beach. No sign of any SES, Army – power said to be out for a fortnight – and electricity poles across the road untouched by human hand.

Refusing to accept nothing can be done, I employ 'shoe leather' (the journalism adage of visiting the scene of the action instead of phoning people). I am rewarded almost instantly. A woman at the petrol station, which we used to frequent for our ice and milk supplies, tells me that the road to Bowen is open. And they have fuel in Bowen. Airlie Beach is out of everything. Of all of the petrol stations I visited the common refrain was: "Fuel maybe in a few days."

We have to get *Providence* out of Airlie Beach. We have a business to run.

Grant and I head to Bowen where we put jerry cans with fuel in the back of Bertha so we can fill up our boat. The holes in her side have luckily not affected her ability to go to sea. Our crew then set sail with our wounded warrior to Townsville. We are one of the first boats up on the slip. $40,000 worth of damage later, we discover, to our relief, that we are covered by insurance. *Providence* sits up on the hard dock in Townsville for a month. Our crew is paid for maintenance and we put them up in an Airbnb. Many in Airlie Beach are finding it hard to get work.

Stories appear in the media with photographs purporting to be coal on a beach south of Abbot Point released by the Australian Conservation Foundation and Australian Marine Conservation

Society. The Murdoch press, in particular, condemns the activists. The Environment Department later confirms it is a naturally-produced substance. Former Mayor and Councillor, Mike Brunker, is photographed on his hands and knees on Dingo Beach a little over halfway between Airlie Beach and Bowen. He is hell-bent on proving that the 'blackness' is a naturally occurring mineral magnetite. Resource Minister, Matt Canavan joins in the ridicule of the activists.

The Mayor of the Whitsundays, Andrew Wilcox, who had reportedly spent so much on the junket to India, also appeared with a magnet on Dingo Beach to do his own scientific experiments.

* * *

In spite of the cynicism about the earlier reports, on 11 August 2017, the newspaper headlines are stark. Adani has been fined $12,190 by the Queensland Government for a stormwater breach before and after Cyclone Debbie – after the company released more than eight times the amount of 'suspended solids' it was permitted to put into the ocean. Although not related to the claims of coal waste on the beaches[150] nearby made by the activists, it confirmed concerns about Adani's lack of responsibility regarding the environment. The company had been given a temporary licence by the Queensland Department of Environment and Heritage Protection to more than triple its suspended solids – up to 100mg per litre of 'suspended solids' between March 27 and 30, just before and after Cyclone Debbie.

A statement from the Department of Environment and Heritage Protection released in August 2017 reads: "Temporary emissions licences and environmental authorities are not taken lightly by the department and there can be harsh penalties for companies that breach their approvals."[151]

Far from being the least bit apologetic, in the same vein as witnessed in India, company denial followed. When the company was confronted with allegations of environmental damage, an Adani spokesman initially claimed that no spill had made its way into the ocean. The spokesman went further, saying the company 'strongly' rejected allowing contaminated floodwaters into the nearby marine environment and said that the company was considering its options about the fine and would be defending the prosecution.

If the release is found to have caused environmental damage, the fine could be $1 million according to Josh Roberts writing in *The Guardian*.[152] In September 2017, a Queensland Government report confirmed that satellite images collected after Cyclone Debbie appeared to show dark waters downstream of the terminal leading into the wetlands. Sampling could not be done immediately by the Department but a preliminary assessment established that there was little evidence that coal 'fines' (tiny coal particles) from Abbot Point had contaminated the wetlands, home to migratory and water birds (up to 48,000 on site during high use times according to the Government Report, some of which are threatened). Some, however, had been sighted near the licensed discharge point. The fact that a large body of water had flowed through the wetlands would have mitigated the impacts from stormwater discharge, the Government Report stated.[153]

The Environment Department also noted further assessment was needed downstream of the licensed discharge point and requested the company to notify the Department within 24 hours of any release from the port going into the wetlands. Commenting on the environmental approvals for the Adani mine in an article entitled: 'Who is Responsible for Monitoring Adani?' Samantha Hepburn, Director of the Centre for Energy and Natural Resources Law at Deakin University, said: "... assessment of the environmental impact of the mine was conducted under a bilateral agreement between both the Federal and State regulatory frameworks. This means that the project has approval under both State and Federal frameworks." The issue, she states, is "a lack of delineation around management, monitoring and enforcement."

The combination of State and Federal scrutiny is supposed to strengthen the protection of our environment. Instead, it reduces it. This overlapping of jurisdictional authority recurs again and again in this story: when protecting groundwater; giving environmental approvals and leases to large mining projects and, more worryingly, any of these authorities' concerns about the effects of irreversible decisions on climate change.

* * *

"How much do you reckon the Great Barrier Reef is worth?"

The local journalist from the *Whitsunday Times* is on the phone. I am about to turn into a petrol station to fill up Bertha and pull over to take the call.

"What are you talking about?"

I google the news before calling him back. It is July 2017. Deloitte Access Economics has just released a Report, which calculates the reef is worth $56 billion and contributes $6.4 billion to the Australian economy.[154] Two thirds of the 1500 respondents consulted for the 90-page report have said they are willing to pay to protect it. The reef is, the Report states, worth $56 billion as an economic, social and iconic natural asset. At $29 billion, tourism is noted as the biggest contributor to the reef's $56 billion value, followed by $23.8 billion from indirect or non-use value (those who haven't yet visited the reef but value knowing it exists). Its value to recreational users ($3.2 billion) makes up the balance. It is worth more than 12 Sydney Opera Houses.

How can you put some economic value on the only living organism to be seen from outer space? It seems like a cheap gimmick. But the journalist argues that politicians and business-people – who after all make the decisions about the future of the reef – will only listen to this kind of argument.

Meanwhile, the public that they are supposed to serve, don't want coal projects at the expense of coral and declare they value the reef. In February 2018, a ReachTEL poll, commissioned by the Australian Conservation Foundation, finds only 6.8% of people supported the idea of using public money to support coal mine projects.

As reluctant as I am to take part in such a ruthless economic exercise I concede the journalist is probably right. Talk the talk of those motivated by profits like billionaire Gautam Adani and the gaggle of politicians who jump for the monetary bean. At least the newspaper headlines are putting the Great Barrier Reef out there again.

Chapter 9

The Ping Pong Politics of Climate Change

In the Whitsundays in 2017 we have the hottest July in 100 years. No rain. Around the airport, the emerald-green lawns the wallabies once fed on are dry as a bone.

"How good is this weather?" say the travel agents in the main street. 'Mexicans' (from across the chilly border – from NSW and Victoria) limber up to the tropics yawning in the warmth of the sun. "What a great season this. How good has the weather been?"

It's a honeymoon after Debbie that lasts and lasts. The tourists love it. I think of the impending summer. That winter, the heat was relentless. No doona-covered nights in the middle of winter. It's still hot enough for a fan. The quilt-lined jackets I've ordered for the crew are still at the uniform shop. The inevitability of coral bleaching is forever in my thoughts. There is now not even an opportunity for the coral to be protected in the cooler months due to global warming.

I dive with my GoPro camera into an ocean that already feels like summer. Warm enough to stay in for 20 minutes or more. A pleasant coolness envelops me, not the biting chill of winter, but a near perfect temperature. Beneath me there is coral. Colours yes. And fish of turquoises and pinks and zebra stripes and a parrot fish. But, somehow, when I look at the photos they seem overexposed and I want to go to 'edit tools' on my iPhone to fix that so the colours dazzle more. The corals seemed more faded than on my snorkel at Blue Pearl the previous winter, which took my breath away. Three quarters of the world's coral can be found on the Great Barrier Reef. In between the sepia-toned colours, the wreckage of coral lies like withered bones in a long forgotten graveyard.

One patch of finger coral is ghostly white. A tiny turquoise fish looks back at me – did I detect an expression of fear? Look what you have already done! What are you capable of doing next?

The coral around Border Island on the way to Whitehaven Beach takes us more than a month to find. After the cyclone we return to places we traditionally offered our guests to snorkel – Dumbell Island – where beneath us, even from the dinghy, the colours used to radiate as we headed closer to shore. It was gone. All gone. "Oh," our skipper said after a few days, adding, "right at the end of the island on the north-east side, there's still some."

Cyclones are the most severe form of mechanical disturbance. On the back of severe bleaching, however, a cyclone can have an even more devastating effect as the coral struggles to recover from structural damage. Fate helped us survive the worst bleaching in 2016. According to GBRMPA, the late summer cooling of ocean temperatures from ex-Tropical Cyclones Winston in February 2016 in Fiji and Tatiana in the same month 1000 kms off the coast of Mackay, helped keep our oceans cool.

These are the kind of conversations we expected might occur if more bleaching did happen and the coral did not recover at all – maybe a decade or so from now, maybe two. We'd all be squabbling over what remained ... but we were already guarding what remained. Boats watched other boats to see where they were taking their tourists to provide the ultimate snorkelling experience. TripAdvisor reviews across most of the tourism operators' ratings are full of complaints. Some people wanted their money back. The response – "There's been a cyclone," did not seem to cut the mustard.

* * *

Tropical cyclones are low-pressure systems that form over warm tropical waters – they are basically a non-frontal low-pressure system according to the Bureau of Meteorology. Cyclones do not form unless the sea surface temperature is above 26.5°C. Cyclones, of course, are naturally occurring phenomena with the potential to wreak catastrophic damage. The Climate Council, however, states that climate change can affect tropical cyclone behaviour in two ways.[155]

Firstly, the formation of tropical cyclones occurs when there are "very warm conditions at the ocean surface and when the vertical temperature gradient through the atmosphere is strong." As the climate continues to get hotter, however, the difference between the temperature near the surface of the Earth and the temperature higher up in the atmosphere, is likely to decrease as the atmosphere continues to warm. As this "vertical temperature gradient" weakens, the good news is fewer tropical cyclones are predicted to form.

However – and here's the catch – the combination of the warmer temperatures of the surface ocean and the upper atmosphere conditions, leads to more intense cyclones because the cyclone draws energy from the surface of the ocean. This, according to the Climate Council, is reflected in terms of maximum wind speeds and the intensity of heavy rainfall that occurs along with the cyclone. Cyclone Debbie is an example of this. The floods that crossed south-east Queensland and as far south as northern New South Wales brought about by heavy rain were responsible for the lives lost in that cyclone.

As the intensity of cyclones increases, damage to the Great Barrier Reef and other reefs worldwide also increases. Damage from Cyclone Yasi in 2011 caused coral damage across 89,000 square kilometres of the Great Barrier Reef Marine Park with 15% of it sustaining some damage and 6% being severely damaged. The ecological impacts of severe tropical cyclones like Cyclones Larry, Yasi and Debbie are likely to be around for several decades according to the Great Barrier Reef Marine Park Authority.[156] As already noted in the 2017 review of GBRMPA, Dr Wendy Craik stated that although in 2016, there had been "a significant co-ordinated response to mass bleaching including the largest ever series of in-water surveys" that "a similar response was not undertaken for the mass bleaching in 2017 due to a lack of resources."

Australian Institute of Marine Science's long-term survey of the reef, which has been running for 30 years, did not survey the damage caused by Cyclone Debbie, as each section of the reef is surveyed on rotation so I was unable to find the kind of detailed report on the effects of Cyclone Debbie on the reef we visit. However, GBRMPA[157/158] has stated that 28% of the total reef area in the Marine Park was within the 'catastrophic damage zone' of the cyclone's path according to its surveys, and Queensland Parks and Wildlife Service revealed that some sites have suffered significant damage (up to 97% coral loss) and are down to very low coral cover, while others received less damage and still have moderate coral cover.

As we can expect to have more intense and more damaging cyclones *because* of climate change, have we got the resources to continue to monitor these disasters so we have more knowledge for the future?

The second aspect brought about by climate change affects the level of storm surge. Storm surges occur because of strong onshore winds and/or reduced atmospheric pressure, states the Report. Storm surges are riding higher now than ever before because of the higher sea levels caused by climate change due to warming oceans and melting ice sheets, according to the Climate Council. The Pacific Islanders who hardly contribute to global warming, are confronting disappearing coastlines and losing their lives and homes as the sea level rises.

Coupled with the rising warmer oceans and acidification causing bleaching, the Great Barrier Reef is struggling against great odds.

On 22 May 2017, the Chair of GBRMPA, Russell Reichelt, warned a Parliamentary Senate Committee that the coral's resistance to such pressures as bleaching, tropical storms and other threats, such as the crown-of-thorns invasions, would not give the coral enough time to recover. He told the Committee that the best science suggested global warming needed to be limited to 1.5°C to allow a good survival rate for coral.

"There had already been a 0.7°C warming over the past century ... I draw the public's attention and the Committee to the fact the unprecedented back-to-back bleaching we've seen is occurring on a fraction of a degree [rise in temperature]," he said.[159] "The safe levels [of warming] for coral reefs, probably we've passed already."

Even delivering the dire news to the lion's den, however, did not seem to make much difference. Reichelt was not the only one with such a devastating warning. Professor Terry Hughes is arguably one of the most informed coral scientists in the world. After responding so swiftly to the global coral bleaching events on the Great Barrier Reef in December 2016, he was named as one of the ten people who mattered most in the world that year. The prestigious science journal *Nature* dubbed him a 'reef sentinel'.[160]

It was Hughes who had reported the chilling facts on the back-to-back bleaching of the reef in 2016/17 in *Nature*[161] stating that some reefs had lost 80% of their corals and that among the casualties were 50- and 100-year-old corals, which would take a long time to be replaced. Importantly, Terry Hughes had named global warming as the central villain in killing the reef and argued that while protecting the reef from run-off and over-fishing was important, immediate action to curb climate change was the *only* thing that would limit damage to the reef. Hughes had used aerial and underwater surveys to document the extent and severity of the 2016 year's bleaching, as well as data from the USA's National Oceanic and Atmospheric Administration (NOAA) satellite data to examine the cause of the increased sea surface temperatures.

Hughes and his team of researchers found bleaching occurred regardless of how protected the reef was from run-off and over-fishing. "The only thing that made the difference was the intensity of the heat," Professor Hughes had told *The Science Show* on ABC's *Radio National* in March 2017 while we were still in India.

"That's an incredibly precarious situation to be in where the health of the Great Barrier Reef at a huge scale depends on a chance weather event."

Significantly, 2016/17 was the first 'back-to-back' bleaching of the reef to occur and it did *not* coincide with El Niño, a weather pattern that has been associated with bleaching events in the past.

"Climate change is already dangerous for the Great Barrier Reef," Professor Hughes said, adding that even a 2°C global temperature rise (1.5–2°C was suggested in the Paris Agreement) "won't be a comfortable place for coral reefs."

"We've got a window of opportunity, but it's getting narrower and narrower to quickly move away from fossil fuels and curb emissions," he said.

Dr Andrew King, a climate scientist from the University of Melbourne who studies climate extremes and variability, said Professor Hughes' research established the strong link between coral bleaching and warmer water.

"These findings, in conjunction with other studies, point to the fact that warmer waters are damaging the reef and climate change means that large parts of the reef won't recover," he said.

Dr King said recent research looking at the frequency of bleaching events emphasised the need for strong action, as, alarmingly, he forecast that it looked like bleaching could occur every second year on average.[162]

* * *

Orpheus Island lies offshore from Lucinda, almost halfway between Townsville and Cairns. James Cook University has a research station there. In 2009, I took a group of life writing students to spend five days on the island. One of my students was a child protection worker who had written a compelling piece about his harrowing career: painting evocative images of seizing children from heroin addicted mothers. My student had had a life threatening disease as a child. Following treatment, he had been told he might never have children of his own. A loving, warm open-faced young man, he unburdened his worst images before the class crafting some beautiful words as he attempted to navigate a pathway through his life story.

Later, we headed to the boat ramp and plunged beneath the surface to see a fairy world of true beauty – some of the best coral I'd ever seen along the eastern coastline. Snorkelling and diving is a solitary experience. An overwhelming, sensory feast. My student had never been snorkelling before. His astonishment and wonder was endearing. Bommie after bommie encrusted with colours that burst forth. Each outdid the other. (A 'bommie' is a submerged reef. It is the colloquial Australian word for the official term bombora.) The myriad fish and giant clams competed with radiating colours that were incomprehensible in vibrancy. But that day, I remember a sense of unease. That what we were looking at could somehow not endure – that it was too perfect. Too precious.

* * *

In the winter months, onboard *Providence*, a 70-year-old woman from England is snorkelling for the first time. Her floating vest is firmly in place and her husband and son are fussing over her as she battles her fear to descend the ladder off the dinghy. Five minutes later, she is in the water clutching a bright pink noodle; a tubular foam to aid swimmers, firmly held by her husband and son.

I take the plunge nearby. "Put your face in," they encourage her.

Jess, our daughter who is our deckie (deckhand) and driving the tender (our support boat), stays nearby on snorkel watch. I am convinced the woman will give up and return to the boat. After ten minutes in the water I swim back to *Providence*. Instead of the woman, it is her husband who arrives back first, beaming.

"I need to get our camera. To record this moment. It's the first time she's ever managed to do it," he explains breathlessly.

Radiant, she is one of the last to get back on board the dinghy.

"I've been to the Isle of Pines in New Caledonia," she gushes. "I've done so many glass-bottom boats but nothing compares to this. Not what I saw down here. Nothing." Our eyes are locked in the experience we have shared. But I know, because I was also snorkelling near her, that no matter how good it is now, it cannot compare with what was.

* * *

The rotten behaviour we had observed in India from the Adani Group is already seeping into the company's Australian operations. After Adani contested the fine for releasing polluted water into the ocean around the time of Cyclone Debbie, the Department of Environment found that, while preparing to defend the fine, the company had falsified records. An article in *The Guardian* reported that a copy of the original laboratory report included a column that had not been included in the document provided to the government by Adani. This column showed suspicions that "an even higher reading of 834 mg/l of coal-laden water had been released."[163]

* * *

In September 2017, I fly to Canberra on a second lobbying trip to that wedding cake in the sky (the Australian Parliament) where those we have elected, govern in our interests. Mid-March 2016 had marked my first official lobbying trip to the nation's capital. Back then I had been accompanied by Charlie Veron who has named nearly a quarter of the world's corals, and Imogen Zethoven, who I was meeting for the first time. I was wholly unprepared by how devastating our visit was.

Days of waiting in opulent corridors filled with original artwork (MPs get to choose their own artwork from the parliamentary catalogue), and soundless plush carpets to wait to see the key men – they are all men – who dominate this debate: Greg Hunt, then Minister for the Environment; Josh Frydenberg, then Minister for Resources, Energy and Northern Australia and later Minister for the Environment and Energy; Matt Canavan, then Minister for Northern Australia and soon to be Minister for Resources and

Northern Australia; Barnaby Joyce, then Minister for Agricultural and Water Resources and Minister for Resources and Northern Australia. This select group of power brokers bat the key energy portfolios with table tennis aplomb between each other and tightly control the debate – as well as the Prime Minister – on climate change.

At the time of going to print, in July 2018, some of them continue to chorus from the recently formed 'Monash Forum', backed by an increasingly vocal former Prime Minister, Tony Abbott, who takes every opportunity to say that we need new coal power plants to be built in Australia. Members of this group, which include 20 backbench MPs, promote the benefits of coal power.

In April 2018, Canavan, then Resources Minister, went further, saying that coal-fired power stations – if replaced with the more efficient 'ultra supercritical technology' – would reduce emissions from current coal power stations by 27% according to articles in *The Australian* and *Guardian,* citing Canavan's own research commissioned from the Department of Industry, Innovation and Science. These numbers were crunched by the Climate and Energy College at the University of Melbourne. Yes, they could, but replacing Australia's coal plants with new ultra-supercritical technology, would cost AU$62 billion and the equivalent energy from renewable energy would be a lot cheaper.[164]

Clean coal became the catch-cry of the government of the day, a particular favourite of Malcolm Turnbull as though all you needed to do was give it a good scrub and it would turn into something more palatable. In her 2017 *Quarterly Essay* 'The Long Goodbye,' Anna Krien comments (p. 102):[165] "As for the cutting-edge technology, most power stations now operating were already super-critical – 'ultra' registers only a minor improvement, with emissions still double those of natural gas."

It is clear who Canavan supports. As if there is any doubt, in July 2017, having stood aside as Minister for Resources and Northern Australia, following accusations about his reported dual-citizenship (Italy and Australia), he revealed his unwavering support for Australian miners on his Facebook page saying how much he had enjoyed serving them during his time in office. "Mining and resources are a uniquely Australian success story. From the small, gambling explorers and prospectors to the large, world-beating multi-nationals, the industry provides rich and diverse experiences that can take you from the smallest towns of outback Australia to the biggest cities in the world. It has been such an honour to represent the Australian mining sector over the past year. It is an industry full of fine, hard-working and innovative people."[166] But what of his constituents?

Meanwhile, Australian Electoral Commission figures reporting on political donations in 2016–17, found that ads spruiking the benefits of coal mining were the biggest political expenditure by third party groups in Australia dwarfing public contributions from unions and GetUp.[167]

* * *

The men we are scheduled to see mostly sent their offsiders to meet us in corridors or noisy coffee shops, rarely in their offices, during our visit to Federal Parliament. They cluster together supporting each other, adamantly pro-coal and anti-climate change. Canavan, then 36 years old and one of the most outspoken MPs, was Chief of Staff to Barnaby Joyce from 2010–13. Between them, and aided and abetted by a compliant Prime Minister, they control the debate on climate change, transparently trumpeting the interests of the mining industry. They make policies that, according to polls, fly in the face of what most Australians want. In our meetings, their offsiders stare into space occasionally nodding, biding out the meeting time when they can go back to their offices. When Greg Hunt was Environment Minister and flew over the Great Barrier Reef in March 2016 after the back-to-back bleaching with Professor Terry Hughes, he still managed to put out a positive spin on such a catastrophic global event. Confronting the third global-scale event since mass bleaching was first documented in the 1980s, he told the media it wasn't as bad as he thought it would be.

In complete contrast, the man who occupied the same plane as Hunt, Professor Terry Hughes, who had flown over 1000 out of the Great Barrier Reef's almost 3000 reefs, was devastated by what he saw in 2016. He told the *Brisbane Times* in April 2016 that 75% of corals north of Cairns "are snow white."[168] Hughes has been scathing about the effectiveness of politicians as stewards of the reef to counteract climate change, warning that politicians are doing little to meet the Paris Agreement target to keep the increase of global average temperature well below 2°C above pre-industrial levels. "Really," he added in a far-ranging interview with Yale Environment 360 published by the Yale School of Forestry and Environmental Studies in April 2017, "what Australia should be doing, in my opinion, as the country responsible for the stewardship of the Great Barrier Reef is taking a leadership role in transitioning away from fossil fuels, but sadly that hasn't occurred."[169]

After a punishing round of lacklustre meetings, Veron and I retreat to one of the multitude of cafés inside this utopian building where the food is heavily subsidised – main courses are around $10. Charlie, whose real name is John, is in his early 70s. His eyes are pale blue and penetrating. His nickname pays homage to his hero Charles Darwin, reflecting his early childhood obsession with collecting specimens. Veron was the first full-time researcher on the Great Barrier Reef, and later Chief Scientist of the Australian Institute of Marine Science. He has been awarded the Darwin Medal for his work on evolution and his life is now devoted to building a Corals of the World website. When David Attenborough made his recent 2015/16 television series on the Great Barrier Reef, Veron was on screen with him. They share a combined historical experience of respective lifetimes on the Great Barrier Reef. Veron wears weariness like a cloak, but whenever he speaks out about the Great Barrier Reef, it is with a fierce passion. He has been diving there for more than 50 years. We place our coffee mugs on the outside table. When I look up, I am shocked. Veron is crying silent tears.

"I'm not going to invest in coming here again," he tells me. "There's no point."

I do not attempt to contradict him. In that moment I see into his soul – the devastation for him – what he has devoted his life to. The powerlessness he feels at failing to protect it. These men we have met have no idea of who Veron is and what he has experienced, nor do they care. It is, he confides later, in his view too late to save the reef. "But, if we say this" – and he leans forward and becomes conspiratorial – "everyone will give up. That," he adds, "is even harder to bear."

During our visit, Veron had spoken at length to Hunt's adviser. This adviser seemed to care and this gave Veron some solace. However, when he returned from our trip, and aired his views in the media, Hunt phoned him and, Veron told me, "accused him" of not coming to Canberra to discuss his concerns. Hunt was not even aware Veron had been there.

* * *

September 2017 marks my second visit to Canberra. My thoughts, as I look down from the plane, are on the baking earth below: dried in the way that fruit dries until they are a shrivelled form of themselves. Criss-crossed cleared fields, below me, are laid bare by man – white man mostly. It is the softly flowing carpeted hills with native vegetation surrounding the bare patchwork that survives this heat. The dark green colours contrast between what was and what is now.

Before white people came to this land, there was human habitation 65,000 years ago.[170] Some of the oldest geological formations in Australia are in the Kimberley region in Western Australia. I once saw cave paintings on Bigge Island that are said to depict Abel Tasman's landing on these shores in the 1640s, reportedly the first white man of any note to visit Australia. The Wandjina art, of which this painting is a part, shows a figure reportedly smoking a pipe. Aboriginal and Torres Strait Islander peoples have fished and hunted its waters and navigated between the islands of our Great Barrier Reef for centuries.

In those intervening years, we have destroyed the landscape rather than preserving it, making a mockery of sustainability. We have one of the highest emissions of carbon dioxide in the world based on the Emissions Database for Global Atmospheric Research (EDGAR) created by the European Commission's Joint Research Centre and Netherlands Environmental Assessment Agency in 2015. EDGAR provides global past and present statistics on greenhouse gas emissions and air pollutants by country and on a spatial grid.

Australia was the second highest country behind Canada for carbon dioxide emissions per capita from fossil fuels and cement production, according to the report, with around 18.6 tonnes of carbon dioxide per capita released in 2015.[171] Little wonder as two thirds of our electricity is generated from coal. The study found that one third of all global carbon dioxide emissions came from coal-fired power plants. More recent figures reveal that there is a continuing rising trend for emissions in Australia, which began around 2011 according to consultants NDEVR Environmental which replicates the Federal Government's National Greenhouse Gas Inventory (NGGI) Reports. While emissions from the electricity sector were the lowest in the last three months of 2017, emissions for transport were at a record high in the same time period continuing a steady rise since the records began in 2001.[172]

In spite of the facts, there are still some scientists who continue to deny what is happening. As the Climate Council recently pointed out, Larry Marshall, CEO of CSIRO, was quoted in the *Australian Financial Review* (AFR) as saying poor water quality is the main cause of the recent back-to-back bleaching on the reef.

Will Steffen, writing for the Council in March 2018 had this to say about Marshall's statement:

"Marshall's comments seem to be aligned to a Federal Government plan to focus on water quality measures. Addressing water quality is just a bandaid solution that is only useful if we also tackle climate change, the root cause of coral bleaching. Yet Australia's greenhouse gas pollution levels continue to rise (by 0.8% the past year) without credible federal climate policy in place."[173]

Marshall was reported as saying to the AFR that it was a common misconception that coral bleaching meant it was too late to save.[174] He said the reef usually grows back two years after a bleaching event, similar to trees after a bushfire, and that the CSIRO had deployed sensors in the reef, which showed most of its problems come from sedimentary run-off from the land, rather than the ocean itself. Steffen, however, said that coral reefs often took decades to repair themselves.

* * *

This time, our visit to Canberra, under the auspices and funded by the Australian Conservation Foundation (ACF), has a different focus. We are to physically deliver a petition of more than 100,000 signatures to Prime Minister Malcolm Turnbull's office, urging the government to reject any funding application from Adani to build the 388 km railway line linking the proposed Carmichael mine with the coal terminal at Abbot Point.

Most taxpayers still appear to be completely unaware that their taxes may potentially be funding the proposed Adani railway line linking the port with the pit. The ACF has made a submission to the Senate Standing Committee in charge of the governance of the Northern Australian Infrastructure Facility (NAIF) urging it to ensure it acts in the interests of northern Australian communities as well as focusing on environmental goals. NAIF was set up by former Prime Minister, Tony Abbott, to approve loans to northern Australian projects of up to $5 billion to encourage development (such as ports, rail, water, communications) in a bid to stimulate growth. By this time, September 2017, there had already been speculation in the media about the lack of transparency in the way that NAIF is governed. The ACF on its website also noted that NAIF had been resistant to FOI (Freedom of Information) requests and that it was "subject to little in the way of checks and balances." Geoff Cousins had already alluded to the responsibility of the Directors of the NAIF Board and their duty to serve the public interest while we were in India.

The ACF has also requested a supporter feedback video from our visit to Canberra, telling compelling stories of self and change. This initiative, I am to find, is all important. It gives people who have committed their time and energy to stop Adani hope that all their hard work is worth it.

Six months after returning from India, the Stop Adani movement is everything Geoff Cousins has said it will be. More than 2 million Australians belong to organisations that have signed up to the Stop Adani Alliance[175] from small environment groups to national organisations leading campaigns against climate change.

It has, quite simply, revolutionised Australian politics, woken up complacency, tumbled supporters out of their living rooms and into the streets and on to the beaches to form human protests photographed from the air and to conduct sit-in protests in banks. Volunteers are getting arrested after tying themselves to railway machinery in the Abbot Point coal terminal; parents are painting murals along school walls in inner city Melbourne.

Crowd-funding sites have sprung up online. Even my octogenarian parents are contributing money from their pension to the fight to stop this coal mine and they have attended a protest in their hometown. The movement is billed by Stop Adani as 'the fight of our times'. 'People power unite' adopted by Stop Adani and ACF is the catch-cry across suburban homes and public gatherings across Australia. The public slumbers no more. #StopAdani is clogging networks everywhere. The giant has awoken.

After the launch, thousands had turned out across Australia to protest against the Carmichael mine on a national day of action in October 2017. Rallies at 40 different locations including Sydney, Melbourne, Brisbane, the Gold Coast and Port Douglas followed an investigative program on ABC-TV's *Four Corners* highlighting Adani Group's shonky financial and environmental history.[176]

There are Stop Adani human signs at various locations including beaches in Newcastle. A new ReachTel poll commissioned by the Stop Adani Alliance in October 2017 reports that the majority of Australians do not want the mine.

Annastacia Palaszczuk rejects these protests claiming that the mine has "the toughest environmental conditions attached."[177] But the protestors appear not to believe her. Continuous public outcry and demonstrations have stopped Australian banks from funding Adani. There is a feeling of euphoria in the air, that if you have a will you can stop anything. Some of the older protestors have not had this feeling since the days of Woodstock and the Vietnam War.

An ebook is released in March 2018 entitled *hope for whole: poets speak up to Adani* edited by Anne Elvey.[178] Among the poems included in the anthology is Michelle Cahill's poem from the future (p. 11):

2030, ADANI, A RETROSPECTIVE

Remember Gujarat? Tidal mangroves were blocked
by bunds & embankments, Chinese MoU,
revenues from aluminium, polysilicon, animal feeds.

The Paris Climate, OECD delegates sipped their lattes,
declaiming coal dust, wastewater choking the fish,
bleached nuggets, burgeoning coral cemeteries.

We, with our winning smiles, tweeting environmental
charities, retweeting memes, protests, petitions, trending,
bracketed clauses in the draft agreement, spineless

politicians, Tourism Australia. Never mind Sir David
or Obama—we needed Murrawah, Amelia, Xiuhtezcatl
to sing the rewilding of grasslands, reefs, native title—

Who knew that Subrata Maity and Claude Alvares
defended the Mundra, or Mormugão Port in Goa from
pollution violations? The permits were not revoked.

When 10 per cent of robots lived in cities compliant
with WHO air quality guidelines, when the black
rhinoceros outnumbered the black-throated finch?

Nevertheless we sweltered, with news analysis full
blast, we dialled up air cons, we talked prophylactic
gene editing, from monkey to pig to homo saps.

We wrote dirges for the third world, prohibiting diesel
& motorcycle distributors, reversing neo-colonialism
with a corporate warrant to drill the Galilee basin.

Everyone was abused; the state's litigations, economic
futures, First nations, mind & memory's quaint algorithms,
poems festering, composed in acid rain; volatile

in smog.

Gautam Adani has re-ignited the politics of protest in a country
which all too often has accepted its fate and where political activity
in the main translates into turning up to vote at the polling booth
every few years.

* * *

The following morning, in my Canberra motel room before visiting
Parliament House, I wake to the incredible radio news that the
Prime Minister, Malcolm Turnbull, wants to keep the aged (opened
in the early 1970s) and closing coal-fired Liddell Power Station in
the Hunter Valley of New South Wales – once the most powerful
generating station in Australia – open.[179] He has even personally
phoned the energy giant AGL Energy's chief, Andy Vesey, to make
the request. AGL had announced it planned to close the power
plant in 2022 and has spent money on a long-running advertising
campaign saying things needed to change and "we are getting
out of coal starting 2022 and ending 2050." One of Turnbull's
acolytes, Josh Frydenberg, has joined in the discussions with AGL.
Although Turnbull has stopped short of saying the Government
will buy the power plant, his voice in the early morning bulletin
sounds close to hysterical. How could this be the same man who

spoke so passionately about "the moral issue of climate change" back in 2011?

* * *

In early September 2017, our group meets for the first time at one of these strange Jetson-like bubbles they call a Canberra coffee shop on the ground floor of an office block close to Parliament House. It is the only commercial food place in the wide streets so empty of traffic, but it does respectable business.

Sharon France is a graphic designer who woke up to environmental consciousness in her 50s, after studying sustainability at university. She works as a volunteer for ACF. One night she had a dream. It was about a giant cheque book. She decided to design such a cheque book asking people to fill in the blank dotted lines with how they would like to see $1 billion spent of taxpayers' money, the amount being considered by NAIF to give to Adani for the proposed rail line. Awaken the Australian public to what the government might be doing with their money, was her idea.

The idea became a reality. The cheque book was stamped: *The People's Bank of Better Ideas*. It had collected 1500 signatures. Sharon France was like many women I met along this journey attracted to the Stop Adani movement who candidly admitted they had never been involved in radical action. Yet, this cause united them. Woke them up. Gave them an identity and purpose in lives where ageing and comfortable monotony threatened. Suddenly they had a new purpose.

Kenny Peters-Dodd, another person in our group, is a Birriah-Widi elder – a 'River man' – "the freshwater people," he tells me, whose lands lie in from the coast in the arid country inland 25 kms from the coastal town of Bowen. His eyes are the colour of green waterholes. He fixes them upon you with a strong no nonsense gaze. He has German forebears but carries a strong Indigenous presence. The proposed Adani rail line will cut through his ancestral lands, waters, ecosystem and cultural heritage.

"To actually stand on country and fight for your country and have that affiliation and spiritual connection to protect your country and advocate for the rights of your country and fight for that – that lineage is broken, you know," Peters-Dodd wistfully tells me later. "With Native Title today we have people signing agreements on country – but they're not considering duty of care or the rights or interests to protect their country – I mean both culturally and environmentally ... These Indigenous people – to me – they are just seeing the opportunity – that these mines may bring jobs and changes to their lifestyle – but they are not standing up as a traditional person, they are not standing up as Birriah people to protect their country. That should be their first interest."

The third member of our party is Clare Johnston, a shy, single mother who loves op shopping and wears colourful skirts and blouses. When in full stride, she belts out her prose like a professional. She is here to tell the politicians the counter-narrative to living in a boom and bust town. She benefits from 'the bust', in her hometown of Mackay on the Queensland coast, she tells them, not the boom, the usual commercial narrative. During the bust she can finally afford to pay the rent pushed up by the miners during the boom, and she has more money to spend on household income to support her son. She is gutsy and passionate, but over the course of the next few days, her eyes regularly fill with tears when she relays her story overcome that people appear to be listening – even politicians. She is a casualty of the lop-sided economy we have created of the 'haves' and the 'have-nots'. The politicians are mostly stunned into silence as she describes her plight. Dr Anne Hoggett, Director of the Research Centre at Lizard Island is one of the last members of our team to join us. She lived through the massive bleaching event on Lizard Island in 2016.

Thomas Kinsman and Basha Stasak from ACF are youthful employees who shepherd us around, providing us with briefs, meeting schedules and enthusiasm. We are here specifically to target the Labor Party that continues to sit on the fence on the

Adani debate under the anaemic leadership of Bill Shorten who has been Opposition Leader since 2013.

Shorten, once a waterside worker and union official and former National Secretary for the Australian Worker's Union (AWU), has predictably chosen to back the Adani mine all in the name of 'jobs'. His favourite garb is a hard hat and 'fluoros' (fluorescent working clothes), to be donned for media opportunities – perhaps a reminder for some of how he was catapulted on to the Australian political stage as National Secretary of the AWU with a self-appointed role of relaying the fate of trapped miners in the Beaconsfield mine collapse in Tasmania in 2006. Shorten is walking the tightrope backing regional jobs in Labor's marginal seats, in cities like Townsville, while at the same time pretending to care about the environment. As Anna Krien wryly points out in her 2017 *Quarterly Essay* (p. 90): "as if the average punter won't be able to put their finger on the dissonance that is a political party ready to fight climate change and happy to open up a new coal seam."[180]

Predictably, though, Bill Shorten stopped short of opposing the Carmichael mine. Making statements about not allowing taxpayers' money to be spent on the rail line meant he could sit on the fence. A critical by-election in the seat of Batman in Victoria favoured a win by the Greens, according to the pre-election polls, that would mean ousting Labor. Labor later did win the seat. After that, Shorten's rhetoric promoting the environment and making disparaging comments about Adani predictably tailed off.

During my first visit to Federal Parliament in March 2016, the Australian Marine Conversation Society delegation had suggested to Bill Shorten's policy advisers that Shorten might consider visiting the Great Barrier Reef where he could launch strong environmental policies, take the opportunity to spruik clean energy, and embrace a strong environmental stance to distinguish Labor from the Liberal/National Party Coalition. He did not take up the invitation. His staffers appeared to be surprised when the idea was broached. But the Australian Labor Party is not radical or left-wing in its views. It has also supported the Government's changes to the Native Title Act, further diluting the rights of Traditional Owners. No wonder there is general agreement that there is little difference between the Government and the Opposition.

The strategy for this visit to Canberra, articulated by the ACF representatives, was based on the reasoning that there was little point convincing Labor to go against the mine as the approvals were already in place. Instead, the strategy was to lobby against the $1 billion proposed NAIF tax loan – yet to be granted. Shorten had already said he would not support it. We were to visit as many Labor MPs as possible.

We begin again with enthusiasm, but soon encounter the same kind of door-shutting tactics I'd experienced during the earlier visit. The ALP MPs are like cattle in the abattoir yard, crowded together with one voice coerced into homogeneity. A small handful seem genuinely interested: Mark Butler, Shadow Minister for Climate Change and Energy, a key figure in the Labor left faction in spite of union roots, is one such person. He has gone further than Shorten stating on the public record in an exclusive interview with *The Guardian*: "I have a very clear view that the economics of Adani don't stack up, and it would not be a positive thing for Australia for the Adani mine to go ahead."[181]

He also said that financial institutions had signalled there was no appetite to build new coal-fired power and that governments would need to indemnify new builds against the risk of a carbon price and against a regulatory risk which would leave taxpayers open "for a massive expense." He said a clean energy target which allowed coal in the mix "was not a clean energy target in anything other than name" and described "'ultra super critical coal' as something out of a Marvel comic, but even awesomely ultra super critical coal is still, by any stretch of the imagination, high polluting electricity."

Two female Labor politicians also stand out. Senator Lisa Singh, on ABC Radio in Hobart in October 2017, described the Carmichael mine as "a huge mistake for this country." Singh had already broken ranks with her own colleagues in her public condemnation of the Adani project. Reportedly, in return for her views, the ALP power brokers had bumped her down to what they presumed was the unwinnable sixth spot on the Tasmanian Senate ticket for the 2016 Federal election.[182] Our aim is to convince her to make a parliamentary statement opposing the Adani rail line project. The other female ALP politician is Terri Butler who has said she doesn't support taxpayers' money being spent on the mine. In October 2017, she is to make a passionate speech to parliament about the effects of climate change on the Great Barrier Reef.

I quiz Terri Butler about how Annastacia Palaszczuk can be so wildly enthusiastic about the Adani project. Her response is enlightening. She says Palaszczuk has been single-minded in her pursuit of the mine and that the rest of the party has gone along with her. There is a grudging admiration for Palaszczuk in the party because of that.

Anne Hoggett is a warm ray of sunshine in our group. Her wealth of knowledge as a scientist, down-to-earth manner and professionalism exudes confidence. She presents some heart-wrenching photographs from the destruction of the coral in the 2016 bleaching event on Lizard Island to the Labor caucus who assemble one afternoon for tea and cakes. Hoggett has lived on the island and has been a joint director of the Lizard Island Research Station with her husband, Lyle Vail, also a scientist, since August 1990. She first visited Lizard Island in 1982 to collect specimens for the Australian Museum where she worked. She gained her PhD on the brittle star family *Ophiotrichidae* in 1991 at the University of Queensland. They home schooled their son Alex on Lizard Island until he was 14 years old.

At the time of the bleaching event, Hoggett hosted a film crew who made the emotionally heart-wrenching, brilliant documentary *Chasing Coral*.[183] The documentary achieved much to engage a world audience with why we should care about the reef beyond just being a tourism destination. A team of divers, scientists and photographers filmed the coral at Lizard Island in its death throes in 2016 shooting more than 500 hours of underwater footage. It won the Audience Award in the USA at the 2017 Sundance Film Festival.

Initially, the documentary team had set up time-lapse cameras off Dunk Island (further south, near Mission Beach), where they had been told bleaching might occur. They had struggled with similar technology in the Caribbean and Hawaii. After days setting up the cameras off Dunk they discovered from NASA that bleaching was in fact occurring further north, off Lizard Island. Abandoning the idea of the time-lapse cameras, they instead marked particular spots on the ocean floor off Lizard Island and headed out each day with handheld cameras to the same spot to record the momentous bleaching event. In the end, young Zach Rago, a self-proclaimed coral nerd, cries on camera as he describes how he witnessed firsthand the same corals he had photographed for three months slowly perishing in front of him. It was like losing old friends, he said.

Lizard Island was visited by many scientists after the bleaching. Justin Marshall, who starred in *Chasing Coral*, a neuro-ecologist from the University of Queensland who had been visiting Lizard Island for 30 years, said he cried underwater after witnessing the coral's demise on the island's Loomis Reef, 270 kms north of Cairns. Writing in *The Huffington Post* in April 2016, Marshall commented that whichever way you looked at the figures, 800 km of deeply distressed and dying reef is "an environmental disaster."

It was Marshall's tears when speaking to journalists on television after the catastrophic bleaching event at Lizard Island that made me take notice. The signs were all there. Professor Terry Hughes admitted after he showed the results of his aerial surveys exposing the amount of damage to the reef, that he had shared the results with his students: "And then we wept."

These scientists are sentinels rising above their customary duties as purveyors of facts on our underwater worlds. Surely we should sit up and take notice. Scientists aren't supposed to cry.

In July 2017, at a public screening of *Chasing Coral* at a local venue in Airlie Beach, I am on a panel describing my views on the threats to the reef. Watching the last bravely colourful display from the corals in their death throes – brighter than any colour that could ever be manufactured – I find myself in tears. *Chasing Coral* was the first time I'd seen coral spawning in that level of detail. I can understand now why scientists call the coral 'animals' instead of just marvelling at their colour and shapes.

Marshall describes the vibrant display as the last sign the 'animals' muster before turning a ghostly white, mostly never to recover. A few months later, David Attenborough's three-part documentary series on the Great Barrier Reef re-screens on television. Charlie Veron sits on a north Queensland beach describing the tragedy, looking distractedly at the camera.

"When the Great Barrier Reef starts to go seriously backwards, what did you do when you had a choice? We're not doing what we should be doing and we are going to pay the price ..." He is crying again. His reaction is so genuine, so endearing, that my eyes fill with tears also.

Attenborough speaks with the same restraint and measured tone we've grown to love as he sums up the state of the reef at the end of the series. He first dived on the reef the year I was born: in 1957. There is plenty of black and white footage of him in baggy shorts and a mop of a brown fringe over a cropped skull as he walks along beaches, delighted with what he is seeing. Back then, he called it "the most spectacular place in the natural world." He had assumed – and why wouldn't he – that it would last forever. His tone in the current series is subdued:

"... the Great Barrier Reef is in grave danger. The twin perils brought by climate change – an increase in the temperature of the ocean and in its acidity – threaten its very existence. If they continue to rise at the current rate, the reefs will be gone in decades. And that would be a global catastrophe. About one quarter of the species of fish in the world spend some part of their lives in the reefs. If the reefs go, the fish will also disappear and that will affect the livelihood and diet of human communities ... worldwide. But there's another reason – the reefs are among the planet's richest most complex eco systems ..."

Beautiful coral landscapes drift by.

"Do we really care so little about the earth on which we live that we don't want to protect one of the world's greatest wonders from the consequences of our behaviour?"

Writing in the 1970s, Judith Wright describes the pristine nature of the Reef when the Reef was threatened with oil refineries. In her book *The Coral Battleground* she wrote (2014, p. 187):[184]

> "I myself had seen only a very small part of it, in the fringing reef of Lady Elliott Island many years before the battle started. But when I thought of the Reef, it was symbolised for me in one image that still stays in my mind. On a still blue summer day, with the ultramarine sea scarcely splashing the edge of the fringing reef, I was bending over a single small pool among the corals. Above it, dozens of small clams spread their velvety lips, patterned in blues and fawns, violets, reds and chocolate browns, not one of them like another. In it, sea-anemones drifted long white tentacles above the clean sand, and peacock-blue fish, only inches long, darted in and out of coral branches of all shapes and colours. One blue sea-star lay on the sand floor. The water was so clear that every detail of the pool's crannies and their inhabitants was vivid, and every movement could be seen through its translucence. In the centre of the pool, as if on a stage, swayed a dancing creature of crimson and yellow, rippling all over like a windblown shawl.
>
> That was the Spanish Dancer, known to scientists as one of the nudibranchs, a shell-less mollusc. But for me it became an inner image of the spirit of the Reef itself."

Writers and scientists have charted the health of the Great Barrier Reef over decades. How can the naysayers continue to ignore such evidence? The climate sceptics? Our grandson, at five-years-old, is too young to snorkel. His children may never experience the sorts of coral underwater landscapes we have taken for granted. Nor the marine creatures that come with it.

* * *

Anne Hoggett's presentation in Canberra is reasonably well-attended, although it is late in the afternoon and after question time. As she posts the last slide on the powerpoint, one of the Labor MPs, who has been sitting half-asleep for most of the presentation, wakes himself and remarks: "Yes, but that is surely caused by cyclones."

Hoggett makes a conscious effort to stop rolling her eyes. It is one thing to have a right-wing conservative Government refuse to budge on climate change and to enable the demise of the Great Barrier Reef, but to have so many MPs from the apparent alternative – the 'left-wing' Labor Party – to be so obstinate in its refusal to embrace the stark future threatening the reef, is to confront despair.

As we cross the entrance to Parliament House I peek between two massive doors into the Great Hall. A mammoth pull-up banner showcases a dark-skinned miner with a hard hat and orange 'fluoros'. The banner is headed *Australian Mining. Making the Future Possible.* I learn later it was launched by the Australian Mining industry whose aim is to "explain the current and future contribution of the mining sector to jobs, living standards and growth to the Australian economy."

The poster seems to make a mockery of why we are here. No matter how hard we try, this age-old mining narrative will continue to be propagated in spite of the facts.

In Parliament this day the focus is on the AU$122 million postal vote asking Australians' opinions on gay marriage. The reef, it seems, hardly registers. I am supportive of the moves towards gay marriage, but the neglect of the reef looms large. "The reef can wait and it's not really that bad after all," seems to be the message from this strangely dislocated space, home to the Government of Australia who have been told by none other than the Great Barrier Reef Marine Park Authority Chair that its ultimate demise is far closer than we all think.

As we leave Parliament House, a baby magpie with ruffled feathers walks up to the entrance hall and pecks at the glass to get in. "Nothing important happens in there mate," I am tempted to pass on. "They are all too full of their own self-importance."

Chapter 10
An About Face

We have entered *Providence V* in the 2017 Whitsunday Tourism Awards in the rather prosaically named category of Major Tour and Transport Operators. The application process was a good opportunity to take stock of our business after more than two years of running tours out of the Whitsundays. We collated statistics off our iPad to find out the type of tourist we attracted as well as where our bookings came from, drew up charts and made monthly comparisons of visitor numbers. We pride ourselves on offering tours that are environmentally friendly, spurning bottled water, providing enviro-friendly toilets and picnic lunches served in lunchboxes to conserve wrapping and waste.

We left for an overseas holiday shortly after making a submission for the awards in mid-September. *MiLady,* our other 54-foot yacht that had been berthed in Greece for four years, beckoned. It was time to move her to Australia and it was our last opportunity to spend time on board. We'd planned to sail from Greece to Malta and then up to Sicily and up the west coast of Italy where we would leave her in Genoa to be loaded onto a ship in November bound for Australia. The day of my birthday in late September, we received a phone call from our skipper, Kieran Burleigh. We'd won the Bronze Tourism Award. Thoroughly chuffed, as it was the first time we had entered, we listened on speaker phone to the excited Glaswegian brogue from Burleigh who had attended the prestigious ball in Hamilton Island on our behalf.

"Only one thing, though," Burleigh said.

"What's that?" I asked.

"You'll never guess who one of the sponsors is ..."

"Who?"

He took a deep breath. "Adani."

The previous elation turned to disbelief. He described how the sponsors' names had been read out to applause, but when Adani's name was mentioned, the room was silent.

We never did see the award. On the way back from Europe, at Rome airport, we emailed the award organisers to let them know we were returning it. While in Sicily, we had visited Corleone, home to a whole host of Mafia bosses as well as the surname of the key fictional character in Francis Ford Coppola's two movies *The Godfather* and its sequel *The Godfather Part II*. In the 1980s and 1990s, the Corleonesi were the most violent and ruthless group ever to take control of the Mafia.

The Anti-Mafia Museum, CIDMA (Centro Internazionale di Documentazione sulla Mafia e del Movimento Antimafia), which opened in 2000, records some of the history. What I remember most was the singular phrase: *"Noi ne parliamo ..."* (*"We Talk About It"*) which sat underneath a photograph of two men: Giovanni Falcone and Paolo Borsellino. The airport at Palermo is named after them. Both judges, they had spent most of their lives trying to bring the Mafia figures to justice. They were both assassinated by the Mafia in two separate bombings. I still remember the black and white photograph in 1987 with the little bubble Fiat in the foreground after the second bomb went off killing Borsellino. He died only 57 days after his best friend Falcone was blown up on the freeway when returning from Rome. Four hundred kilograms of explosives had been placed in a culvert under the highway.

The museum includes a Room of Pain including black and white photographs of the body of a woman whose family was killed by the Mafia and who then committed suicide. Her dark expressionless eyes still resonate. Many of the images and court documents exposing the wrongdoings of the Mafia mirrored the same decade I spent as a crime reporter with the corrupt Darlinghurst police in Sydney and other luminary figures in the underworld reminding me of how dangerous it is to speak the truth. But, without truth what kind of a world can we live in?

Truth had always been my mantra as a journalist. The thought of keeping an award that had been sponsored by Adani – for the reportedly small sum of $2000 – to reward us for our efforts in excellence as Tourism Operators seemed obscene to both of us. We penned a piece on our Facebook page stating we were handing the award back. We were unprepared for the response. Our Facebook page was inundated with well-wishers congratulating us for returning the award. Some said they would choose our tour over others; others offered help. Many said they would spread the word.

There were perhaps two comments in the hundreds we received from all around Australia that complained about what we had done. Australians were speaking out. They had had enough of politicians foisting this coal mine upon us. After the uproar, Tourism Whitsundays apparently decided that any offers from non-tourism sponsors (like the Adani company) had to be officially approved by the Board. No decision was made, however, to send Adani's money back.

* * *

It's 29 October 2017. Annastacia Palaszczuk had just announced the Queensland State election. She's going to an early election full of promises, egged on by her regional supporters like Townsville Mayor, Jenny Hill, who is delighted that in June 2017, Adani declared Townsville would become its regional headquarters. Jobs are in the air. Queensland will be great again. Mining will return. Palaszczuk's first stop outside of Brisbane is Airlie Beach.

The day before she arrived I got a call from one of our drivers, Alison Mason. I had met her some months previously while addressing a Stop Adani rally in Townsville. She was looking for work. Mason is heavily involved in the Stop Adani movement, regularly visiting the frontline Adani camp set up near Collinsville, an inland coal mining town. She also sells wares at the local markets to fundraise for those who have received fines during frontline action activities.

Mason, 56, was in the UK when she first read in the *Daily Telegraph Travel Magazine* that Australian governments had given the go-ahead for the Carmichael mega-coal mine. "See the Great Barrier Reef on your bucket list before it is too late," she remembers the magazine message. She dropped everything and headed home. A former Murdoch journalist and sub-editor, Mason devotes her life to worthy causes. Campaigning against fossil fuels is a high priority.

"Do you know where Palaszczuk will be tomorrow for the start of her election campaign?" she asks me that afternoon.

"No idea," I reply.

She calls again later.

"She's going to be at the waterfront," Mason informs me.

"The waterfront in Airlie Beach?" I say. Like looking for a needle in a haystack, I am thinking. There is waterfront everywhere in Airlie Beach.

En route to picking up our *Providence V* guests early the next morning, Mason hears on media coverage that Palaszczuk is already in Airlie Beach and giving media interviews. She drives down to the lagoon – the heart of Airlie Beach – and hits the jackpot. Palaszczuk is on a podium doing a stand-up to a bevy of cameras: Sky News, ABC, Channel 7. Mason waits her turn. As the Premier finishes her stand-up with Channel 7, she notices Mason, the only member of the public present so early in the morning. Palaszczuk's itinerary has not been widely publicised. There are no other protestors in sight.

"Annastacia Palaszczuk, fancy meeting you here. Why are you doing nothing to save the Great Barrier Reef?" she begins.

"I love the Great Barrier Reef," Palaszczuk counters.

"Well ... why don't you try to protect it?"

"We all do ..." continues Palaszczuk faltering.

"You said you would protect it last time you were elected."

"We are spending $100 million on it."[185]

"What are you spending $100 million doing?"

"On water quality and the farms ..."

"You are putting it on water quality?" Mason is getting angry. "What are you doing to stop Adani putting eight times the legally allowable particulate in the water pre-Cyclone Debbie?"

"That's not true ..." Palaszczuk says, adding, "That was investigated."

Mason is taken aback. The Premier, she is thinking, does not know her facts. It was true, as Adani had been fined, even if they had appealed.

"It was thoroughly investigated," Palaszczuk answers.

"And your own government fined Adani $12,000 ..."

Palaszczuk moves a step closer placing her right hand on Mason's shoulder.

"I'm not going to argue with you ..."

As soon as Palaszczuk places her hand on Mason's shoulder, two of Palaszczuk's minders approach. The Premier returns to the podium to continue her media standups.

"You've had your say Ma'am."

"Are you security?"

'Yes, we are."

"You've had your say. You've had a good say. You're getting agitated and you're starting to interrupt," one of them tells her.

"I am not agitated," Mason is quietly efficient.

"I can see you're upset. Your lips are quivering. Your eyes are quivering. Ok? So, I can see you're upset. So how about we cool down and maybe talk about it?" one man adds.

"Do you understand that I'm not upset?" Mason says quietly.

Mason tells me later she well knew these men were employing tactics to provoke her.

"You've had your chat," he continues.

Mason counters: "Well ... people of Queensland are upset about this because they don't want the Adani mine. They see people like you – heavy security – trying to suppress their words ..."

"You've had your chat."

"Everyone in Queensland. Everyone in Airlie Beach is against the mine."

"We understand that."

"We've signed petitions. We're not standing in the middle of the street yelling at the Premier."

The men continue to stand next to her.

"She doesn't seem very well-informed," Mason continued in a reasonable voice.

Neither the men nor Mason are aware that Channel 7 has continued filming the aftermath of the media conference including the exchange with the security men. This is far more active footage than the humdrum, predictable pre-election speak issued by the Premier from the podium.

In spite of the intimidation, Mason is cucumber cool. The men are still standing close to her ... Police are supposed to be there for the security of the Premier, not to quell free speech. Mason fumes inwardly. She is aware of the existence of the Queensland Fixated Threat Assessment Centre set up by Palaszczuk's predecessor, Campbell Newman, which allows Queensland police officers and clinicians from the Forensics and Mental Health Service to declare those who focus on Government officials and the public a 'fixated person'.

The clip from the Channel 7 footage goes viral with almost 10,000 hits, especially when it is linked to a story in the regional newspaper *The Daily Mercury* in Mackay.[186] Bullying is not the kind of behaviour the Premier wants to see go to air on the first day of her election campaign. But it is clear from the multitude of comments that's how the public perceives it. Even shock jock Alan Jones, known for his anti-Adani stance, reportedly applauds Mason's nerve. Jones also took part in a TV advertisement seeking to 'stop the taxpayer loan to Adani'.

After social media goes viral, Mason later identifies herself on Twitter as 'the upset woman' as she's been titled on the clip. Later that morning, Mason with the rest of the community action group Reef Action Whitsundays (RAW), obtain police permission to mount a placard action on the roadway leading out of Airlie Beach towards the small sleepy sugar cane town of Proserpine – the administrative hub of the Whitsundays which the Premier is visiting. Mason follows the official entourage, who are in rented people movers, in her own car. In Proserpine, she plays cat and mouse as the police try to throw her off the trail.

First Palaszczuk attends the Labor candidate's campaign office. Getting out of her car in the main street, Mason immediately spies what she describes as 'the goons' hiding in shop doors and begins to photograph them on her phone. Their reaction is swift. One begins photographing Mason whereupon she applies lipstick turning one side towards them. "That's my better profile," she quips. She trails them through town while they try to wave her on. She is pulled over twice by police that morning and subjected to licence checks. Later, Palaszczuk drives to the hospital where she is to make an announcement. RAW have set up a picket line at the front of the hospital. The Premier is forced to leave through a back door.

Mason guesses her next destination after lunch will probably be the airport and heads there herself. Arriving at the airport she pulls in to a driveway leading to the hangar and sees what she believes is Palaszczuk's government jet sitting on the tarmac. Another jet is nearby which looks ready to depart. The pilot is standing waiting, holding a bag of ice. A dual-cab ute pulls in behind Mason. From her rear-view mirror, she spots an unlikely passenger – Gina Rinehart, sitting in the front seat. She appears to be laughing. Of course Mason has no idea why. But she does know Rinehart has one of the other major mining projects seeking an opening in the Galilee Basin and presumes she is delighted that the focus is on Adani rather than her.

Rinehart has, by now, got other interests. She recently joined the export beef industry and, in 2017, bought the Kidman cattle empire with Chinese real estate partner Shanghai CRED. But she has retained interests in fracking and gas exploration. In June 2018,[187] Atlas Iron's board approved her $390 million cash bid to take over the company through Hancock Prospecting. "One of Atlas' key assets is its stake in the North West Infrastructure joint venture, which controls potentially valuable rights to one of the world's largest iron ore ports, Port Hedland."[188] Rinehart's company Hancock Prospecting owns 70% of Roy Hill, an iron ore mine which recently ramped up to 55 million tonnes a year (the largest single ore mine) and is 250 kms east of Port Hedland. Iron ore is known as one of the biggest contributors to greenhouse gas (GHG) emissions. Iron ore used to produce a tonne of steel creates an average of about two tonnes of GHG.[189]

When the Premier's entourage arrives, Mason quizzes journalists accompanying Palaszczuk on their next destination but no one will reveal it. Only a local journalist, who joins the contingent late, eventually confirms that the Premier's destination is Townsville. Mason immediately rings the Stop Adani supporters in Townsville. "The Premier," she tells them, "is on her way."

So continues an election campaign where Palaszczuk is dogged by protestors. Everywhere she goes, the Premier is forced to confront the issue of the Carmichael mine. No matter how many sweeteners the media offers in return, such as filming Palaszczuk walking the Strand in Townsville while chatting to supporters with elderly pooches, the question is always asked: "Why do you so strongly support the Adani mine?" All that time ago in India, Geoff Cousins had been right. Public opinion has turned. Even councils are releasing public statements about their opposition to the Adani mine. The Douglas Shire north of Cairns that includes the Wet Tropics' Daintree Forest and Cape Tribulation is one such council. It reminds the Government on its website about the value of tourism to the Shire. Many others will follow.

* * *

A few days after her visit to Airlie Beach, Palaszczuk's electioneering takes a dramatically unexpected swing. On 3 November, late one Friday afternoon, she calls a last minute media conference. She tells the assembled media that she will veto the $1 billion

Adani loan from NAIF, thus effectively killing any possibility of the Adani group receiving taxpayers' funds to build the railway line. As *The Australian* comments on 4 November 2017, "For constitutional reasons, a loan from the Commonwealth's Northern Australia Infrastructure Facility (NAIF) can only be made to the Indian conglomerate via the Queensland Government."

Shocked headlines follow. And there is plenty to write about. Less than three weeks before the election, Palaszczuk is announcing in an outraged voice that her reputation has been besmirched by those foul opponents of hers – Liberal senators in Canberra. These despicable people have tried to smear not only her reputation, but also the reputation of her partner, Shaun Drabsch, with whom she has been in a relationship since 2014 and has known for two decades it later transpires. Her opponents are dragging both their names through the mud. For what reason, the bemused media asks, still presumably wondering what this has to do with a veto of the NAIF loan. These senators, she tells them, are alleging there is a conflict of interest.

Then she drops the bombshell. Drabsch has been employed by Price, Waterhouse Cooper (PWC) as a part-time adviser on infrastructure and has been working on the Adani loan bid application to NAIF to promote Adani's chance of securing taxpayers' funds for the railway line for the Carmichael mine. She tells the media she first heard about her partner's 'real' job only days before, on 31 October through her Chief of Staff David Barbagallo. According to an *Australian Women's Weekly* article published in July 2017, Drabsch often worked from Palaszczuk's home.

"Shaun has always told me he's worked at PWC, working on infrastructure, and that is it," she informed *The Guardian* newspaper.[190] She told the media that she has just found out Drabsch had been engaged on the Adani application since May 2016. He had kept his work a secret from her under his 'commercial-in-confidence' obligations. Palaszczuk said she had been assured by PWC that any conflicts of interest between Drabsch's work and her role as Premier would be managed. She also said Drabsch was only working "at a Federal level" and pointed out that he had been employed on the project after the Adani mining leases had been approved in April 2016. Nor did she have any role in the Federal Government's NAIF loan assessment process, she added.

Thundering at the waiting cameras, she turned the focus instead on her opponents who she claimed had been attempting to undermine *her integrity* and the integrity of her partner. And ...? And, she now had no choice but to *veto* the NAIF loan to Adani to prove her impartiality, save her reputation, and that of her partner. She said she would write to the Prime Minister to let him know what she had done "to neutralise the conflict."

As it turned out, the Queensland Integrity Commissioner, Nikola Stepanov, had *not* recommended a veto of the loan, but had strongly suggested Palaszczuk simply sit out of any Cabinet Budget Review Committee meetings (the state's approving authority involving Adani's NAIF application) to manage the conflict. Palaszczuk, however, decided to go one step further. In what was to be a masterly move, she not only managed to deflect criticism that she might have a conflict of interest by making the announcement herself, she also was now in a position to challenge votes for the Greens for the upcoming state election, especially from those disillusioned with the Labor party for supporting the Adani mine. This from a Premier who had done more to secure the future of the Carmichael mine for the Adani Group than any other member of parliament.

Vetoing the NAIF loan would be one of the first issues she would handle, if her government were re-elected when parliament resumed after the election, she assured the media. The media hardly dwelt on the minutiae of the story, nor, it seemed, asked many questions about how the Premier had no idea what her partner's job entailed. That is apart from a few columnists, including right-wing Sky News commentator Andrew Bolt who accused her of undermining the Adani mine through her actions.

Drabsch's *LinkedIn* profile stated that he was "Assisting the National Infrastructure Advisory team to facilitate the assessment and procurement of, or bidding for, major projects." Palaszczuk clearly knew Adani was one of those seeking funds from NAIF. The *LinkedIn* entry states that Drabsch's job with PWC ended in December 2017.

The motivation for Palaszczuk's passionate defence of Adani has been a frequent conversation in the halls of parliament, party rooms and suburban shopping malls. I cast my mind back to her reaction when we had spoken about the number of jobs Adani would create in October 2016. How surprised she had appeared when I told her an Adani representative had said it was fewer than 1500 and not 10,000. Anna Krien, in her *Quarterly Essay*, echoes my sentiments. "Is it possible she is unaware of evidence given under oath by Adani's own handpicked expert, Jerome Fahrer, in the Queensland Land Court?"[191] Krien asks (p. 12), after writing about Palaszczuk announcing that Townsville would be the base for Adani's regional headquarters: "You can't get the smile off my face."

What other sources had she been relying upon when she rushed through critical infrastructure status for the Adani project, offered free groundwater, and discussed waiving royalties for Adani and ignoring the company's dubious environmental and financial history? In spite of more recent commitments in May 2018 to funding for the Great Barrier Reef, Palaszczuk seems to be focused on the notion of 'Make Queensland Great' at the expense of the environment by pursuing the Adani mine with such single-mindedness. Encouraging coal mining, a major villain in the climate change drama, can only have the most catastrophic impact on the reef's future.

As to the identity of the LNP Senators who engaged in such "truly and utterly disgusting behaviour," according to Palaszczuk, none of the media appeared to have revealed their names. Federal resources minister Matt Canavan was on the record saying he had canvassed senators and no one had owned up to the allegations made by Palaszczuk. She had explained that her federal colleagues had alerted her to allegations being raised in parliament about 'a conflict of interest' involving a Queensland minister but it was never clear that it was Palaszczuk herself. It *was* clear to any observer of Queensland State party politics, however, that there was considerable conflict within the party about the Adani mine. Canavan also commented that the [Queensland] Government had been "all over the shop" on Adani. Palaczscuk's Deputy Premier, Jackie Trad, had been on the record saying that the Labor Government would not participate in any NAIF loan and would block Federal funding.

This was contradicted the following day by the Queensland Treasurer Curtis Pitt. Strategists had suggested to Labor that supporting the Adani loan was a critical step towards retaining marginal seats in regional Queensland, especially Townsville, even though polls showed a majority in the state, as well as nationally, opposed Adani receiving a government loan.

Writing in *The Australian* on 9 December 2017,[192] Sarah Elks said that the announcement of the veto was the "turning point for the election" and she described it as "political gold," saying the decision diverted attention from green activists. It was politically crucial to Palaszczuk's career. Her electioneering had been continually hijacked by Stop Adani supporters. By vetoing the loan, Elks wrote, she gained powerful support from the group GetUp (that has over a million members and targets people from all walks of life with its aims to seek wider participation in democracy).

According to Elks, Labor had been holding focus groups across the state, including the North Queensland capital, Townsville. Labor held three seats in Townsville which were under threat from the right-wing political party, One Nation, and the LNP. The focus groups had confirmed these constituents did not want taxpayers' money going to an 'Indian billionaire.'

Palaszczuk's resounding win on 25 November 2017 proved the clout of the Adani issue. Many voters, it seemed, were prepared to vote for whoever stood against the mine. Palaszczuk's Liberal

National Party opponent, Tim Nicholls, had already pledged that under his leadership the Carmichael mine would go ahead. Barnaby Joyce, the blustering National Party MP and then Deputy Prime Minister, gave his own version about Palaszczuk's motives to *The Australian* published on 9 November 2017: "I think it's weak as water. If that's a conflict of interest then everything that they've ever been involved with is [a] conflict of interest. Maybe their relationship is a conflict of interest," he told the Murdoch newspapers a few days after her announcement.

"Weasel things like that annoy people. You're getting out of Adani, not because of conflict of interest. You're trying to get green preferences and [Deputy Premier] Jackie Trad is your conflict of interest, not your partner."

After the announcement of the veto, Palaszczuk's relationship with Grabsch only lasted a further three months. On 10 February 2018, the pair, the media dutifully reported, had amicably split.

Chapter 11
The Carbon Bomb is Ticking[193]

The Galilee Basin, a 247,000 square kilometres thermal coal basin, isolated and around 400 kms inland, is one of the largest untapped coal reserves on the planet. In October 2015, the Queensland Government released the Galilee Basin State Development Area Development Scheme[194] to regulate the development of the area. Its strategic vision included facilitating 'infrastructure corridors' between the basin and Abbot Point to transport coal for export; it discussed landscaping for mining precincts and its objectives stretch to 'minimise potential impacts on water quality'. Climate change is not mentioned throughout its bureaucratic jargon as an issue that plays any role in either its strategic vision or objectives. Ensuring we continue to live on a viable planet is not, after all, what the objectives are to mine this wilderness. The short-term goal is, and always has been, to make money.

During 2015-16, Queensland mines produced 242.2 million tonnes of saleable coal through 37 open cut mining operations and 13 underground mines. Asia buys 85% of Queensland coal. The royalties brought in around AU$1.59 billion in the same time period according to the Government Report. And that money has not even started to be earned through the Galilee Basin. The reef, however, as already outlined in this book, has been assessed by Deloitte Access Economics as being worth $6.5 billion per year to the Australian economy.

Nine mega mine projects[195] (among them Alpha, GVK Hancock Coal, Hancock Galilee, Macmines Austasia – a Chinese based company – and Palmer's Waratah Coal) are proposed for the Galilee Basin which will make it the second biggest fossil fuel expansion proposed anywhere in the world after Western China. At the time this book goes to print in July 2018, Adani was the only company to have its application granted. At full production, estimates are that the Galilee Basin projects will double Australian coal exports and produce more than 600 million tonnes a year. Australia is already the biggest net exporter of coal in the world.

As already mentioned earlier, in March 2018, Clive Palmer declared he would be going ahead with his $6.5 billion Waratah Mine later in the year regardless of whether the Adani Carmichael mine begins construction or not. But he will still need a railway line to transport his coal to Abbot Point. According to the Department of State Development, Manufacturing, Infrastructure and Planning website,[196] the Environmental Impact Statement (EIS) status for the Carmichael rail project is approved for a 310 km standard gauge greenfield rail line connecting the basin with the port. The applicant is Carmichael Rail Network P/L, a wholly owned subsidiary of Adani. The Isaac Regional Council and Whitsunday Regional Council are the local governments involved.

In June 2018, the Queensland Crime and Corruption Commission (CCC) announced there were no grounds for an investigation into Adani bankrolling the jobs for local government staff tasked with assessing activities around its mine proposal. The deal involved paying up to $1.15 million in wages, housing and vehicle costs for Isaac Regional Council employees to deal with the 'extraordinary workload' created by the Carmichael coal project. The Council has stated it is to spare ratepayers from bearing the brunt of the cost of processing.[197] At the time of writing Adani had not paid the Council any money.

Collinsville, 87 kms south-west of Bowen, is in the coal-rich Bowen Basin, which runs almost parallel to the Galilee Basin but is much closer to the coast and more accessible. Collinsville has three coal mines. A rich belt of coal bearing land, it is the largest coal reserve in Australia and produces around 70% of Queensland's coal. The basin contains almost all of the State's hard coking coal.[198] Queensland's oldest coal mine, Glencore

– Collinsville's open cut mine – is only four kilometres west of Collinsville and has been operating for more than 100 years. Mining began in Collinsville in 1912. Up until 1921, the town was named *Moongunya*, an Aboriginal word which means 'place of coal'.

Entering the town from Route 77, the only road into town from Bowen, coal trains regularly pass by on the adjacent railway line. The town, with a population of around 1500 people has a time-standing-still weariness. You can still buy a house here for $49,000. The corner store has newspaper sandwich boards, which today scream with the *Townsville Bulletin* moral panic headlines 'Addicts Swamp Health Services' and 'Growing Ice Scourge'. The corner store doubles as a takeaway shop, offering the usual small town fare of hamburgers with chips and schnitzels.

A large arresting mural on one building in town is a grim snapshot of mining life. Four miners carry their mate on a stretcher who has a breathing apparatus strapped to his face. Pit ponies, Clydesdale horses that used to haul coal from the underground mines, also feature on another mural. The last one retired to pasture in 1990.

Collinsville is struggling to rid itself of its mantle of coal. But according to John Cole, the director of Australian renewable energy company Edify Energy, the town has the potential to become the solar capital of Australia. In August 2017, the company[199] announced it would provide $9.5 million to its 69 MW Whitsunday Solar Farm and RATCH-Australia Corporation's 43 MW Collinsville Solar Project.

'Camp Nudja' is on the Bogie River on the way into Collinsville from Bowen, around 80 kms southwest of Abbot Point. The *Townsville Bulletin* has described it as a 'guerilla camp' whose aim is to train activists. Frontline Action On Coal (FLAC), a movement that started in 2012 out of Australia's first mine blockade, runs the camp.

A yellow handwritten sign on the gate is the only advertisement: 'Warning. Trespass is an Offence. Admittance to this property is only by invitation or prior appointment. Authority, High Court of Australia'. The dirt driveway meanders to the headquarters past some small dome tents pegged into the dry scrub. I am invited by Alison Mason, our driver.

At the entrance to the white colourbond house with a small verandah is a big bold yellow sign with large red writing: 'Camp Nudja Past Present Future. Know Understand Remember'. A turning circle runs around two slender trees and a collection of outhouses flanks the side of the property, which includes an outdoor kitchen. Plastic chairs form a makeshift dining room. It is the week before Christmas 2017. In the outhouses two men, one called 'Sooty', are building a Santa sleigh which will have a large Christmas wish: 'Ho Ho Ho. Adani must go' inscribed on it. There is a pervading sense of busyness. Daily agendas are set, tasks are allotted and activities planned.

Inside the house, a young woman is at the computer designing a flyer with the 'Twelve Gifts of Christmas' from Adani, among them:

- Free unlimited depletion of Qld's groundwater (rather than paying like locals do).
- An obsolete project in a declining global coal economy (instead of investment in the growing renewables sector).
- Disposable short-term FIFO workforces (instead of secure, long-term community employment).
- Increased likelihood of black lung disease (rather than creating healthy communities).
- Destruction of arable land (rather than support local agriculture).
- A project that's consistently struggling to lock-in financial backing and taxpayer funds (rather than standing on its own two feet).
- A project whose contractors keep walking away (instead of long-term partnerships).
- A project consistently forced into legal battles (rather than adhere to environment legislation and social norms).

- Reef pollution through discharge of run-off (instead of ensuring a stable tourism industry).
- Extreme climate and weather events (instead of contributing to a more stable future for all).

On the verandah, at a long table, a young woman with a green headband is drafting a media release. Today's activities are planned to coincide with Adani's welcome barbecue that will be held at the Lion's Park in Collinsville. The purpose of the Adani barbecue is to engage the community and to discuss potential jobs on Mining Camp 3 – a construction camp in Collinsville to be used if the rail line between the proposed mine and Abbot Point goes ahead.

Stop Adani and FLAC are preparing their own barbecue, also to be held at the Lion's Park where the Twelve Gifts flyer will be distributed. Outside the earth bakes. One young protestor lies prone on the verandah zapped by the heat. Most of these protestors are from interstate attracted by the invitation to actively engage in what they believe in, to trade their urban landscapes and move bush. Many are students on a break from university. An article in Byron Bay's *Echo*[200] lists the occupations of a group of protestors who had recently returned from the Collinsville camp: a naturopath in her 40s; a filmmaker, a former builder and a former schoolteacher both in their 60s. Around \$120,000 in fines and 95 arrests have already been incurred at the time of writing in various actions.

The call to frontline action has seized the imagination of many disenchanted young people from major cities as far away as Hobart and Perth. Photographs on the group's website portray them standing on top of trains brandishing fists or lying next to rail lines with posters declaring 'Veto loan for Aurizon' (Aurizon is the company that operates the Queensland coal freight network and, at the time, was applying for a NAIF loan to build the Adani railway line, but withdrew after Adani did not get the NAIF loan).

Participants in frontline action are invited to pledge to take part "in dignified, peaceful civil disobedience to protect the climate, reef and everyone's future by stopping the construction of Adani's coal project in Queensland." The group has been involved in many actions including locking themselves onto a barrel of concrete placed on the Aurizon railway line, thus blocking Aurizon coal trains for up to six hours. In January 2018, five FLAC campaigners shut down the Adani Abbot Point Coal Terminal by pulling the safety cord and locking themselves onto the conveyor belt which transports coal to a freighter ship. 'Locking on' means placing their forearms on to large metal cylinder and chaining their hands together inside. It is a technique known as 'sleeping dragon.' Police response, according to one activist, reported in the media, was to deprive the activists of food and water until they agree to be unlocked. Another activist, a 20-year-old student from Sydney sat in a cot suspended from a tree with the only rope supporting her tied to the tracks 20 m below. The only crew qualified to bring her down safely had to be flown up from Brisbane.

* * *

Stop Adani has changed the face of Australian politics. Protest, by dictionary definition means "an expression or declaration of objection … often in opposition to something a person is powerless to prevent or avoid." Up until Stop Adani, large-scale protests were something of the distant past – belonging in the 1970s and 1980s when there were protests for peace, women's liberation, gay liberation, Indigenous rights and protests against the Franklin Dam and the US military base Pine Gap. Clive Hamilton, in his 2016 book *What Do We Want! The Story of Protest in Australia,* writes that 200,000 people marched against the Vietnam War at the 1970 Vietnam moratorium rallies around Australia.[201] In 2003, when former Prime Minister, John Howard deployed troops to fight in Iraq, 600,000 people marched in protest, to no avail. "Despite the massive size," writes Hamilton, "the protests were simply ignored."

The protests against the Franklin Dam remain the biggest and most significant environmental campaign in Australian history. The dam was proposed to be built on the Gordon River in Tasmania to generate hydro-electricity and in December 1982 the site was occupied by protestors. It was the same day that the UNESCO Committee in Paris was due to list the Tasmanian Wild Rivers as a World Heritage site. The Franklin campaign, as it came to be known, was said to have brought down the Liberal Coalition Government led by former Prime Minister, Malcolm Fraser, because Bob Hawke, his Labor opponent, promised not to build the dam if elected to government. A landmark High Court ruling in 1983, following a battle between the Tasmanian and Federal Governments, voted in Labor Federal Government's favour stating that they had the right under the constitution to stop the dam based on their international obligations under the World Heritage Convention.[202]

The area had been declared a World Heritage site in 1982, coincidentally a similar time period to the Great Barrier Reef. The same issues surfaced decades ago about the Franklin as applied to the WHA listing of the Great Barrier Reef in 1981. The listing recognised its unique status but could not prevent the dam going ahead. To stop the dam needed an incorporation of the protected status to be written into Australian law. The World Heritage Properties Conservation Act was passed in 1983. Written at a time when climate change was barely on the drawing board as an issue, it seems to have had little effect on protecting the Reef.

Throughout January 1983, a total of 1217 arrests including of celebrities, were made following blockades. Full-page colour advertisements featuring the wilderness photographer Peter Dombrovskis' images 'Morning Mist' and 'Rock Island Bend' also helped draw attention to the cause.

Arguably, now, one of the most potent weapons to help focus on issues and igniting the desire for people power is GetUp whose slogan is 'Take Action Now'. The group embraced the fight to stop the Adani coal mine along with Stop Adani, the Australian

Conservation Foundation, the Australian Marine Conservation Society, 350.org, a global grassroots climate movement and many other community environmental groups.

As testimony to this new wave of political action, when 13 FLAC activists faced the Bowen Magistrate's Court on 13 March 2018 after shutting down part of Adani's North Queensland coal port, the Magistrate, Simon Young, struggled with what ABC reporter, Josh Robertson, described in his report as "the first known cases of an obscure charge – intentionally or recklessly interfering with a port's operation." No one, not the magistrate, defence or prosecution could find a relevant case law for the charge, reported Jessica Lamb in *The Whitsunday Times* on 14 March 2018.

The proceedings marked a legal precedent, setting a benchmark for future cases heard under the legislation. Several rolling actions have since been carried out at Abbot Point. One group twice stopped operation of the Abbot Point coal terminal and halted two coal-carrying Aurizon trains. Ten anti-Adani protestors were arrested in September 2017 after blockading the road to Abbot Point. Workers were allowed to leave, but not to gain access to the port.

* * *

The Santa sleigh is almost ready. Mason agrees to drive down to Collinsville to the Lion's Park (or the Lion's Den) and do a reconnaissance on the Adani barbecue before the cavalcade with the sleigh leave. I go with her. The town is full of police cars: patrol cars and paddy wagons. Other than that, there's no one about. We drive through the main street past the swimming pool to the park. At the barbecue at the back of the Lion's Park near a fence are the orange fluoro shirts of some workers and Adani banners. There are no more than a dozen people. Many seem to be Lion's Park members. We park on the same side as the park to get a closer look. Mason then does a U-turn to head back to the camp and is immediately pulled over by a paddy wagon.

She winds down her window.

"What's this all about?" she asks irritably. She tells me later she recognised the police officer, as he had already pulled her over.

"Just doing a licence check."

"I can't see you stopping anyone else?"

Nevertheless she produces her licence. The young uniformed cop goes through the motions and then hands the card back. We drive off.

As we head back towards the road to Bowen, the frontline camp car approaches looking for all the world like a refugee boat. Santa's sleigh is strapped to the roof.

Later, there are complaints in the local Bowen newspaper that there are not enough police to oversee local crime as police resources are being deployed to take care of Adani activists. Out of 27 officers at Bowen police station, more than $18,000 worth of overtime has been claimed since the protests began according to a story in *The Whitsunday Times*.[203] With the heavy police presence in Bowen that day – no wonder.

The presence of this camp and the activities of its occupants have stirred locals from Collinsville to Bowen. In the ensuing months, only days after a mass school shooting in the USA, George Christensen, the Federal National Party member and vocal Adani supporter posts a photo on social media of himself aiming a handgun which states: "You gotta ask yourself, do you feel lucky, greenie punks?" And this from an elected member of Federal Parliament.

The *Townsville Bulletin*[204] in January 2018 reports shaken Adani protesters were confronted by a local Bowen man threatening that they may get hurt by their actions. Adani, meanwhile, has managed to have its name included in the Bowen Adani Offshore Superboat Carnival run in April 2018 as though naming rights permit it to become part of the community.

So highly charged is the tension that in early January 2018, Mackay Superintendent, Bruce McNab, warns the local community not to take vigilante action against the protestors. Weeks after my visit, dead wallabies shot through the head are found in the driveway to the camp.

* * *

Ken Peters-Dodd's house is past the camp off the main road and down a dirt road that snakes through the dry bush. It is mid-afternoon when Mason and I arrive back from the Lion's Park Adani barbecue. The peachy light softens the eucalypts and the ironbarks that surround the collection of buildings, home to Peters-Dodd and his wife Maria. He greets us at the front door wearing a bandana and a black polo shirt proclaiming Birriah people. I haven't seen him since our trip to Canberra three months ago. Around his wrists are bracelets of shells and leather. Maria, who is clearly a source of strength for Ken, is a small woman with long dark hair. They have both been long outspoken about the proposed Adani mine and feel strongly that it ignores and disrespects the feelings of Indigenous people.

While their land is around 70 kms from the proposed railway line, Peters-Dodd, an elder of the Birriah people, is quite articulate as to why the mine should be refused.

His people, he reminds me, are from the fresh river country, one of several Aboriginal groups in the Bowen district. His coastal neighbours, the Ngaro people in the Whitsundays, are "the salt-water people."

"We're the freshwater people. We're the inland people, the Birri. Our country starts in the Clarke Ranges part of the Great Dividing Range near the Bogie River and out west to Belyando and then it crosses down near Midge Point and back up to Charters Towers up north."

In the 1860s, Peters-Dodd's land was carved up into cattle stations. White settlers arrived in force. The Aboriginal population began to decline dramatically in the Bowen district. Indigenous people were removed from their land to work on the cattle stations for white settlers or killed through conflict or disease. Peters-Dodd's great-grandparents were part of 'the great roundup' that continued through the late nineteenth and into the twentieth century. His grandfather was taken at the age of six in 1915 from his birthplace at Strathmore Station, a cattle station further west. His parents had witnessed the first clearing of the land for the cattle stations. Many of the Indigenous population were moved on to Christian missions as far as Coen in Cape York in the far north and Mission Beach on the Far North Queensland coast. Some of Peters-Dodd's ancestors even ended up on Palm Island, an Aboriginal community which is the main island of the Greater Palm Group of islands 65 kms north west of Townsville.

After the displacement of Aboriginal people from mainland Queensland, the island became a home for many Indigenous groups and attracted the focus of powerful Australian literature. Thea Astley in *The Multiple Effects of Rainshadow*[205] wrote a novel based on true events about a psychotic super-intendent, a Kurtz-like figure who tried 90 years ago to kill the white staff on the island.

Ken Peters-Dodd was born in Rockhampton, 520 kms south from the land of his forebears.

Unbelievably, it was not until April 2016 that the Federal Court finally recognised the Birriah people as Traditional Owners of 9845 square kilometres of land between Mackay and Townsville in North Queensland. The Birriah people signed an ILUA with Adani in 2014.

Almost 100 years since his ancestors were forcibly taken off their land, Peters-Dodd made the decision to 'return to country': the land his people come from. About 20 years ago, after living in Sydney where Ken was an artist and a performance artist of traditional song and dance, he and Maria returned.

"It was a calling. It was right to come back to country. Spiritually, it's a calling for our people. We come home because we know it's right. We're guided by our ancestors to protect the rest of our country. It was time to go home and reconnect with our lands ... through our bloodlines. We need to come back – the importance of country for our own spirit and bloodline ... There was a big pull to sit on country and protect country."

Peters-Dodd takes me to the old railway station house that he now uses as his artist retreat. The traditional weatherboard was once the homestead of the railway master. The train line is only around five kilometres away at the back of the house. This railway line, Peters-Dodd tells me, will link with the proposed Adani railway line.

The afternoon light spreads into the old railway house highlighting the artwork – stencils of hands against the beige weatherboard; waterholes, serpents and totems in paintings of all shapes and sizes. Massive turtles with patterned backs and totem poles are on canvasses around the walls. A dominating canvas of a solitary Indigenous man with a mobile phone. An empty yoghurt pot acts as a water container. The walls are rainbow-coloured, a complete departure, I imagine, in this transported place that once housed the railway station master. By the window are stands containing jewellery made from ironbark and porcupine quills gathered from the property. The porcupine quill[206] is Peters-Dodd's totem from his ancestors. His children come and go up the ramp to the gallery. Meting out a gruff but affectionate discipline to his daughter, Ruby, it is clear they respect him.

The proposed rail line will first cross the land belonging to the Juru people, whose cultural heritage includes the ocean north of Bowen to the Burdekin River near the present day township of Home Hill and then through Birri country across rivers like the Bowen and Bogie. Peters-Dodd says the Birriahs share boundaries with the Yanggas, their neighbouring skin group. The proposed Carmichael mine will be built on Wangan and Jagalingou (W&J) people's country in the south-west in central-western Queensland.

About six months ago, Peters-Dodd's house was the FLAC and Stop Adani headquarters before the property was bought nearby. 'Camp Nudja', which the new camp was named after its original namesake, he tells me, means "to know, understand and remember past present and future."

"This place here," his arms circle out to embrace his home and the land. "It was significant to buy this place as a healing place. It's a place of cultural knowledge – a place where environmental people have come and scientists and researchers."

When Ken and Maria moved back to country, there was no Adani, but there were other environmental threats – mostly related to the precious commodity of water. Even though it has been two generations since his family had lived on country, Peters-Dodd knew where his traditional land was along the Bogie River.

"Our land has been impacted massively since white settlement," he explains. "Now they're starting to encroach into the lowest environmental eco-system waterways and mining in areas where they shouldn't be. It is of great concern for us that this country has survived for thousands of generations. We are witnessing our lands being destroyed and there will be no sustainability in the practices that they are doing. Our people have walked here for years."

He once met the Australian writer, Alex Miller, when Miller was researching his novel *Journey to the Stone Country* that was published in 2002 and subsequently won the Miles Franklin award.[207] The novel is about a white university lecturer from Melbourne whose parents were cattle farmers. He reconnects with an old childhood friend who happens to be the grandson of a Murri Aboriginal woman. Presciently, they become romantically entwined after being sent on a mission to survey cultural artefacts in a country that has been earmarked for coal mining.

Miller had worked in the Bowen Basin on a cattle station when he was a young man. Coincidentally, I had read the novel when journeying to North Queensland from Tasmania. I was struck by its authenticity. It opened up the country for me in a way that would not have been possible if I had relied on the tourist tracts. Morag Fraser writes in a review in *Reading Australia* and *Australian Book* Review, "The land registers their approach: it shivers with apprehension."[208] Peters-Dodd echoes similar sentiments to the themes traversed in the novel.

"Some people say we've sacrificed a lot by coming back and living on country. But it's been a major strength for our families. We're respected on country by communities. We've really stood on the front line for not just our own family but for all people to be able to walk as sovereign people on their own lands ... the law of the land is still there. It's written in the land. There it is. The history is still there. The occupation sites and mountains of significance, rivers, walks, passages, it's all still written in the land. That's why it's important for our people to come back to country and walk that line ... open up those songlines ... them old dreaming tracks ... where our ancestors used to walk."

Peters-Dodd is adamant that many traditional owners do not support the Adani mine or other mines and says there are other alternatives. His son has recently started working 35 kms away at a solar power plant, one of two projects in renewable energy nearby. He is hopeful this is where the future lies.

"The whole agreement that Adani is trying to push us people into is further assimilation through the Government process. 'Forget about your people. Just get assimilated.' It's easy to sign away something you've never had a connection to or an understanding of. The advantage of taking a poor race of people that have never had money who are quick to sign agreements giving them a false sense of wealth or opportunity – you can see how these projects get passed quickly through traditional owners. We are not just about mining. We want to transition from mining and see all other areas where we can protect our country."

* * *

Since the Adani mine has come closer to reality, the tussle to win the hearts and signatures of the Traditional Owners has been raging. Adani, of course, understands the need to swiftly win over locals, particularly Indigenous ones, as the Mundra and Hazira locals in India discovered when signs were allegedly posted around Mundra proclaiming their land had already been subsumed by the Adani SEZ.

The Wangan and Jagalingou Family Council represent 120 members and key stakeholders in W&J land. The Native Title rights to 2750 hectares of this land must be extinguished in order for the Adani Group to build the Carmichael mine. This group has mounted a remarkable struggle against the mine. As in India, however, they are discovering that the Government at both State and Federal level seems intent on giving their land to Adani and spurning their rights to ownership of the land.

Back in 2004, a few families had put in a Native Title claim detailing bloodlines and connections to their country. However, a few years later, their land was eyed up as a potential money earner. Writing in the 2017 *Quarterly Essay* 66, *The Long Goodbye*, Anna Krien notes that in 2009, Linc Energy announced on the Australian Stock Exchange that it had drilled four holes, 120 metres deep (p. 34): "There was, on Wangan and Jagalingou land, a shitload of coal."[209]

Adani has continued to employ tactics of divide and conquer with the W&J people. In 2012 and again in 2014 they had approached the W&J people to try to negotiate an Indigenous Land Use Agreement (ILUA) under the provisions of the 1993 Native Title Act. In April 2016, the company tried a different approach, inviting a few hundred Indigenous people to a meeting to discuss the ILUA. Adani maintained it gained overwhelming support from the Traditional Owners at that meeting in central Queensland, which the company said was 294 to 1 in favour of the project going ahead thereby authorising the agreement. The ILUA was then certified by the Queensland South Native Title Services (QSNTS). However, the W&J Family Council hotly dispute the result, saying it was a sham. The Council did not attend the meeting and said a vast majority of those attending the meeting appeared not to be members of the Native Title group.[210]

In December 2017, the National Native Title Tribunal registered the ILUA and authorised the Queensland Government to approve the mining leases to Adani but that has been the subject of an ongoing legal battle with the W&J Traditional Owners Family

Council. The Council representing 12 families from W&J has filed several court challenges to the mine.

The ILUA presented by Adani would allow the company to undertake all works associated with the project including an airstrip, a workers' village, and a washing plant. In return, the Traditional Owners were promised jobs and economic security. Tim Elliott, writing in *The Good Weekend* in 2017, describes a similar tactic the company allegedly employed with Mundra fishermen. He interviewed Budha Ismael who had been fishing in Mundra for most of his life and who is head of the fishing settlement at Tragadi Bandar, three kilometres from Adani's power plant. Ismael told him that people from the Adani company and a fishing notary offered him a one-off payment of 20,000 rupees (around AU$400) to leave his fishing site. Ismael said the money was worth "about two days of fishing."

The ILUA is critical for Adani to gain finance for the mine, as it shows Indigenous consent without which most of the world's banks, under the Equator Principles,[211] will not invest in resources projects. Under an ILUA Native Title, claimants can surrender land in return for benefits, but the extinguishment of Native Title may be irreversible, even if the ILUA is found to be illegitimate.[212]

A February 2017 Federal Court full bench decision provided a ray of hope confirming that the Native Title Act[213] required *all* registered Native Title claimants to sign an ILUA and the agreement could not be registered unless this happened. The W&J Family Council moved quickly to have Adani's ILUA struck out. However, as our plane was touching down in Australia back from New Delhi in March 2017, both houses of Federal Parliament were also swiftly working on amendments[214] to ensure previously signed ILUAs did *not* need a majority of signatures as long as the ILUA had been approved by the claim group. This explains why Malcolm Turnbull was so confident in telling Adani back in April 2017 that he had reportedly 'fixed' Native Title and Indigenous objections to the Carmichael mine. The parliamentary amendments, supported by the Queensland Labor Government, were a triumph for the mining industry, yet again proving its clout with both levels of Government and the Governments' dismissal of the rights of Traditional Owners.

The Adani ILUA had been signed by seven out of 12 W&J stakeholders. However, in June 2017, one of the members, Craig Dallen, a W&J representative, who had originally backed the agreement, reversed his position leaving the W&J people locked six in favour and six against.

Traditional Landowner, Adrian Burragubba,[215] from the W&J Family Council, alleged in the Federal Court that some of the attendees of the original meeting were paid $2000 to attend, and was critical of Adani for not making enough effort to identify W&J stakeholders. Burragubba has also claimed that Patrick Malone, the spokesperson for those who supported the deal with Adani, had later said he was coerced into the ILUA agreement by the Queensland Coordinator-General, who reportedly told him that Native Title would be extinguished for W&J people unless they agreed to the deal with Adani. Burragubba steadfastly claims his 120 members had met four times and each time rejected the ILUA. Malone said the claims some people were paid to attend the meeting was "nonsense."[216]

In August 2017, the Full Court of the Federal Court of Australia dealt two further blows to the actions against the Carmichael mine. It dismissed appeals from the W&J people questioning the legality of the ILUA signed with Adani as well as an appeal by the Australian Conservation Foundation (ACF) to stop the mine going ahead. The ACF had sought to argue that Environment Minister, Josh Frydenberg, had not considered the effect of the mine's emissions on the Great Barrier Reef under the Environmental Protection and Biodiversity Act.

Burragubba stated after this that the Federal Court of Australia's decision effectively proved that any challenge on the basis of environmental or Indigenous rights over the land was worthless. After losing the appeal, ACF campaign director, Paul Sinclair, told the *Brisbane Times*[217] that environmental laws did not stand up to scrutiny.

"Our national environmental laws don't require our Environment Minister to properly evaluate the impact of 4.6 billion tonnes of pollution on the Great Barrier Reef and other world heritage areas."

He added, "It's like approving a mine for asbestos without having to consider the impact of that asbestos on the health of human people."

After Adani moved to access the land for the Carmichael mine in December 2017, the W&J Family Council were granted an injunction to stop the land being surrendered. In February 2018, however, their claim to extend the injunction was dismissed. They appealed against this decision and the interim injunction remains in place.

On 8 March 2018, the W&J Council held a smoking ceremony outside Queensland Parliament requesting Premier Palaszczuk and her Government to rule out extinguishing Native Title for the W&J people. The appeal was heard in March 2018. The presiding judge, Justice John Reeves, has reserved his decision.

In June 2018, *The Guardian* published an article querying the cultural assessment process[218] when it revealed that a North Queensland Indigenous organisation had kept secret $2 million in payments from Adani in 2014 to develop the land around Abbot Point and that the organisation had paid its directors up to $1000 in cash a day to conduct now invalidated cultural assessments for Adani. The Federal Court ruled that a different group, called Juru Enterprises should have been the nominated people to decide on land-use agreement with Adani. In July 2018, *The Guardian* reported that Adani would, nevertheless, proceed with construction work at Abbot Point with or without support from Juru Traditional Owners after Juru Enterprises lodged an application to stop the work going ahead.[219]

* * *

The rally outside Federal Parliament House on 5 February 2018 marks my third visit to the nation's capital on this mission. The rally is to coincide with the first sitting of Federal Parliament for 2018.

The host for my stay in Canberra is Anna Nolan. The text message description she has sent me so I recognise her at the airport is apt. Not that I need to know she had short curly grey hair and glasses. She stands out in the arrivals hall in her black Stop Adani t-shirt with the slogan in red.

Nolan represents so many middle-aged women who have taken up the fight against Adani. Within minutes she is telling me that she was arrested during the week of blockade action in Abbot Point in September 2017. Her quiet pride as we drive from the airport is obvious.

"Some of us decided we wouldn't follow police requests to leave when asked and we were consequently arrested for trespass and brought up for a hearing in the Bowen Magistrate's court." She adds, "It was a way of giving Adani a warning that this is a foretaste of what to expect if that mine gets into action ... Even if it wasn't Adani, we'd be determined to stop them as it's coal. It's fossil fuel."

The next day, over a breakfast of porridge and yoghurt – the same breakfast she says she has had for 20 years – and some beautifully brewed Lady Grey and Arctic flowered tea, she provides the backstory. She is a retired psychologist. Her late husband who died of cancer was an active climate campaigner and she has vowed to continue his work.

"I've been concerned about the climate emergency for a decade now – just following the science. I wanted to get active. I didn't want to be a whinger. I wanted to do something to make the difference. We need to – along with all the other strong, committed people – force the Government to change. Change policy. Get out of fossil fuels. Stop Adani is the way to go."

She first became involved when the movement had its Canberra launch in 2017, which was coincidentally the day I arrived back into Australia from India. "I guess I felt I would have to go all the way and do whatever was necessary. There were all these young people who were willing to put their body on the line ..."

The movement has, she says candidly, shaped her identity.

"It's like a kind of conscious matter – if I and ordinary people like me don't get into action, we will have to give an answer to our children and grandchildren one day about what were we thinking. Why didn't we save our climate for them? I just don't want to face having no answer so ..."

She pauses, as though considering this for the first time: "It is defining. It's the biggest issue I've ever faced in my life ... ever," she adds for emphasis.

There is no doubt it's given her life new purpose.

"I've made great friends in this movement. It's so diverse. I love the fact that I'm shoulder to shoulder with people from every walk of life, every age group and that's a sign in a way that it has got strength. We're not a homogenous group. It's something I have to keep working at."

For Nolan, the call to action was also when she was alerted to attempts by the Federal Government to 'siphon' $1 billion of taxpayers' money to Adani.

"That was pretty crucial."

People like Nolan have never been in trouble with the law. They've paid taxes all of their adult life. They own their homes. Many have superannuation squirrelled away. They tend not to be a burden on the state. The Stop Adani action has made them feel alive again after so many decades buried under the tag 'complacent voter'. 'There is no more need for apathy' is their simple message. They are among a growing number of Australians whose opinions and views do not appear to count before a Federal Government that only governs because of a one-seat majority and is only elected because it governs with another party in a mismatched Coalition.

* * *

On the lawns in front of Parliament House the following day, the mood is buoyant. Bill Shorten, the Opposition Leader, who plays his own apathetic role in this story, at that time is facing the threat of losing an established Labor seat at a by-election in Batman, Melbourne, Victoria. Sensing a potential victory by the Greens, he has belatedly begun to cast doubt on Adani. The Stop Adani protest is well-timed.

A group of supporters in red is rehearsing a dance that will follow on from the speakers. Three people have donned uncannily accurate giant caricature masks of Adani, Palaszczuk and Turnbull. They dance around like macabre clowns: a parody on the seriousness of the mission. Palaszczuk waves a banner emblazoned with '60 Years Unlimited Free Water'. Adani with his characteristic wide grin holds hands with the Prime Minister, Malcolm Turnbull, who is gripping a giant bag of cash labelled 'Your Taxes $1b'. Behind them, others are holding up a massive red banner Stop Adani next to a large black flag with hashtag #StopAdani. There are several hundred people gathered. Aboriginal flags flash black, red and yellow.

The speakers include a Pacific Islander Warrior, 350.org Pacific representative Zane Sikulu; Climate Change Council of Australia scientist Will Steffen; John Hepburn from The Sunrise Project whose mission is to grow social impetus to drive the change from fossil fuels to renewable energy, me and community organiser of the Mackay Conservation Group, Maggie McKeown.

When I am invited to the podium I ask Bill Shorten to 'wake up' and have the guts to stand up for the Great Barrier Reef. To stop prevaricating. I talk about the Great Barrier Reef and its continuing struggle for survival. How we must unite to protect it and stop the Adani mine. I speak briefly of what I saw in India and how the same tactics are being played out in Australia by a company who cannot be trusted.

Geoff Cousins is one step ahead. Presumably prompted by the pressure on the Labor party due to the growing dissent to the Adani mine which could play out at the Batman by-election, Shorten had requested a meeting with Cousins just before Christmas telling him that he wanted to know more about the reef and the effects of climate change. He was planning, according to Cousins, to firm up a policy position on Adani – unsurprisingly given the by-election in Victoria was looming.

After Shorten's request, Cousins agreed to take him on a trip to the reef in late January. Other guests included Imogen Zethoven and Professor Terry Hughes.

Shorten also flew from Cairns to the Carmichael River and the nationally important wetland area of Doongmabulla Springs to look at the threat posed by the Carmichael mine as well as the proposed site of the mine. In late February 2018, Cousins appeared on the ABC's *7.30 Report* telling host Leigh Sales that Shorten had told him during the trip that if Labor won Government in the next election, it would revoke the Adani mine licence. Cousins also said that after spending two days with him, Shorten had reportedly assured Cousins that he was going to take a lead over his party and take it to Shadow Cabinet.

According to a report in *The Guardian* newspaper, Cousins had also provided Shorten with legal advice obtained by the ACF which argued that the Federal Environment Minister had discretion to revoke the approval for the mine under the Environment Protection and Biodiversity Conservation (EPBC) Act on "at least two grounds." The first ground involved "new information of the consecutive bleaching of the Great Barrier Reef indicating increased sensitivity to greenhouse gas emissions," and the second related to the survival of the endangered Black-throated finch. The advice from the Environmental Defenders Office Queensland was that revocation would not trigger a 'sovereign risk' issue nor leave the Government open to a compensation claim from Adani.

It was at the end of the trip that Cousins told *The Guardian* that he advised Shorten to have a clear policy about Adani and take 'appropriate action' which involved revoking the licence. He said he told Shorten: "What you need to say is the following: 'When we are in Government, if the evidence is as compelling, as we presently believe it to be regarding the approval of the Adani mine, we will revoke the licence as allowed in the act.'" Shorten had replied that: "I get it. I understand" and had told Cousins that he would say this in Queensland the following week.[220]

Cousins said this had not happened and he was speaking out to the *7.30 Report*[221] to "increase the pressure" on Labor to make a decision and that he believed there was "some sort of resistance in his [Shorten's] party to him leading on this issue." But a spokesperson for Bill Shorten in response to the ABC's *7.30 Report* denied agreeing to ban the Adani coal mine if his party was elected. The spokesperson, declared Shorten was "deeply sceptical of the Adani coal mine," but "Labor does not rip up contracts and we don't create sovereign risk."

Politicians, such as Matt Canavan, had been using the term 'sovereign risk' to suggest that the Australian Government could not allow the Carmichael mine to *not* go ahead as it would jeopardise future investment prospects. However, economist Saul Eslake, writing in *The Sydney Morning Herald* in May 2018,[222] has since pointed out that the term has been misused. Its correct usage, Eslake suggests, is more about a Government defaulting on its debts, and that politicians had been 'completely' abusing the term. Richard Denniss, Chief Economist at the Australia Institute, also derided the way that 'sovereign risk' was being used especially by the mining industry to disallow the Labor party to revoke Adani's license, should it be elected to Government. Denniss said that *any* Federal Government could withdraw approval for a project if a proponent failed to meet its obligations, or if that proponent relied on false, inaccurate or misleading information to gain that approval. Denniss pointed out that Bill Shorten was not "threatening to change the law but threatening to enforce it" by relaying some of the inaccuracies already put forward by Adani.[223]

* * *

Bill Shorten is nowhere to be seen at the protest in front of Parliament House. The audience is enthusiastic and some television cameras stop by to cover the protest. One TV reporter advises the organisers to put the activities back half an hour as there are a few things happening in the House.

I notice the rhetoric from other speakers, especially John Hepburn from the Sunrise Project, has subtly turned from saying 'No' to Adani to saying 'No to coal.' I think of our driver Mason's description of Gina Rinehart laughing at the airport in Proserpine. Maybe she was struck by the irony that the three coal mines she has invested in that are earmarked for the Galilee Basin will reportedly produce the same amount of coal as Adani. However, there are multiple media reports especially in the Indian media about her Indian partner, GVK Reddy and the level of debt the company now faces. Tim Buckley from IEEFA noted that in March 2016, the company reported a fourth consecutive annual loss with a net debt rising another US$435 million to US$3.5 billion such that he concludes the financial distress at GVK is clear and extreme.[224] No one, it seems, at this time though, is paying the other Galilee mines much attention. Everyone is focusing on Adani. The Alpha mine also threatens to remove reportedly 176 billion litres of groundwater over 30 years according to Coast and Country, the community group that tackled the mine in the Queensland Land Court. This threat to the Great Artesian Basin was Bruce Currie's constant focus when we were in India. There is so much at stake.

* * *

The crowd at the rally is upbeat and defiant. A folk singer who has written anti-Adani songs performs ballads. Everyone joins in the chorus.

June Norman is amongst the participants. Dressed in her colourful op shop hat made out of sacking which she picked up for $5, she is a ray of sunshine and hope. Her brightness is contagious. She is a formidable contributor to the Fight for the Reef. Now 77 years old and a great-grandmother, she has been an activist since 2005, 12 years before the Stop Adani movement started.

We set up on camp chairs outside her camper van (her home) at the Aboriginal Tent Embassy in the lawns outside old Parliament House. One of Norman's triumphs was walking all the way from Cairns to Gladstone "around 1400 kms of road – only half the reef I know," she confesses. She and other campaigners ignited local communities along the way, but Norman was the only one to walk the entire way.

"We do the walk for $10 a day – that covers everything. We call into all of the communities in the towns along the way – "Please feed us ... give us somewhere to stay, we've got our own tents. Sometimes in a space in people's yards. We'd talk to people about the threat to the reef. This is big business. This is Government. What can we do?"

"It's a big empowerment movement," we tell them. "It's only us who's going to stop this ... You didn't know this was a threat? If you do nothing you are going to be part of the problem. You don't have to do the walk. Donate money, join a conservation group, write a letter to your MP."

Having once walked from London to Geneva, a distance of around 1600 kms to protest against nuclear power, she became convinced that taking this kind of action was "the best way to make a difference."

"Not in my Backyard ...," she gives a mock astonishment expression. "The reef's everyone's backyard. We had trolleys with big wheels on the walk. I pushed one of those with all our food and water, clothes and tent. And we had a dog. We had to get up before 4 am and off the road by 10 am because of the heat. That's what started it. I came back from that walk and people said: 'Where have you been?'"

Norman represents the new wave of politics that empowers ordinary people. She challenges the notion that Australian politics is a stagnant swamp – and says that instead of doing nothing, we should do everything we can to influence Local, State and Federal Governments. She puts us all on notice that we can't just fall back on the old adage: since we can do nothing, why bother? It's hard to resist her simple take on what is wrong with the world, especially when you look at her successes.

The expansion of Abbot Point and the dumping of the dredge on the Great Barrier Reef revived her commitment to campaigning. She had already been arrested in 2005 with a three month good behaviour bond when she campaigned against the Talisman Sabre, a joint biennial military training activity between Australia and the USA off the coast at Shoalhaven Bay near Rockhampton in Queensland. Norman describes it as 'War Games' and says their exercises included dropping bombs on the precious ocean.

Back then she challenged the whole idea of war and those who ignored the people who had paid the ultimate sacrifice. Along with other activists, she made coffins with the Christian cross and the Muslim emblem to commemorate those killed in the Iraq war. The protest named more than 1000 people who had been killed which included American soldiers and civilians.

Norman was part of the community group Coast and Country Association of Queensland, who took on Gina Rinehart and the Indian conglomerate's proposed coal mine in the Galilee. She tells me she is already committed to losing her family home to fight for the environment if costs are ever awarded against activists in her fight.

Norman's walk from Cairns to Gladstone kick-started the Whitsunday Residents Against Dumping (WRAD), a small community group that in June 2017 took Adani to the Supreme Court challenging the Queensland's Department of Environment and Heritage Protection approval for the extension of the Abbot Point coal terminal. WRAD failed in the bid and had Adani's costs awarded against it. WRAD is no longer active but Reef Action Whitsunday has taken up the challenge to save the reef.

Norman considers herself "lucky enough to be divorced" by the time she was 50, but admits she was initially "devastated" when her husband left her for another woman.

"I was engaged at 17. Married at 19. Brought up to believe you get married you have kids – that's your role in life – to support a

man who I thought, thought the same thing. We had five kids …
I loved being a mother, it was absolutely amazing and then, after
31 years, he goes off with someone else. I didn't know what to do.
I didn't have a career. I had to start again."

At the time, she had lived in Canberra for 24 years and had
never seen the Tent Embassy, now one of her favourite stomping
grounds and her 'home' when she comes to town. It was after she
moved to East Timor that her passion for activism was stirred.

"It's only people power that's going to do it. If there's enough
of us, they have to do what we want," she says unwavering in her
determination.

She is proud of her arrests, saying she was the first person
arrested in Australia over the protests against coal seam gas
extraction.

In June 2017, she was one of ten protestors arrested for sitting
in the Commonwealth Bank protesting against the bank funding
Adani. The bank has since ruled out lending any funds to Adani.

"We got inside – this other guy and I. We had hundreds of
people outside the bank protesting. They put us in a police car,
took us to the station and then had us unarrested. The bank didn't
want us arrested. So they let us go."

Norman's determination has sure had some wins.

While on a 500 km walk from Dalby to Gladstone in 2012
protesting against the Queensland Gas Company's coal seam gas,
LNG pipeline and the X-Strata coal corridor into Gladstone, she
was contacted by someone from Parliament House in Canberra.
They told her she had been invited to talk to the UNESCO
representatives in Gladstone who had come to investigate the
issues facing the reef. When she arrived at the meeting, the host
introduced her by saying that some people had got to the meeting
by boat, some had flown, others had driven "but we have someone
who has walked. She's walked 500 kms to be at this meeting."

Norman said Fanny Dupré from UNESCO immediately jumped
up to welcome her, telling Norman she had heard of her exploits
"before I got on the plane in Paris."

* * *

At the National Museum in Canberra, I am lying flat on my back on a communal couch in a semi-circle shared with around 20 other visitors. The rally is over. On the six-metre dome above us is a starry sky. Not the kind Don McLean wrote about in his world renowned *Starry, Starry Night* commemorating Vincent Van Gogh. This sky is an Indigenous sky. Midnight blue and black with a myriad of stars morphing into an apricot dawn. Eucalypts appear around the circular periphery. A bird begins to sing and the comforting throb of the didgeridoo pervades the dome. It's like looking through the eye of the birth canal and seeing the birth of the first dawn. Crackling fire and the sky above creates a sensory experience as the slowly lightening darkness fills the space. An Indigenous voice speaks.

Transported from the busyness of twenty-first century life to another realm, we see the dawning of the new day. We see it as Indigenous people have witnessed it for tens of thousands of years long before electricity and the industrial revolution, before greenhouse gases began to destroy our planet, when the Great Barrier Reef was pristine and bountiful, when time was suspended.

Billed by the museum as an exhibition "of pursuit and escape, desire and magic and the power of family bonds," the story is the experience and the story of the Seven Sisters. It is called *Songlines: Tracking the Seven Sisters.* Cave Hill – the inspiration for the dome – is a real location, which is called Travelling Kungkangkalpa. The Walinynga (Cave Hill) Experience. The cave is in the Anangu, Pitjatjatjara and Yankunytjatjara (APY) Lands of remote north-west South Australia.

The *Songlines* exhibition includes paintings, sculptures and other works by more than 100 artists from the Martu, Ngaanyatjarra, Pitjantjatjara and Yankunytjatjara lands of Australia's Central and Western deserts. The cave's artwork had never been visited by white people until the National Museum undertook an archaeological exploration. The exhibition was seven years in the making and curated by Aboriginal women.

Akin to astral travelling, we are transported as the Seven Sisters are transformed into boulders and new sisters are born. Songlines are part of the knowledge system of Indigenous Australians. Songs and dances connect people to the land, to knowledge of past changes in climate, to seasonal knowledge and to the stars in the sky as they shift through the seasons. Noel Pearson, the Aboriginal lawyer, academic, land rights activist calls them 'Australia's Book of Genesis': a dreaming track that can be on the land or in the sky. Songlines entered the popular lexicon after Bruce Chatwin's book of the same name was published in 1987.

Singing keeps the land alive and it was singing that was used in Aboriginal Creation myths to bring all the beings into existence. Kenny Peters-Dodd told me about the songlines that brought him back to his ancestral land. Adrian Burragubba describes it as his people's spiritual connection to the land which has evolved through songs and dancing. "Our law comes back to the time immemorial. In the beginning when the Great Spirit made the sun ... the sun shone through the water and the Rainbow Serpent Mundunjudra carved up the mountains." His people paint themselves with white ochre to represent water and spirit and they sing "and that's the rhythm of the land – It's in that time when we sing it, we know we're connected. This is a place of our dreaming. The spirits remain there indefinitely."

If the Carmichael mine goes ahead, however, it would, according to Burragubba's words written on the W&J website,[225] "... tear the heart out of the land. The scale of this mine means it would have devastating impacts on our native title, ancestral lands and waters, our totemic plants and animals, and our environmental and cultural heritage. It would pollute and drain billions of litres of groundwater, and obliterate important springs systems. It would potentially wipe out threatened and endangered species. It would literally leave a huge black hole, monumental in proportions, where there were once our homelands. These effects are irreversible. Our land will be 'disappeared.'"

Burragubba told the Queensland Supreme Court in an affidavit that the Adani mine will "prevent me from keeping my songlines alive" and that "the land around the mine would be both culturally and physically barren."

* * *

Didgeridoo and tin drums throb and fill the dome. Disoriented, many of us strangers lie on the communal couch, united by our decision to attend this exhibition. We are captive to the dome above seeking signifiers to understand what we are watching guided by the voice of the narrator. A series of Indigenous artworks fill the dome as the sisters battle with Wati Nyiru the snake, a carpet python who is an ancestral being, a shape shifter and a man who wants to possess and hurt them. Singing, they throw the snake up to the sky. Then the sisters dig a hole to catch the snake. They cook and eat it. It makes them sick for three days. They fly over the spinifex country. Then they morph into the circle, and, still chased by Wati Nyiru, escape into the sky to become stars. The story continues in the night sky as the dome darkens again – turning midnight blue and darker still. The sisters reappear as a sparkling cluster of stars. The ancient Greeks called these stars Pleiades in the constellation of Taurus. Dazzling aeons away is their pursuer who has become Orion.

I wander through the rest of the exhibition in a daze struck by how Governments can ignore the rights of Indigenous people to land they have owned for tens of thousands of years. How can Australia, particularly its Governments who are not accountable and the world (through bodies such as UNESCO who still has not declared the Great Barrier Reef as endangered) stand by and allow a mine like Adani's Carmichael mine to proceed? A mine, that along with other proposed mines for the Galilee Basin, will undoubtedly contribute through global warming to escalating the destruction of the only living organism to be seen from outer space as well as so many other reefs around the world, all because of our continued dependency on fossil fuels?

As I am nearing completion of this book, James Bradley, in a book review in *The Weekend Australian* (May 19-20, 2018), writes that, "We inhabit a moment of profound planetary crisis ... Meanwhile our demands on the planet continue to escalate." Commenting on recent figures that the five hottest years on record have all occurred in the past decade, he states, "... we have somehow willed ourselves into ignoring the scale of the disaster that is bearing down on us. Like addicts on the world's biggest bender, we are burning through our children's and our children's children's inheritances so fast it should make our heads spin, yet nobody talks about it."

Those who aided and abetted the approval of these massive coal mines in Australia will find no comfort by re-stating they are looking after a handful of jobs for those alive today. Their actions will live forever in the disappearing beauty of what our current generation may be the last to see.

* * *

On the ABC news - ironically on the eve of the first anniversary of Cyclone Debbie, 28 March 2018 - the television screen is filled with powerful images. Thousands of young people, some who saw 17 classmates killed in a shooting at a Florida high school are taking to the streets and marching on Washington in a protest they call 'March For Our Lives' to reclaim the safety of their classrooms. In Sydney, horses with Stop Adani on their saddles take part in the Time2Choose rally demanding clean air, energy and water for New South Wales stating that the combined impacts of 11 new and expanded coal mine projects in New South Wales is bigger than Adani's mine in Queensland. Thousands have gathered from around the state to choose protection for people, culture, farmland and water resources over the damage of coal seam gas.

On 25 March 2018, *The Guardian* online newspaper[226] publishes figures from the International Energy Agency (IEA, set up in 1974 in the wake of the oil crisis with the aim of ensuring reliable, affordable, renewable energy) which shows that global emissions from energy (the total amount of energy used by human civilisation) have jumped back to an historic high with global energy largely driven by Asia growing by 2.1%, more than double the rate of 2016. More than 70% of the growth comes from fossil fuels. Coal, the most carbon-intensive fuel, having experienced two years of declining usage (2015–16) is up by 1% in 2017 as coal burning in China, India and South Korea has grown. Australia's contribution is sobering. Earlier, an Australian Associated Press (AAP) account on 15 February, also reprinted in *The Guardian*, points out that while Australia has cut the emissions intensity of its electricity sector by 15% since 2005, it has still the highest emissions of *any* IEA member country and double the average of any other member country. In spite of pledging to cut emissions under the Paris climate agreement, citing the four-yearly review of IEA countries' energy policies, the IEA found that Australia had "not yet come forward with durable climate change policies after 2020," nor had we named a long-term goal.

Fossil fuels remain our absolute enemy. Renewables, the IEA 2017 report states, put a brake on emissions, but renewables don't stop coal, oil and gas from being dug out of the ground. The world's carbon budget for 1.5°C, the agency predicts, will be exhausted by 2022 and for 2°C by 2034.

The most sobering statistic in the Agency's research is that 81% of global energy comes from fossil fuels. And it's been the same for the past three decades.

Even more alarmingly is the later article in *The Guardian* published on 5 April 2018[227] that accuses the IEA of undermining the global shift towards renewables, claiming it is influenced by the oil industry and is undermining the targets of the Paris Climate Agreement. Citing a study from NGO Oil Change International, the article warns that the agency's investment projections are massively skewed towards oil and gas encouraging Governments to overshoot emission targets and worsen climate change.

If the Adani Carmichael mine goes ahead and the other large mines planned for the Galilee Basin follow, our current Australian politicians, both Federal and State, will have played a major role in contributing to the world's greenhouse gases. Adani's mine alone, according to the Joint Report to the Land Court of Queensland on Climate Change Emissions, by Associate Professor Chris Taylor and Associate Professor Malte Meinshausen from the University of Melbourne,[228] will leave a legacy of a massive 4.6 billion tonnes of carbon footprint if it mines 2.3 billion tonnes of coal during its 60-year operation. This is the contribution to the global footprint of fossil fuels whether it's burnt far away from Australia or not.

Other mines in the Galilee are proposing similar outcomes for production. The authors of the Joint Report claimed the mine's cumulative emissions would be "among the highest in the world from any individual project."

According to environmentalist, Kathryn Kelly[229] who gave evidence at the Queensland Land Court, farmers and environmentalists' challenge to Gina Rinehart's partly owned multi-billion Alpha coal mine in 2013, if all of the proposed nine or ten mine projects go ahead in the Galilee Basin, they will produce the equivalent of more than 700,000 million tonnes of carbon dioxide a year once they are in full production. Gina Rinehart is one of those who does not accept the science of human-caused climate change. "This," Kelly said "would exhaust the carbon budget in a flash."[230] There is, however, apparently no requirement under Australian law to outline the impact of approving mining leases on climate change, nor do environmental approvals need to take that into consideration. As Kelly told the court, as though the court needed this explained, "This is a decision of global importance." As the ACF found when it went to the High Court, climate change really is not a factor we have bothered to incorporate into our legal framework.

Importantly, the IEA identifies weakening Government policy as one of the major issues that affects global energy demand.

The goals set by nearly 200 governments in Paris in 2015 are far from being reached. India, where I began this story, is the coal industry's last great hope – and, in particular, the Australian

Government's main hope in its greed for royalties and supposed jobs.

There is some good news though but it remains to be seen whether it's all too late. China has added as much solar power in a single year as the total installed capacity across France and Germany combined. The USA, in spite of Donald Trump's first year as President, recorded the steepest drop in emissions as new renewable energy generation came on-line. The seeds for this increase, presumably, would have predated Trump's rise as President. Internationally, there has been, thankfully, a faster than expected rise in solar power, squeezing out coal projects. Even in India. On 3 June 2017, Modi was photographed hugging French President Emmanuel Macron during an official visit to Paris where they both pledged to achieve emissions reductions beyond what their nations had promised under the Paris Agreement.

According to an article in *The Conversation*[231] on 9 June 2017, India is expecting to reach 40% renewables by 2027 instead of 2030 and is laying out aggressive plans for investments in solar and wind. India's installed capacity for solar energy has tripled in the past three years to 12 GW and is expected to jump to 175 GW before 2030. It is, according to *Forbes Magazine*,[232] because of Modi that Gujarat attracted investment in industries such as solar power offering a nearly 24-hour electricity statewide compared to, between 2011 and 2014, the country running a power deficit of up to 9%. From January 2016, the cost of producing utility-scale solar electricity in India fell from 4.34 rupees per kilowatt-hour in January 2016 to 2.44 rupees in May 2017, which makes it cheaper to produce than coal.

Coal, however, accounts for almost 60% of India's installed electricity generating capacity of 330 GW. Thermal energy power plants (those powered by coal) were cancelled by the Indian Government in Gujarat, Odisha and Uttar Pradesh with a combined capacity of almost 14 GW of power according to the article. It is, of course, still about money, but if the traditional power sources are more expensive, renewables surely will come into their own.

Even Adani has joined the bandwagon. Adani Solar in Mundra is already operational and its Australian project – a 100–200 MW solar plant near Moranbah in the Bowen Basin is to begin its first phase in October 2018. In February 2018, eight renewable energy companies were short-listed in Newcastle (New South Wales) to put in tenders for a five MW solar farm on a former landfill site at the coal town. In Gladstone, Queensland, the place where so much environmental destruction has occurred in the past decade, five companies have been short-listed to tender for the job of developing an up to 450 MW renewable energy hub at the fossil fuel shipping port which is home to a 1680 MW coal-fired power station. It will be the largest electricity generator in Queensland.

In our own backyard – the Whitsundays – plans are afoot for what is claimed to be Australia's first co-operatively owned concentrated solar thermal power plant between the farmlands and the reef. Billed as 'Not for Profit Public Power', the SolReflection Concentrated Solar Thermal Power Plant is working on a sustainable model of renewable energy power stations that can be replicated by other communities Australia-wide.

Renewable energy sources are expected to increase in Australia substantially with more than 49 projects either constructed, under construction, or having secured funding and proceeding to construction. Australia's first Renewable Energy Index produced by Green Energy Markets,[233] funded by GetUp, released its initial Report in August 2017. It estimated that in 2016 and 2017, Australia generated enough renewable energy to power 70% of the country's households. A decade ago, renewables made up only about 7% of national electricity output. Once the wind and solar projects in the pipeline are complete at the end of 2018, enough energy should be generated to power 90% of the country's homes according to the Index. This reduction is the carbon pollution equivalent of taking more than half of all cars in Australia off the roads, a major source of carbon emissions.

Less than 2% of this renewable energy will come from large solar farms, which, the Reports states, means "the best is yet to come from this arm of the renewables industry which has an array of large-scale projects underway."

The Index notes that Queensland is taking its share of jobs from this new growth with 2625 jobs created by mid-2017 – a thousand more than the Adani spokesman had said in the Land and Environment Court in April 2015. The 46 large-scale energy projects that were under construction by July 2017, the Index stated, helped the renewable sector to employ 10,000 people full-time for a year. Most jobs were in New South Wales (3018), thanks largely to wind farms, while Queensland was next, with 70% of the renewable sector's jobs (2625) coming from solar farms.

As for the Great Barrier Reef, however, according to the scientists and environmentalists and our most famous of all commentators, David Attenborough, the predictions are dire. In spite of warnings from people like Attenborough that we should have acted back in the 1980s, countering fossil fuel is one major reason we are in the predicament we are in now.

Back then, according to Oreskes and Conway in their 2010 book, *Merchants of Doubt*,[234] when American scientists forecast to the powers that be in Washington that carbon dioxide levels would double in 50 years and would have major impacts on the planet, they were told to come back in 49 years. "But in forty-nine years it would be too late," Oreskes and Conway wrote (p. 174). We would be 'committed' to the warming. Perhaps 'sentenced' might have been a better word.

After writing this book, I still cannot understand why we have elected Governments who control our environmental future by making dangerous decisions for our planet. After the US 1978 National Climate Act, Oreskes and Conway note, Congress began looking into climate change and established a national climate research program. More research was needed. Good move. We could have been tackling the issue straight after the diagnosis. Instead today, the country historically responsible for more emissions than any other country in the world[235] – the USA – walked away from the Paris climate deal in June 2017. The economists, however, won the debate when the scientists might have changed government policies way back then.

The chapters in the ensuing 1983 'Changing Climate: Report of the Carbon Dioxide Assessment Committee,'[236] ordered by the US Congress and written by natural scientists, mostly agreed that global warming would occur with serious physical and biological ramifications. One scientist, Roger Revelle, wrote about sea level rise and warned of the possible disintegration of the West Antarctic Ice Sheet, which (p. 23) "would release about 2 million kms of ice before the remaining half of the ice sheet began to float." The resulting worldwide rise in sea level would be between five and six metres. The likely result (p. 442): "The oceans would flood all existing port facilities and other low-lying coastal structures, extensive sections of the heavily farmed and densely populated river deltas of the world ... and large areas of many of the world's major cities." Revelle warned that if temperature increases of 2°C to 3°C were reached by mid-century, thermal expansion alone would produce a 70 cm of sea level rise and a further two metres would occur by 2050 if the ice sheet began to fail.

Ironically, the results from the most comprehensive study of the Antarctic have just been released. In June 2018, two studies from scientists in the UK and the USA, using satellites to collect data were both published in *Nature* magazine. One confirms that the Antarctic ice sheet has accelerated threefold in the last five years and is now vanishing faster than any other time on record and the second study found that unless urgent action is taken against global warming in the next decade, the melting ice could contribute more than 25 cm to a total global sea level rise of more than a metre by 2070. This would result in the collapse eventually of the entire West Antarctic ice sheet, which would result in a 3.5 metre sea level rise. Reported in *The Guardian*,[237] one study found that before 2012, the Antarctic lost ice at a steady rate of 76 billion tonnes per year, but since then there had been a sharp increase with a loss of 219 billion tonnes of ice per year. The second study assesses the state of Antarctic in 2070 under two different scenarios – the first where urgent action on greenhouse gas emissions is taken and the second where emissions continue to rise unabated and the Antarctic is exploited for its natural resources. The study found that much of the change the continent had experienced already was irreversible.

Blindly ignoring these calamitous predictions, back in the early 1980s, Oreskes and Conway wrote, the economists began by agreeing with all that had been said by the scientists, concluding, according to one of them, Yale economist, William Nordhaus, that the only solution was to impose "a large permanent carbon tax" but he added, "that would be hard to implement and enforce."[238]

"Rather than confront their own caveat that changes might happen much sooner than their model predicted – and thus be much more costly than prevention – the economists assumed that serious changes were so far off as to be essentially discountable," the authors observed.

Worse, in the final chapter of the 1983 Research Report, economist Thomas Schelling – much like the politicians I've encountered in the writing of this book – although agreeing that climate change was the real issue and the impact of carbon dioxide needed to be assessed with all sorts of "other climate-changing activities" such as dust, land use changes and natural variability – advised against making carbon dioxide the major focus. Schelling argued against controlling carbon dioxide.

"It would be wrong to commit ourselves to the principle that if fossil fuels and carbon dioxide are where the problem arises, that must also be where the solution lies," Schelling argued (in Oreskes and Conway, 2010, p. 179).

Oreskes and Conway countered that Schelling's attempt to ignore the cause of global warming was "equivalent to arguing that medical researchers shouldn't try to cure cancer, because that would be too expensive, and in any case, people in the future might decide that dying from cancer is not so bad," the authors observed (p. 180).

That was almost 40 years ago. As those scientists predicted in 1979, the temperatures are warming mostly because of generated human carbon dioxide. Back then, there had been discussion about the cost of fossil fuels going up and so usage of these fuels would go down and this would permit conversion to alternative energy sources at a lower cumulative carbon dioxide concentration BUT – and here's the message we well and truly knew 40 years ago – the sooner we begin the transition from fossil fuels, the easier the transition will be. Ironically, economists such as Schelling suggested this was a good reason to do nothing. Market forces, after all, would take care of it, so no need to regulate fossil fuels.

Renewables worldwide are finally on the brink of being economically viable, without government subsidies, according to the IEA, so market forces have come into play. In the UK alone, an estimated £20 billion worth of wind and solar farms will be built without subsidies between now and 2030. But even if we are developing cheaper renewable energy as an alternative, is it all too late?

As I wind up the writing of this book in mid-2018, an 'upbeat' story heads the news about a solution to the Reef's demise. A 'sun shield'[239] 50,000 times thinner than a human hair has been designed to sit at the surface of the water, directly above corals. The thin film is meant to be like an umbrella that blocks as much as 30% of the sun's rays. The shield is biodegradable and is made of calcium carbonate, the same component that coral skeletons are made of. The project has been created by the University of Melbourne and the Australian Institute of Marine Science. Other projects from the same source include creating hybrids and growing multiple generations of the coral's microscopic algae under heat-stress conditions – but they've not yet prevented bleaching.

Other researchers are refining the cryopreservation process (snap-freezing) to produce algal seed banks with an option of flying planes across the more than 2000 kms of the Great Barrier Reef and spraying heat-tolerant symbionts[240] across the bleached reefs. This is described as an aerial first-aid for corals. And the even older idea of covering the reef with a shadecloth is raised as something to consider for future ocean management plans. But how could we ever find one big enough?

These kinds of geoengineering band aid solutions underline how desperate we are to right the wrongs. How much easier it would have been if we had done the right thing decades ago and kept fossil fuels in the ground.

Denial and doubt are still doing a good trade. In March 2018, a glossy few pages on Lizard Island appear in *The Australian* in its *Weekend Magazine*: 'What lies beneath?'[241] The tone is light and bubbly and full of bustling reef photographs and beautiful metaphors from the journalist who also lists what she ate on the menu at the Resort. There's no mention of its more recent catastrophic history. All is good. Of the 33 comments readers made at the end of the article, most of them criticise those who believe in climate change. "Told you, it's fine," is the general tone of the commentaries. "Much ado about nothing."

In June 2018, a report on the impacts on tourism of the 2016/17 bleaching events on the Great Barrier Reef is handed down. Produced by Central Queensland University and the Reef & Rainforest Research Centre, the report has a sober analysis pointing to the fact that "the GBR is the key destination pull factor for international tourists in Cairns, Port Douglas and the Whitsundays"[242] and "further coral bleaching may lead to a significant decline in international tourism, with resultant economic impacts."[243] It warns that "coral dependent tourism destinations are unprepared for a future decline in reef tourism."[244] The report includes research from the GBRMPA which states that ".... bleaching events are expected to increase in frequency and severity as a result of climate change."[245]

* * *

In May 2018, we embark on a homeward journey to the Whitsundays bringing our dark-blue hulled 54DS Jeanneau *MiLady* who has been shipped from Genoa from her faraway European home in Greece to another ancient continent, home to the world's largest coral reef system. Lady Elliot Island is said to be the real beginning of the 2900 individual reefs and 900 islands that make up the 2300 km Great Barrier Reef. The island is described in our cruising guide as 'an upturned saucer'. We first notice it about ten nautical miles away. Only around 46 nautical miles away is Gladstone, once a farming and tourist town, now branded far and wide through journalistic headlines as a poisonous relic of industrialisation.

Later, we anchor in a massive lagoon at Lady Musgrave Island (like so much of the reef appropriated by a colonial namesake): 14 hectares of coral cay. An eight-nautical mile natural coral wall encircles us with its narrow entrance which is carefully charted by red and green channel markers. The evening light after our arrival is shimmering. Around us, the sea is calm, protected by the Great Barrier Reef. But at 4 am, our *Four Women Wandjinas*, a painting by Robyn Woolagoodja we bought from the Kimberleys five years ago, flickers in the red light from the saloon cabin. The women Wandjinas are our erstwhile harbingers of weather. Robyn is a cousin of Donny Woolagoodja, a Wororra elder responsible for the design and creation of Namarali, the king of the Wandjinas, a giant laser-projected Wandjina that towered five metres high over Sydney's 2000 Olympic games. Wandjinas, according to Valda Blundell and Donny Woolagoodja's 2015 book *Keeping the Wandjinas Fresh* are "the spirit in the cloud." [246]

The Wororras are one of three tribes in the North West Kimberley region of Western Australia where the Wandjinas are found in caves. Both human in form and cloud-like, their elaborate head-dresses not only represent the hair of the Wandjinas, but the lightning in the clouds of the Wandjina spirit. Rather than being inherited works of art, many Indigenous people believe the

Wandjina spirits left their images in the caves, like the ones I saw on Bigge Island.

By 4.15 am the wind howls and moans. We are at anchor. Unlike the other boats in the lagoon we were not lucky enough to secure a mooring. The cruising guide had warned us of the perils of being stuck there in rough weather. With no internet or weather forecast, the sudden change has caught us offguard.

The night is spent with Grant anxiously checking the anchor line until daybreak. If we drag here, we have nowhere to go, not to mention about what we might do to the coral.

When the wind thankfully abates by lunchtime the following day, we head for a 14-hour sail to Great Keppel Island. After dropping anchor at 4 am, in the first light of morning, I see a rainbow bouncing across the face of each Wandjina. The day is picture perfect with fringing reefs a stone's throw away. *MiLady* is only a few days away from her new home. She will be the second boat we have brought to the Whitsundays. We harbour a kernel of hope that the coral will survive for at least our lifetime. More than that, we will do everything in our power to help it survive even longer.

Professor Terry Hughes should perhaps have the last word. After all, he and his team have witnessed firsthand over many years what is happening to the Great Barrier Reef. In a new study from the ARC Centre of Excellence Coral Reef Studies, published in *Nature*, Hughes points out that while we've now lost close to half of the corals in shallow-water habitats across the northern two-thirds of the Great Barrier Reef due to back-to-back bleaching over two consecutive years, "that still leaves a billion or so corals alive, and on average, they are tougher than the ones that died. We need to focus urgently on protecting the glass that's still half full, by helping these survivors to recover."

Hughes previously has noted[247] that it might take several decades for reefs to recover especially the oldest and largest colonies and, of course, that depends on whether there will be further bleaching, not to mention other threats like crown of thorns starfish and water quality. Bleached coral, points out Hughes, has lower reproductive output. But we can't, no matter how hard, give up. Researchers from the Institute for Energy Economics and Financial Analysis (IEEFA) published in their Report that the dropping profits from the oil and gas markets outline the increasing frailty of the profit margins around fossil fuels.

As Bill McKibben, a Schumann Distinguished Scholar at Middlebury College and founder of 350.org writes in *The Guardian*,[248] the increasing viability of renewables through their affordability is helped by the climate movement, according to IEEFA. That movement is a material financial risk to those who profiteer from fossil fuels. That, and the fact that the climate activists have joined with such an increasingly diverse set of allies – particularly the Indigenous Rights Movement to make corporations accountable by targeting banks and financial institutions. The Report details a series of recommendations on how to hurt the industry most by creating delays that "turn a marginal project into a cancelled one" to "strategic litigation" and "changing the narrative."

We need to wake up to our predicament. Keep fighting.

Stanley Douglas, the Indigenous narrator of *Songlines* whose knowledge has been passed on from his forebears, describes what is meant by *Tjukurpa*. This Indigenous word, which refers to the creation period, echoes in the present. It is about religion, law and identity. An Indigenous person who loses their *Tjukurpa* loses their past, present and future and becomes unstuck from their place in the world.

His words might just as well be describing our plight.

Endnotes

Chapter 1: The Courting of a Mining Magnate

1   Long term warming trend continued in 2017; <https://climate.nasa.gov/news/2671/long-term-warming-trend-continued-in-2017-nasa-noaa/>

2   Magnate who plans to ship coal through Reef accused of exploitation; <https://www.afr.com/business/mining/coal/magnate-who-plans-to-ship-coal-through-reef-accused-of-exploitation-20140905-jer1m>

3   According to an ABC article, none of the other mayors published the details of any gifts or hospitality online. Adani bought India flights for Queensland mayors of councils paying $30m for airstrip; <http://www.abc.net.au/news/2017-10-30/adani-bought-india-flights-queensland-mayors-funding-airstrip/9100332>

4   Turnbull was referring to the Full Federal Court decision in 2017 in the McGlade case which upheld that under the Native Title Act all traditional owners who were registered claimants needed to sign an Indigenous land use agreement or the agreement was invalid. This put in doubt 126 projects including the Adani mine.

5   According to *The Australian Financial Review*, Adani had requested Turnbull to 'fix' Native Title laws in order to clear the way for the Carmichael mine. Malcolm Turnbull tells Adani native title issues will be 'fixed'; <https://www.afr.com/news/politics/malcolm-turnbull-tells-adani-native-title-issues-will-be-fixed-20170410-gvi6i3>

6   Indigenous recognition in our Constitution matters – and will need greater political will to achieve; <https://theconversation.com/indigenous-recognition-in-our-constitution-matters-and-will-need-greater-political-will-to-achieve-90296>

7   An internal investigation by the Federal Environment Department later found in February 2018 that in omitting to reveal this fact Adani "may have been negligent." Government considered prosecuting Adani over CEO's link to company convicted over environmental disaster; <http://www.abc.net.au/news/2018-02-13/government-considered-prosecution-against-adani/9423152>

8   In response to a further story by Willacy about the issue, an Adani spokesman told the ABC that the company and Mr Janakaraj stood by their earlier comments that Mr Janakaraj was committed to proactive good environmental management.

9   A review of the Adani group's environmental history in the context of the Carmichael coal mine approval; <https://envirojustice.org.au/sites/default/files/files/envirojustice_adani_environmental_report.pdf>

10 The Brief also commented "especially given the current lack of an emergency response plan or availability of emergency funding for dealing with damage to coral reefs following a shipping incident in the GBR, as demonstrated by the Shen Neng 1 coal ship grounding, which was still not cleaned up six years later."

11 Goa's pollution control board issues notices to MPT, two port operators; <https://www.business-standard.com/article/pti-stories/gspcb-issues-notices-to-mpt-two-port-operators-115122400130_1.html>

12 Adani: Remote Prospects Carmichael Status Update 2017; <http://ieefa.org/wp-content/uploads/2017/04/Adani-Remote-Prospects-Carmichael-Status-Update-2017_April-2017_SN.pdf>

13 Tim Buckley, authorised personal communication to author, June 2018.

14 Tim Buckley and Simon Nicholas: Adani Godda Power Project: Too Expensive, Too Late and Too Risky for Bangladesh; <http://ieefa.org/wp-content/uploads/2018/04/Adani-Godda-Power-Project-April_2018.pdf>

15 Adani's Carmichael Mine is unbankable says Queensland Treasury; <https://www.smh.com.au/business/companies/adanis-carmichael-mine-is-unbankable-says-queensland-treasury-20150630-gi1l37.html>

16 Digging Into Adani; <http://www.abc.net.au/4corners/digging-into-adani/9008500>

17 Coal from Carmichael mine "will create more annual emissions than New York"; <https://www.theguardian.com/environment/2015/nov/12/coal-from-carmichael-mine-will-create-more-annual-emissions-than-new-york>

18 Impassioned Turnbull defends climate change science; <http://www.abc.net.au/news/2011-07-22/turnbull-climate-speech/2805536>

19 Naomi Oreskes and Erik M. Conway (2010) *Merchants of Doubt: How a Handful of Scientists Obscured the Truth on Issues from Tobacco Smoke to Global Warming.* Bloomsbury Publishing, London.

20 Sources of Greenhouse Gas Emissions; <https://www.epa.gov/ghgemissions/sources-greenhouse-gas-emissions>

Chapter 2: The Dirty Truth

21 Air pollution killed 81,000 in Delhi and Mumbai, cost Rs 70,000 crore in 2015; <https://timesofindia.indiatimes.com/city/mumbai/air-pollution-killed-81000-in-delhi-mumbai-cost-rs-70000-crore-in-2015/articleshow/56656252.cms>

22 The American Geophysical Union journal Earth's Future; <https://agupubs.onlinelibrary.wiley.com/doi/full/10.1002/2017EF000542>

23 India: A huge electrification milestone with big questions – 10 industry leaders weigh in; <https://medium.com/energy-access-india/india-a-huge-electrification-milestone-with-big-questions-10-industry-leaders-weigh-in-d343f5b3833a>

24   Living in the Dark: 240 Million Indians Have No Electricity; <https://www.
     bloomberg.com/news/features/2017-01-24/living-in-the-dark-240-million-
     indians-have-no-electricity>

25   Low ash, low sulphur and low phosphorus used to create coke for iron and
     steel making.

26   Burned for steam to run turbines to generate electricity. The coal is ground to
     a powder and fired into a boiler to create steam.

27   Coal exports by country; < http://www.worldstopexports.com/coal-exports-
     country/>

28   G20 Governments propping up fossil fuel exploration; <https://www.odi.
     org/g20-fossil-fuel-subsidies>

29   Energy Policies of IEA Countries; <http://www.iea.org/publications/
     freepublications/publication/EnergyPoliciesofIEACountriesAustralia2018R
     eview.pdf>

30   This report gives a detailed analysis of Australia's energy policies.

31   The Finkel Review at a glance; <https://theconversation.com/the-finkel-
     review-at-a-glance-79177>

32   The geographical distribution of fossil fuels unused when limiting global
     warming to 2°C; <https://www.nature.com/articles/nature14016>

33   For a comprehensive timeline of events see Carbon tax: a timeline of its
     tortuous history in Australia; <http://www.abc.net.au/news/2014-07-10/
     carbon-tax-timeline/5569118>

34   A snip at $22m to get rid of PM; <https://www.smh.com.au/business/a-snip-
     at-22m-to-get-rid-of-pm-20110201-1acgj.html>

35   Mark Butler (2017) *Climate Wars*. Melbourne University Publishing,
     Melbourne.

36   How Australia bungled climate policy to cerate a decade of disappointment;
     <https://www.theguardian.com/australia-news/2017/jul/05/how-australia-
     bungled-climate-policy-to-create-a-decade-of-disappointment>

37   David Richardson and Richard Denniss (2011) 'Mining the truth: the rhetoric
     and reality of the commodities boom'. The Australia Institute, Canberra.

38   Labor Market Information Portal – Mining; <http://lmip.gov.au/default.
     aspx?LMIP/GainInsights/IndustryInformation/Mining>

39   How Many People Work in the Coal Industry; <https://www.investopedia.
     com/news/how-many-people-work-coal-industry/>

40   Company profits surge as wages fall; <http://www.abc.net.au/news/2017-
     02-27/company-profits-surge-as-wages-fall/8307178>

41   The tip of the iceberg: Political donations from the mining industry; <http://
     www.tai.org.au/content/tip-iceberg-political-donations-mining-industry>

42   Clive Palmer faces '$1.4bn clean-up' for nickel refinery; <https://www.
     theaustralian.com.au/news/investigations/clive-palmer/clive-palmer-
     faces-14bn-cleanup-for-nickel-refinery/newsstory/8519cc717df186a77691e
     2980a2935dd>

43   Clive Palmer's assets frozen by Brisbane Supreme Court; <https://www.
     afr.com/news/clive-palmers-assets-frozen-by-brisbane-supreme-court-
     20180525-h10k4p>

44 Great Barrier Reef pollution: FOI documents in full; <https://www. theguardian.com/environment/interactive/2014/feb/12/great-barrier-reef-australia>

45 Clive Palmer's nickel refinery pumped toxic waste into Great Barrier Reef park; <https://www.theguardian.com/environment/2014/feb/12/cliver-palmers-nickel-refinery-pumped-nitrogen-great-barrier-reef-park>

46 Clive Palmer company 'approves' reopening of nickel refinery; <https://www.smh.com.au/business/companies/clive-palmer-company-approves-reopening-of-nickel-refinery-20180606-p4zjpi.html>

47 According to Tim Buckley and Simon Nicholas' Report 'Adani: Remote Prospects' (Carmichael Status 2017 Update), Adani acquired the coal deposit for a collective $A680 million. Buckley and Richardson state that initially Adani paid $500 million in August 2010, then in August 2014 paid A$155 million for the A$2/tonne coal royalty rights and paid A$25 million for the adjacent EPC 1080 from Mineralogy Pty Ltd tenement; <http://ieefa.org/wp-content/uploads/2017/04/Adani-Remote-Prospects-Carmichael-Status-Update-2017_April-2017_SN.pdf

48 Former Linc energy head ordered to clean up site of controversial gas project; <http://www.abc.net.au/news/2016-05-26/former-linc-energy-head-ordered-to-clean-up-site-of-gas-project/7448588>

49 Linc Energy trial hears company 'did nothing' to stop its alleged contamination continuing; <http://www.abc.net.au/news/2018-01-30/linc-energy-trial-hears-company-didnt-act-to-stop-contamination/9374900>

50 Linc Energy fined $4.5 million for serious environmental harm at underground coal gasification plant; <http://www.abc.net.au/news/2018-05-11/linc-energy-fined-$4.5-million-for-serious-environmental-harm/9751154>

51 Linc Energy; <https://www.ehp.qld.gov.au/management/linc-energy/>

52 Insolvency Law Update – an insolvent company's environmental obligations: the case of Linc Energy Ltd; <https://www.listgbarristers.com.au/publications/insolvency-law-update-disclaiming-an-insolvent-companys-environmental-obligations-the-case-of-linc-energy-ltd-in-liquidation>

Chapter 3: 'The Custodians' of the Great Barrier Reef

53 Unpublished and Untitled Research Paper, James Cook University, Townsville.

54 Report on the Reactive Monitoring Mission to the Great Barrier Reef (Australia), 6–14 March 2012; <https://whc.unesco.org/en/documents/117104>

55 Investigation of contaminant levels in green turtles from Gladstone: final report; <http://www.gladstoneconservationcouncil.com.au/web/wp-content/uploads/2013/04/Entox-Report-Investigation-of-contaiminanr-Levels-in-Green-Turtles-from-Gladstone.pdf>

56 Department of State Development Annual Report 2014-2015; <http://statedevelopment.qld.gov.au/resources/publication/annual-report/dsd-annual-report-2014-15-part-6.pdf>

57   Ban on capital dredge material disposal; <http://www.gbrmpa.gov.au/ managing-the-reef/how-the-reefs-managed/Managing-multiple-uses/ ports/ban-on-capital-dredge-material-disposal>

58   Review of Governance of the Great Barrier Reef Marine Park Authority; <https://www.environment.gov.au/system/files/resources/6a038c9a-34dd-42cb-a0b4-a688bd284658/files/final-report-review-governance-gbrmpa. pdf>

59   Half-a-billion dollars for the Great Barrier Reef; <https://www.smh.com.au/ politics/federal/federal-budget-half-a-billion-dollars-for-the-great-barrier-reef-20180428-p4zc6p.html>

60   Marine Turtle Conservation, Research and Monitoring Strategy; <https:// www.ehp.qld.gov.au/wildlife/pdf/marine-turtle-conservation-research-monitoring-strategy.pdf>

61   Unpublished and Untitled Research Paper, James Cook University, Townsville.

62   Marine (dugong and turtle) strandings update 2017; <https://www.ehp.qld. gov.au/wildlife/caring-for-wildlife/marine-strandings-update.html>

63   Links Between Water Quality and Marine Turtle Health; <https://www. researchgate.net/publication/304424778_Links_Between_Water_Quality_ and_Marine_Turtle_Health_TropWATER_Report_No_1405>

64   Great Barrier Reef turtles exposed to thousands of chemicals; <https:// www.uq.edu.au/news/article/2015/09/great-barrier-reef-turtles-exposed-thousands-of-chemicals>

65   High metal levels found in Queensland turtle blood; <https://www.uq.edu. au/news/article/2017/02/high-metal-levels-found-queensland-turtle-blood>

66   The Reef 2050 Plan; <http://www.environment.gov.au/marine/gbr/long-term-sustainability-plan>

67   State of Conservation – Great Barrier Reef; <https://whc.unesco.org/en/ soc/3658>

68   Queensland Resources Council denies urging Great Barrier Reef experts to ignore climate change; <http://www.abc.net.au/news/2017-08-02/lobbyists-deny-urging-reef-experts-to-ignore-climate-change/8766412>

69   Bessell-Browne, P. *et al.*, (2017) 'Impacts of turbidity on corals: The relative importance of light limitation and suspended sediments'. *Marine Pollution Bulletin*; <http://dx.doi.org/10.1016/j.marpolbul.2017.01.050>

Chapter 4: The Midas Touch – Gujarat Open For Business – At What Cost?

70   Meet the landholders of the Galilee Basin; <http://www.abc.net.au/ radionational/programs/breakfast/meet-the-landholders-of-the-galilee-basin/7096062>

71   Gina Rinehart flew MPs to India for lavish wedding; <https://www.theage. com.au/national/gina-rinehart-flew-mps-to-india-for-lavish-wedding-20110616-1g5zf.html>

72 Coalition MPs in 'overseas study' claim for wedding; <https://www.smh.com.au/politics/federal/coalition-mps-in-overseas-study-claim-for-wedding-20131005-2v13w.html>

73 Alpha Coal Mine Case; <http://envlaw.com.au/alpha-coal-mine-case/>

74 Adani Carmichael coal mine Land Court objection; <https://www.edoqld.org.au/adani_carmichael_land_court_objection>

75 Adani Carmichael Supreme Court EA Judicial Review; <https://www.edoqld.org.au/adani_ea_judicial_review>

76 *Hancock Galilee Pty Ltd v Currie & Ors* [2017] QLC 35; <https://archive.sclqld.org.au/qjudgment/2017/QLC17-035.pdf>

77 Alpha coal mine Court of Appeal challenge; <https://www.edoqld.org.au/alpha_coal_mine_court_appeal>

78 Alpha Coal Mine Case; <http://envlaw.com.au/alpha-coal-mine-case/>

79 Narendra Modi 'allowed' Gujarat 2002 anti-Muslim riots; <https://www.bbc.com/news/world-south-asia-13170914>

80 National Board for Wildlife to be toothless; <https://www.business-standard.com/article/economy-policy/national-board-for-wildlife-to-be-toothless-114072500169_1.html>

81 Modi Government's Environment Policy Endorses Everything that Bodes Well for Business; <https://thewire.in/environment/modi-government-environment-policy>

82 In March 2018, Hurun's Global Rich List stated Gautam Adani was the only Indian who saw "a massive growth in his fortunes," adding his wealth doubled to US$14b in 2017. India has the world's third-largest number of billionaires; <https://www.sbs.com.au/yourlanguage/hindi/en/article/2018/03/05/india-has-worlds-third-largest-number-billionaires-adani-doubles-wealth-14bn>

83 Carmichael coal mine magnate Gautam Adani: from school dropout to $12bn empire; <https://www.smh.com.au/lifestyle/carmichael-coal-mine-magnate-gautam-adani-from-school-dropout-to-12bn-empire-20171106-gzfobl.html>

84 Large amounts of money in India are often written in terms of crores. One crore is ten million rupees. 15,000 crore is 150 billion rupees (almost US$2.3 billion). Crore can also be used to refer to large numbers of other things e.g. people.

85 *The Adani Brief*; <https://envirojustice.org.au/sites/default/files/files/Submissions%20and%20reports/The_Adani_Brief_by_Environmental_Justice_Australia.pdf>

86 NGT lambasts Adani group for environment damage in Hazira; <https://www.thehindu.com/news/national/other-states/NGT-lambasts-Adani-group-for-environment-damage-in-Hazira/article14001610.ece>

87 Hazira Port; <https://www.sourcewatch.org/index.php/Hazira_Port>

88 Hazira Port; <https://www.prwatch.org/cmd/index.html>

Chapter 5: Confronting the God Adani

89 David Ritter (Ed) (2018) *The Coal Truth: The fight to stop Adani, defeat the big polluters and reclaim our democracy,* UWA Publishing, Perth.

90 The Salt Farmers of the Rann of Kutch; <https://thediplomat.com/2016/10/the-salt-farmers-of-the-rann-of-kutch/>

91 Worth their Salt: A Fascinating Glimpse into the World of the Hardworking Salt Farmers of Kutch; <https://www.thebetterindia.com/73603/agariyas-salt-farmers-rann-of-kutch/>

92 Adani solar plant guzzles illegal fresh water in drought-hit Tamil Nadu; <http://www.newindianexpress.com/states/tamil-nadu/2017/jun/06/adani-solar-plant-guzzles-illegal-fresh-water-in-drought-hit-tamil-nadu-1613326.html>

93 Solar Power and Water Consumption; <https://www.energymatters.com.au/renewable-news/em426/>

94 Annastacia Palaszczuk: Queensland's accidental premier; <https://www.smh.com.au/lifestyle/annastacia-palaszczuk-queenslands-accidental-premier-20150402-1mdq2e.html>

95 Adani's Galilee Basin project mine leases approved; <https://www.brisbanetimes.com.au/business/companies/adanis-galilee-basin-project-mine-leases-approved-20160403-gnx016.html>

96 The Adani lobbyist and Labor insider who smoothed the way for mega mine; <http://www.abc.net.au/news/2017-11-23/the-labor-insider-who-lobbied-for-adani/9181648>

97 Following Palaszczuk $1m for chickpea funding, in January 2018 an article in Brisbane's *Courier Mail* said that India had "slapped a surprise and costly 30% tariff on the superstar crop."

Chapter 6: The Coal King of the World

98 Carmichael coal mine magnate Gautam Adani: from school dropout to $12bn empire; <https://www.smh.com.au/lifestyle/carmichael-coal-mine-magnate-gautam-adani-from-school-dropout-to-12bn-empire-20171106-gzfobl.html>

99 The Alchemist; < https://www.outlookbusiness.com/specials/super-seven/the-alchemist-1113>

100 How Adani Group is moving towards corporate responsibility from controversies; <https://economictimes.indiatimes.com/industry/transportation/shipping-/-transport/how-adani-group-is-moving-towards-corporate-responsibility-from-controversies/articleshow/53642896.cms?utm_source=contentofinterest&utm_medium=text&utm_campaign=cppst>

101 'Adanis' (sic) Game Plan for Mundra ship-breaking yard; <http://www.downtoearth.org.in/news/adanis-game-plan-for-mundra-shipbreaking-yard-42050>

102 Violations of the Environment Clearance Conditions of the Waterfront Development Project of the MPSEZ Ltd, Mundra, Kutch (Gujarat); <http://env-compliance.in/media/uploads/report/8/WFPD-evidence-report.pdf>

103 Adani Mundra project: First, Rs 200-crore fine cancelled. Now, officials find company did no wrong; <https://scroll.in/article/869582/adani-mundra-project-first-rs-200-crore-fine-cancelled-now-officials-find-company-did-no-wrong>
104 APSEZ gets green nod to set up ship recycling facility at Mundra; <https://www.livemint.com/Companies/WAO1fKb8ezGnG95fapfGeL/APSEZ-gets-green-nod-to-set-up-ship-recycling-facility-at-Mu.html>
105 Photos: Shipbreaking on the Beaches of Alang; <http://gcaptain.com/photos-shipbreaking-in-alang-india/>
106 The alchemist; <https://www.adani.com/docs/MrGautamAdaniThe Alchemist>
107 Post Gujarat elections, spotlight is back on Tata, Adani Mundra plants; <https://www.business-standard.com/article/companies/post-gujarat-elections-spotlight-is-back-on-tata-adani-mundra-plants-117123000743_1.html>
108 Adani signs 1.65 bn coal-import deal with Indonesia; <https://www.livemint.com/Companies/dPB47fpY7ogaufPeiR7eWN/Adani-signs-165-bn-coalimport-deal-with-Indonesia.html>
109 Post Gujarat elections, spotlight is back on Tata, Adani Mundra plants; <https://www.business-standard.com/article/companies/post-gujarat-elections-spotlight-is-back-on-tata-adani-mundra-plants-117123000743_1.html>
110 Adani project in Mundra has violated environmental norms rules MoEF committee; <https://www.cseindia.org/adani-project-in-mundra-has-violated-environmental-norms-rules-moef-committee-4925>
111 Minister's Briefing Note; <http://services.dip.qld.gov.au/opendata/RTI/DSD/documents-for-publication-RTIP1617-030.pdf>
112 Chapter 6 Impact of Industrial Expansion in Mundra Coast; <http://www.ceeindia.org/cee/pdf_files/impactofindustrial_expansion_in_mundra_coast.pdf>
113 Violations of the Environment Clearance Conditions of the Waterfront Development Project of the MPSEZ Ltd, Mundra, Kutch (Gujarat); <http://env-compliance.in/media/uploads/report/8/WFPD-evidence-report.pdf>
114 The Gulf of Kutch Marine National park and Sanctuary: A Case Study; <http://aquaticcommons.org/2077/1/Kutch.pdf>
115 How India's first Marine National Park is faring; <https://www.livemint.com/Leisure/2deHepvduSFEZv8byR2eZJ/Marine-National-Park-A-shift-in-the-tide.html>
116 Adani Mundra project: First, Rs 200-crore fine cancelled. Now, officials find company did no wrong; <https://scroll.in/article/869582/adani-mundra-project-first-rs-200-crore-fine-cancelled-now-officials-find-company-did-no-wrong>
117 Mundra SEZ: Adani Group secures in-principal approval to divert 1552 hectares forest land; <https://indianexpress.com/article/business/companies/mundra-sez-adani-group-secures-in-principle-approval-to-divert-1552-hectares-forest-land-5083425/>

118 US Supreme Court will hear Landmark Case Challenging World Bank Group Immunity; <https://earthrights.org/media/u-s-supreme-court-will-hear-landmark-case-challenging-world-bank-group-immunity/>

119 Doing Big Business In Modi's Gujarat; <https://webcache.googleusercontent.com/search?q=cache:y9hVI6la5YcJ:https://www.forbes.com/sites/meghabahree/2014/03/12/doing-big-business-in-modis-gujarat/+cd=1&hl=en&ct=clnk&gl=au>

120 Supreme Court's Order on 'Compensatory Tariff' Powers Accountability and Strengthens Competition; <https://thewire.in/business/supreme-courts-order-compensatory-tariffs-accountability>

Chapter 7: Digging up the Dirt on Adani

121 Kachchh – Central Ground Water Board; <http://cgwb.gov.in/District_Profile/Gujarat/Kachchh.pdf>

122 Study on groundwater salinization and formulation of management strategies for the coastal aquifers of Mundra region Kutch district Gujarat state; <http://hdl.handle.net/10603/58602>

123 Kutch Coast-People, Environment; <http://env-compliance.in/media/uploads/report/43/Kutch%20Coast%20Study%20-%20new%20-%20Copy%20copy.pdf>

124 Chapter 6 Impact of Industrial Expansion in Mundra Coast; <http://www.ceeindia.org/cee/pdf_files/impactofindustrial_expansion_in_mundra_coast.pdf>

125 Sazina Bhimani (2014) 'Study on groundwater salinization and formulation of management strategies for the coastal aquifers of Mundra region, Kutch district, Gujarat state.'

126 Report of the Committee for Inspection of M/s Adani Port & SEZ Ltd; <http://www.moef.nic.in/sites/default/files/adani-report-290413.pdf>

127 Doing Big Business in Modi's Gujarat; <https://www.forbes.com/sites/meghabahree/2014/03/12/doing-big-business-in-modis-gujarat/2/#7cdc91a9398f>

128 Report of the Committee for Inspection of M/s Adani Port & SEZ Ltd; <http://www.moef.nic.in/sites/default/files/adani-report-290413.pdf>

129 GABWRA overview; <https://www.csiro.au/en/Research/LWF/Areas/Water-resources/Assessing-water-resources/GABWRA/Overview>

130 Adani ground water plan could permanently drain desert oasis; <http://www.abc.net.au/news/2018-03-21/adani-groundwater-plan-risks-permanent-damage-to-desert-springs/9569184>

131 How Adani Group is moving towards Corporate Responsibility; <http://economictimes.indiatimes.com/articleshow/53642896.cms?utm_source=contentofinterest&utm_medium=text&utm_campaign=cppst>

132 What makes Kutch's Kharai Camels Truly Remarkable; <https://weather.com/en-IN/india/science/news/2018-05-27-kutch-kharai-camel-remarkable>

133 Mayor says Rocky won't pull their funds for Adani's airport; <https://www.themorningbulletin.com.au/news/mayor-says-rocky-wont-pull-their-funds-for-adanis-/3444153/>

134 Townville Major Jenny Hill gives Adani six months deadline; <https://www.theaustralian.com.au/national-affairs/state-politics/townsville-mayor-jenny-hill-gives-adani-sixmonth-deadline-for-coalmine/news-story/659b938b3aa239ef8048c00c4ff76c2d>

135 Opposition to Coal in India; <https://www.sourcewatch.org/index.php/Opposition_to_coal_in_India>

136 Countries with the Biggest Coal Reserves; <https://www.mining-technology.com/features/feature-the-worlds-biggest-coal-reserves-by-country/>

137 Adani Godda Power Plant: Too Expensive, Too Late and Too Risky for Bangladesh; <http://ieefa.org/wp-content/uploads/2018/04/Adani-Godda-Power-Project-April_2018.pdf>

138 Coal exports to help India lower trade deficit in energy; <https://www.livemint.com/Industry/QFDUYTcvc4aGf4TUoELFSJ/Coal-exports-to-help-India-lower-trade-deficit-in-energy.html>

139 Coal 2017 – International Energy Agency; <https://www.iea.org/coal2017/>

140 Coal Vision 2030; <https://www.coalindia.in/DesktopModules/DocumentList/documents/Coal_Vision_2030_document_for_Coal_Sector_Stakeholders_Consultation_27012018.pdf>

141 World's biggest coal company closes 37 mines as solar power's influence grows; <https://www.independent.co.uk/news/world/asia/coal-india-closes-37-mines-solar-power-sustainable-energy-market-influence-pollution-a7800631.html?source=Snapzu?source=Snapzu>

142 Malcolm Turnbull talks up coal in Delhi despite India's aim to stop imports; <https://www.theguardian.com/environment/2017/apr/11/malcolm-turnbull-talks-up-coal-delhi-india-stop-imports>

143 Adani coal 'welcome' part of India's future electricity supply; <http://www.abc.net.au/news/2017-06-13/adani-coal-imports-relunctantly-welcomed-in-india/8611970>

144 Adani Loses Nearly All Its Investment On Mundra Power Plant; <https://www.bloombergquint.com/business/2017/09/04/adani-loses-entire-investment-in-mundra-indias-biggest-thermal-power-plant>

145 Adani Godda Power Plant: Too Expensive, Too Late and Too Risky for Bangladesh; <http://ieefa.org/wp-content/uploads/2018/04/Adani-Godda-Power-Project-April_2018.pdf>

146 Galilee Basin mines will slash coal output, jobs elsewhere; <http://www.abc.net.au/news/2017-07-06/galilee-basin-mining-project-will-reduce-coal-output:-research/8682164>

147 In March 2018, a year after this interview, Modi had promised to raise the solar power generation capacity fivefold to 100,000MW and with tariffs reaching R2.44 per unit.

148 India is home to 70% of tigers in the world.

149 In October 2017, Reuters reported that Indian resource conglomerate Adani and Vedant were considering bidding for a $9 billion diamond project abandoned by Rio Tinto, said to hold around 32 million carats of diamonds. The area is a corridor between the Panna Tiger Reserve and the Navardehi Wildlife Sanctuary; <https://www.reuters.com/article/uk-india-mining-

exclusive/exclusive-vedanta-adani-may-bid-for-9-billion-indian-diamond-
mine-left-by-rio-idUKKBN1CV2XI>

Chapter 8: The Swirling Dervish

150 Listed in the Directory of Important Wetlands in Australia and home to
    several threatened species.
151 Adani fined $12,000 for Abbot Point coal terminal stormwater breach;
    <https //www.smh.com.au/business/companies/adani-fined-12000-for-
    abbot-point-coal-terminal-stormwater-breach-20170811-gxtxmd.html>
152 Adani's Abbot Point coal spill contaminated wetlands, Report finds;
    <https://www.theguardian.com/business/2017/sep/20/adanis-abbot-
    point-coal-spill-contaminated-wetlands-report-finds>
153 Caley Valley Wetlands; <https://www.ehp.qld.gov.au/management/pdf/
    caley-valley-wetlands-assessment-impacts-cyclone-debbie.pdf>
154 Deloitte Access Economics. (2017) At what price? The economic, social and
    icon value of the Great Barrier Reef; <https://www2.deloitte.com/content/
    dam/Deloitte/au/Documents/Economics/deloitte-au-economics-great-
    barrier-reef-230617.pdf>

Chapter 9: The Ping Pong Politics of Climate Change

155 Climate Council. (2017) Tropical Cyclones and Climate Change: Factsheet.
    p. 1; <https://www.climatecouncil.org.au/uploads/3cf983377b8043ff1ecf15
    709eebf298.pdf>
156 Independent Review of Governance of the Great Barrier Reef Marine
    Park Authority; <http://www.environment.gov.au/marine/gbr/authority-
    governance-review>
157 Significant coral decline and habitat loss on the Great Barrier Reef; <http://
    www.gbrmpa.gov.au/media-room/latest-news/coral-bleaching/2017/
    significant-coral-decline-and-habitat-loss-on-the-great-barrier-reef>
158 Reef health. Updated: 29 June 2017; <http://www.gbrmpa.gov.au/about-the-
    reef/reef-health>
159 Significant coral decline and habitat loss on the Great Barrier Reef; <www.
    gbrmpa.gov.au/media-room/latest-news/coral-bleaching/2017/significant-
    coral-decline-and-habitat-loss-on-the-great-barrier-reef>
160 Global warming transforms reef assemblages; <https://www.nature.com/
    articles/s41586-018-0041-2>
161 Terry Hughes, P. James, T. Kerry et al (2017) 'Global warming and recurrent
    mass bleaching of corals' in *Nature*, Vol. 543, pp. 373–377, 16 March; <https://
    www.nature.com/articles/nature21707>
162 Coral bleaching: Extreme heat pushes parts of the Great Barrier Reef
    beyond recovery; <http://www.abc.net.au/news/science/2017-03-16/coral-
    graveyards-grow-as-bleaching-becomes-the-new-normal/8353030>
163 Suspicions Adani altered lab report; <https://www.theguardian.com/
    business/2018/feb/02/suspicions-adani-altered-lab-report-while-
    appealing-fine-for-abbot-point-coal-spill>

164 Turnbull slammed, rebuffed by industry, over clean coal; <https://thenewdaily.com.au/news/national/2017/02/02/turnbull-slammed-clean-coal/>

165 Anna Krien (13 June 2017) *The Long Goodbye: Coal, Coral and Australia's Climate Deadlock, Quarterly Essay 66*. Black Inc. Publishing, Melbourne.

166 Sorry, Matt Canavan, no one believes coal magic means everyone wins; <https://www.theguardian.com/australia-news/2018/mar/31/sorry-matt-canavan-no-one-believes-coal-magic-means-everyone-wins>

167 Coal lobby ads biggest third-party political expenditure in Australia; <https://www.theguardian.com/australia-news/2018/feb/01/coal-lobby-ads-biggest-third-party-political-expenditure-in-australia>

168 Great Barrier Reef coral bleaching: Queensland tourism body downplays damage; <https://www.brisbanetimes.com.au/national/queensland/great-barrier-reef-coral-bleaching-queensland-tourism-body-downplays-damage-20160404-gny9nr.html>

169 A Close-Up Look at the Catastrophic Bleaching of the Great Barrier Reef; <https://e360.yale.edu/features/inside-look-at-catastrophic-bleaching-of-the-great-barrier-reef-2017-hughes>

170 Aboriginal settlement in Australia was planned migration: study; <https://www.smh.com.au/national/aboriginal-settlement-in-australia-was-planned-migration-study-20180521-p4zggl.html>

171 Trends in Global CO_2 Emissions, 2016 Report; <http://edgar.jrc.ec.europa.eu/news_docs/jrc-2016-trends-in-global-co2-emissions-2016-report-103425.pdf>

172 Australia's emissions rise again in 2017, putting Paris targets in doubt; <https://www.theguardian.com/environment/2018/mar/29/australias-emissions-rise-again-in-2017-putting-paris-targets-in-doubt>

173 CSIRO Chief Ignores Scientific Evidence Of Climate Change as Biggest Threat to Reef; <https://www.climatecouncil.org.au/2018/03/12/csiro-chief-ignores-scientific-evidence-of-climate-change-as-biggest-threat-to-reef/>

174 US and Asian growth planned as CSIRO 'moonshots' take shape; <http://www.afr.com/technology/us-and-asian-growth-planned-as-csiro-moonshots-take-shape-20180213-h0w23b>

175 Stop Adani Alliance; <http://www.stopadanialliance.com>

176 Digging into Adani – *Four Corners*; <http://www.abc.net.au/4corners/digging-into-adani/9008500>

177 Adani: Palaszczuk and business groups brush off allegations of company's corruption, negligence; <http://www.abc.net.au/news/2017-10-03/queensland-government-defends-adani-amid-damning-allegations/9010532>

178 Anne Elvey (Ed) (2018) *hope for whole, poets speak up to Adani*. Rosslyn Avenue Productions, Melbourne; <https://plumwoodmountain.files.wordpress.com/2018/03/hope_for_whole_poets_speak_up_to-_adani-ebook050318.pdf> With kind thanks to Michelle Cahill and Anne Elvey for permission to republish this poem.

179 On April 30, 2018 *The Sydney Morning Herald* reported that Alinta Energy had put in a $250 million bid to buy the power station and that Federal Environment and Energy Minister, Josh Frydenberg had regularly been on the phone to Alinta encouraging its bid; <https://www.smh.com.au/business/companies/alinta-lobs-250m-bid-for-agl- s-liddell-power-station-20180430-p4zcdg.html> but in May 2018 AGL announced it had knocked back Alinta's bid; <https://www.smh.com.au/business/the-economy/agl-rejects-alinta-offer-for-liddell-power-station-20180521-p4zghf.html>

180 Anna Krien (13 June 2017) *The Long Goodbye: Coal, Coral and Australia's Climate Deadlock, Quarterly Essay 66.* Black Inc. Publishing, Melbourne.

181 Adani mine 'not a positive thing for Australia', Labor's Mark Butler says; <https://www.theguardian.com/australia-news/2017/jun/22/adani-mine-not-a-positive-thing-for-australia-labors-mark-butler-says>

182 An unprecedented grassroots campaign meant Lisa Singh was re-elected in the 2016 Federal Election, which was the first time a candidate has been elected on the below-the-line votes since the Senate voting system was introduced in 1984.

183 *Chasing Coral*; <https://www.chasingcoral.com>

184 Judith Wright (1977, re-published 2014) *The Coral Battleground.* Spinifex Press, Mission Beach and Geelong.

Chapter 10: An About Face

185 In May 2018, Annastacia Palaszczuk announced $40 million new funding in the upcoming budget which included $26 million in extra funding for a Joint Field Management Program for reef protection and a further $13.8m over the next four years for water quality. Minister for the Environment and the Great Barrier Reef, Leeanne Enoch, said that further investment for the reef needed to be backed by a national climate change policy and said that was the 'number one challenge facing the reef right now'. The Palaszczuk Government also has a 50% renewable energy target with net zero emissions by 2050; <http://statements.qld.gov.au/Statement/2018/5/23/palaszczuk-government-injects-more-funding-for-great-barrier-reef>

186 'Upset' Adani protester goes at premier in Airlie Beach; <https://www.dailymercury.com.au/news/upset-adani-protester-goes-at-premier-in-airlie-be/3252238>

187 Gina Rinehart celebrates Roy Hill ramp up in blaze of pink; <https://www.afr.com/news/gina-rinehart-celebrates-roy-hill-ramp-up-in-blaze-of-pink-20180502-h0zk5c>

188 Atlas Iron backs Gina Rinehart's $390 million takeover offer; <http://www.abc.net.au/news/2018-06-21/atlas-iron-backs-gina-rinehart-takeover-390-million/9893448>

189 The Boom: Iron ore and Australia; <https://theconversation.com/the-boom-iron-ore-and-australia-1847>

190 Palaszczuk says she will veto federal Adani loan as she accuses LNP of 'smear'; <https://www.theguardian.com/australia-news/2017/nov/03/palaszczuk-says-she-will-veto-federal-adani-loan-as-she-accuses-lnp-of-smear>

191 Anna Krien (13 June 2017) *The Long Goodbye: Coal, Coral and Australia's Climate Deadlock, Quarterly Essay 66.* Black Inc. Publishing, Melbourne.
192 Queensland Election: how Palaszczuk's Adani veto turned tide for ALP; <https://www.theaustralian.com.au/national-affairs/queensland-election/queensland-election-how-palaszczuks-adani-veto-turned-tide-for-alp/news-story/fd0e162c2a784a745e0af37bfda712ad>

Chapter 11: The Carbon Bomb is Ticking

193 On 17 May 2018, environmental writer, Peter Hannam wrote about Clive Palmer's proposed Alpha North mine in the Galilee Basin under the headline: 'Carbon bomb': Clive Palmer seeks nod for mine twice the size of Adani's; <https://www.smh.com.au/environment/climate-change/carbon-bomb-clive-palmer-seeks-nod-for-mine-twice-the-size-of-adani-s-20180515-p4zfe5.html>
194 Galilee Basin: State Development Area Development Scheme; <http://statedevelopment.qld.gov.au/resources/plan/cg/galilee-basin/gbsda-development-scheme-oct-2015.PDF>
195 Cooked by Coal: The Global: Significance of Australia's Galilee Basin; <https://www.greeninstitute.org.au/wp-content/uploads/2017/05/Galilee-Basin-backgrounder-March-2015.pdf>
196 North Galilee Basin Rail Project; < https://www.statedevelopment.qld.gov.au/assessments-and-approvals/north-galilee-basin-rail-project.html>
197 Adani to pay for Isaac council staff working on Carmichael mine activities; <http://www.abc.net.au/news/2018-05-28/adani-to-pay-for-isaac-council-staff-working-on-carmichael-mine/9801988>
198 Queensland coal – mines and advanced projects; <https://www.dnrm.qld.gov.au/__data/assets/pdf_file/0011/238079/coal-mines-advanced-projects.pdf>
199 Other stakeholders include the Queensland Government, Wirsol (which has 94.9%) and Whitsunday Regional Council and Federal Government ARENA (Australian Renewable Energy Agency).
200 Dispatches from the Adani frontline; <https://www.echo.net.au/2018/01/dispatches-adani-frontline/>
201 Clive Hamilton (2016) *What Do We Want! The Story of Protest in Australia.* National Library of Australia Publishing.
202 Tasmanian Dam Case; <http://envlaw.com.au/tasmanian-dam-case>
203 Adani claims anti-coal activists cost company $7.5 million; <https://www.whitsundaytimes.com.au/news/adani-claims-anti-coal-activists-cost-company-75m/3360423/>
204 Furious Bowen local in viral spray at Adani activists involved in North Queensland protest; <https://www.townsvillebulletin.com.au/news/furious-bowen-local-in-viral-spray-at-adani-activists-involved-in-north-queensland-protest/news-story/5c82017cd99f1c82032fc403340b9ec6>
205 Thea Astley, *Multiple Effects of Rainshadow* (1996) Viking Press, Melbourne.
206 Porcupine is Aboriginal English for echidna. Barrbira is the Birri people's word for what they call porcupine.

207 Alex Miller (2002) *Journey to the Stone Country*. Allen & Unwin, Sydney.

208 Reading Australia: 'Journey to the Stone Country' by Alex Miller; <https://www.australianbookreview.com.au/reading-australia/alex-miller/journey-to-the-stone-country-by-alex-miller?tmpl=component&print=1>

209 Anna Krien (13 June 2017) *The Long Goodbye: Coal, Coral and Australia's Climate Deadlock, Quarterly Essay 66*. Black Inc. Publishing, Melbourne.

210 The attendance register for the meeting indicates that 60% of the participants had never attended any of the prior claim group meetings and were not recorded in a database of Wangan and Jagalingou members maintained by Queensland South Native Title Services (QSNTS) encompassing the then 12 years of the claim. Others still did not name an ancestor from whom they were descended. 'Killing Country (Part 5): Native Title Colonialism, Racism And Mining For Manufactured Consent'; <https://newmatilda.com/2018/01/30/native-title-colonialism-racism-adani-and-the-manufacture-of-consent-for-mining/>

211 The Equator Principles (EPs) is a risk management framework, adopted by financial institutions, for determining, assessing and managing environmental and social risk in projects and is primarily intended to provide a minimum standard for due diligence and monitoring to support responsible risk decision-making.

212 Adani mine: Traditional owners aiming to block native title ruling on mine site; <http://www.abc.net.au/news/2017-12-03/adani-mine-traditional-owners-want-to-block-native-title-ruling/9221256>

213 Native Title law came into effect through the 1993 Native Title Act, to the celebrated 'Mabo case' in which Eddie Koiki Mabo and other Murray Islanders from the Torres Strait asserted ownership of their island. The 1992 Mabo v Queensland (No 2) High Court case decided in favour of the islanders, overturning the idea of terra nullius (land of nobody) as a legal fiction, thereby altering the established land ownership recognised previously through settler land law in Australia.

214 Native Title Amendment (ILUA) Bill 2017.

215 Adrian Burragubba, 'High Noon in the Galilee: Wangan and Jagalingou Law and Order' in *The Coal Truth* by David Ritter (Ed) (2018), UWA Publishing, Perth.

216 Adani mine: Traditional owners aiming to block native title ruling on mine site; <http://www.abc.net.au/news/2017-12-03/adani-mine-traditional-owners-want-to-block-native-title-ruling/9221256>

217 Federal Court rejects latest bids to stop Adani; <https://www.smh.com.au/business/companies/federal-court-rejects-latest-bids-to-stop-adani-20170825-gy47iq.html>

218 Indigenous group hid more than $2m in payments from Adani mining giant; <https://www.theguardian.com/australia-news/2018/jun/22/indigenous-group-hid-more-than-2m-in-payments-from-adani-mining-giant>

219 Adani port faces possible 'stop order' after traditional owners object; <https://www.theguardian.com/environment/2018/jul/05/adani-coal-port-faces-possible-stop-order-after-traditional-owners-object>

220 Geoff Cousins reveals how Bill Shorten wavered on Adani mine; <https://www.theguardian.com/environment/2018/feb/28/geoff-cousins-reveals-how-bill-shorten-wavered-on-adani-mine>

221 Geoff Cousins said Bill Shorten told him Labor could revoke Adani licence; <http://www.abc.net.au/7.30/geoff-cousins-says-bill-shorten-told-him-labor/9490962>

222 Stopping Adani mine would pose no 'sovereign risk' to Australia, says economist Saul Eslake; <https://www.smh.com.au/politics/federal/stopping-adani-mine-would-pose-no-sovereign-risk-to-australia-says-economist-saul-eslake-20180520-p4zgea.html>

223 Richard Denniss: 'Sovereign risk' econobabble has lost all meaning; <https://www.smh.com.au/opinion/richard-denniss-sovereign-risk-econobabble-has-lost-all-meaning-20180309-h0x8r3.html>

224 The Indian newspaper *Business Standard*, in September 2016 reported that GVK Reddy failed to pay the final tranche of $560 million to Gina Rinehart. GVK fails to pay $560 million for mines in Australia; <https://www.business-standard.com/article/companies/gvk-fails-to-pay-560-million-for-mines-in-australia-116040700060_1.html>

225 Stop Adani destroying our land and culture; <http://wanganjagalingou.com.au/our-fight/>

226 Good news about renewables: but the heat is still on to cut fossil fuel use; <https://www.theguardian.com/environment/2018/mar/25/renewables-good-news-heat-on-cut-fossil-fuel-use>

227 IEA accused of undermining global shift from fossil fuels; <https://www.theguardian.com/environment/2018/apr/05/iea-accused-of-undermining-global-shift-from-fossil-fuels>

228 Draft Joint Report – Environmental Law Australia; <http://envlaw.com.au/wp-content/uploads/carmichael14.pdf>

229 Assessment of selected aspects of the Alpha Coal Project with respect to climate change; <http://envlaw.com.au/wp-content/uploads/alpha23.pdf>

230 Professor Roger Jones, Centre for Strategic Economic Studies, Victoria University, expert witness for Kelly said that the Alpha mine and three other mines' total emissions could be 2% and 5% of total global emissions by 2040.

231 To slow climate change, India joins the renewable energy revolution; <https://theconversation.com/to-slow-climate-change-india-joins-the-renewable-energy-revolution-78321>

232 Doing Big Business In Modi's Gujarat; <https://webcache.googleusercontent.com/search?q=cache:y9hVI6la5YcJ:https://www.forbes.com/sites/meghabahree/2014/03/12/doing-big-business-in-modis-gujarat/+&cd=1&hl=en&ct=clnk&gl=au>

233 Renewable Energy Index – Green Energy Markets; <http://greenmarkets.com.au/images/uploads/Resources/RE_Index/Renewable_Energy_Index_2016-17-_Benchmark_report.pdf>

234 Naomi Oreskes and Erik M. Conway (2010) *Merchants of Doubt: How a Handful of Scientists Obscured the Truth on Issues from Tobacco Smoke to Global Warming.* Bloomsbury Publishing, London.

235 The US is the Biggest Carbon Polluter in History. It Just Walked Away From the Paris Climate Deal; <https://www.nytimes.com/interactive/2017/06/01/climate/us-biggest-carbon-polluter-in-history-will-it-walk-away-from-the-paris-climate-deal.html>

236 Changing Climate. Report of the Carbon Dioxide Committee; <http://www.nap.edu/read/18714/chapter1#iii>

237 Antarctic ice melting faster than ever, studies show; <https://www.theguardian.com/environment/2018/jun/13/antarctic-ice-melting-faster-than-ever-studies-show>

238 Naomi Oreskes and Erik M. Conway (2010) *Merchants of Doubt: How a Handful of Scientists Obscured the Truth on Issues from Tobacco Smoke to Global Warming.* Bloomsbury Publishing, London.

239 Floating sunscreen-like film could protect the Great Barrier Reef; <http://www.nationalgeographic.com.au/australia/floating-sunscreen-like-film-could-protect-the-great-barrier-reef.aspx>

240 The amazing biological fixes that could help save the Great Barrier Reef; <https://www.smh.com.au/opinion/the-amazing-biological-fixes-that-could-help-save-the-great-barrier-reef-20170930-gyrzad.html>

241 What lies beneath?; <https://www.theaustralian.com.au/life/weekend-australian-magazine/lizard-island-resort-great-barrier-reef/news-story/9d8e25ce1832e5daaf583ff52d55efb5>

242 Page vii, Impacts of the 2016 and 2017 mass coral bleaching events on the Great Barrier Reef tourism industry and tourism-dependent coastal communities of Queensland; <http://rrrc.org.au/wp-content/uploads/2018/06/RRRC-Impacts-2016-17-Coral-Bleaching-on-GBR-Digital.pdf>

243 Page vii, Impacts of the 2016 and 2017 mass coral bleaching events on the Great Barrier Reef tourism industry and tourism-dependent coastal communities of Queensland; <http://rrrc.org.au/wp-content/uploads/2018/06/RRRC-Impacts-2016-17-Coral-Bleaching-on-GBR-Digital.pdf>

244 Page 85, Impacts of the 2016 and 2017 mass coral bleaching events on the Great Barrier Reef tourism industry and tourism-dependent coastal communities of Queensland; <http://rrrc.org.au/wp-content/uploads/2018/06/RRRC-Impacts-2016-17-Coral-Bleaching-on-GBR-Digital.pdf>

245 Page 25, Final Report 2016 Coral Bleaching Event on the Great Barrier Reef, Great Barrier Reef Marine Park Authority, Townsville; <http://elibrary.gbrmpa.gov.au/jspui/bitstream/11017/3206/1/Final-report-2016-coral-bleaching-GBR.pdf>

246 Valda Blundell and Donny Woolagoodja (2015) *Keeping the Wandjinas Fresh,* Fremantle Press, Perth.

247 How will the Barrier Reef recover from the death of one-third of its northern corals?; <https://theconversation.com/how-will-the-barrier-reef-recover-from-the-death-of-one-third-of-its-northern-corals-60186>

248 Some rare good climate news: the fossil fuel industry is weaker than ever; <https://www.theguardian.com/commentisfree/2018/jun/21/climate-change-fossil-fuel-industry-never-been-weaker>

Other titles available from Spinifex Press

The Coral Battleground
Judith Wright

In the late 1960s, the Reef was threatened with limestone mining and oil drilling. A small group of dedicated conservationists in Queensland – John Büsst, Judith Wright, Len Webb and others – battled to save the Ellison Reef from coral-limestone mining and the Swain Reefs from oil exploration. The group later swelled to encompass scientists, trade unionists and politicians throughout Australia, and led in 1976 to the establishment of a guardian body: the Great Barrier Reef Marine Park Authority. That it still survives is a legacy of activists, artists, poets, ecologists and students. In 1967 they were branded as 'cranks'; now they should be recognised as 'visionaries'.

"It will come as a surprise to most people that so many of the issues confronted in the 1960s by the doughty campaigners against drilling for oil on the barrier reef are still alive. We will have to be as determined and as persistent as they if we are to protect what is now a World Heritage Site from pollution, dredging, dumping, coral bleaching and pest species."
—Germaine Greer, author of *White Beech*

ISBN: 9781742199061

Trauma Trails, Recreating Song Lines: The Transgenerational Effects of Trauma in Indigenous Australia

Judy Atkinson

Shortlisted in The Australian *Awards for Excellence in Educational Publishing, 2003*

I was running a workshop in the Kimberleys, and in the circle a woman began to speak from a place of deep pain and despair. She described herself as bad, dirty, ugly, words she had taken into herself from childhood experiences of abuse. I leant forward and sang her a song. 'How could anyone ever tell you, you are anything less than beautiful?' While sitting with her, as the words settled into her soul, another woman said to the circle: you are re-creating song lines - from trauma trails. I was honoured by this description of my work. Providing a startling answer to the questions of how to solve the problems of generational trauma, *Trauma Trails* moves beyond the rhetoric of victimhood, and provides inspiration for anyone concerned about Indigenous and Non-Indigenous communities today. Beginning with issues of colonial dispossession, Judy Atkinson also sensitively deals with trauma caused by abuse, alcoholism, and drug dependency.

"I recommend this complex, well-composed and emotionally satisfying book to anyone who has an interest in improving the quality of Australian psychological work."

—Craig San Roque, *Aboriginal History*

"*Trauma Trails* is a remarkable book by any standards ... [it has] much to say about diagnosis and treatment, of individuals and whole social groups. It is a substantial reconciliative achievement and should encourage others to bridge the cultural divide in imaginative ways."

—Antonia Esten, *Journal of Australian Studies*

ISBN: 9781876756222

The Lace Makers of Narsapur

Maria Mies

Spinifex Feminist Classic

The Lace Makers of Narsapur is a sensitive and groundbreaking study of women at the beginning of the process of globalisation. Maria Mies looks at the way in which women are dispossessed by producing luxury goods for the Western market and simult-aneously not counted as workers. Instead they are defined as 'non-working housewives' and their work as 'leisure-time activity'. The rates of pay are far below acceptable levels resulting in accelerating pauperisation and a rapid deterioration in their position in Indian society.

"This classic breakthrough feminist text was of considerable influence in my research. So little has changed concerning the valuing and vulnerability of women's work it resonates as rigorously in 2012. Mies has made significant contributions to feminist scholarship, and the *Lace Makers* is iconic."

—Marilyn Waring, author of *Counting for Nothing*

"... a graphic illustration of how women bear the impact of development processes in countries where poor peasant and tribal societies are being 'integrated' into an international division of labor under the dictates of capital accumulation."

—Chandra Talpade Mohanty, author of *Third World Women and the Politics of Feminism*

ISBN: 9781742198149

Locust Girl: A Lovesong

Merlinda Bobis

Winner, 2016 Christina Stead Award for Fiction,
NSW Premier's Literary Awards

Most everything has dried up: water, the womb, even the love among lovers. Hunger is rife, except across the border. One night, a village is bombed after its men attempt to cross the border. Nine-year old Amedea is buried underground and sleeps to survive. Ten years later, she wakes with a locust embedded in her brow. This political fable is a girl's magical journey through the border. The border has cut the human heart. Can she repair it with the story of a small life? This is the Locust Girl's dream, her lovesong —

>   For those walking to the border for dear life
>   And those guarding the border for dear life

"It's allegorically pertinent not just to the question of refugees but also to how the future might play out if climate change is as disastrous as some of the modelling suggests."

—Ed Wright, *The Australian*

"There were many fine and stylistically accomplished works among this year's entries, but the distinctiveness, sweep and visual power of this short novel set it apart."

—Christina Stead Judges' Report

"It is no surprise that a dystopian novel about climate change has won the Christina Stead Prize for Fiction in the NSW Premier's Literary Awards."

—Susan Wyndham, *Sydney Morning Herald*

ISBN: 9781742199627

Earth's Breath

Susan Hawthorne

Shortlisted Judith Wright Poetry Prize

It's an eye that radiates out from the personal to the communal, tracking its subject matter through the lenses of history and myth. Susan Hawthorne's poetry shifts with seismic intensity, from tranquility to roar, bureaucratic inertia to survival, and the slow recovery from destruction to regeneration.

"*Earth's Breath* depicts a vast historical and emotional landscape through meticulous attention to detail. In this case, much of the detail reflects the poet's love of the natural world."

—Carolyn Gage, *Lambda Literary*

"Hawthorne's work reveals poetry so vivid, so exquisite, so sensitive to the wind and its effects, it has made me determined to find out some more about some of our barely reported global catastrophes."

—Robyn Peck, *poam*

"Susan Hawthorne has captured the essence of the moment and the lingering toll a natural disaster takes on those who have lived through it. Hawthorne delivers legend, fable and emotion as well as reflections on humanity, nature and science."

—Melanie Busato, *Townsville Bulletin*

ISBN: 9781876756734

*If you would like to know more about
Spinifex Press, write to us for a free catalogue, visit our
website or email us for further information
on how to subscribe to our monthly newsletter.*

Spinifex Press
PO Box 105
Mission Beach QLD 4852
Australia

www.spinifexpress.com.au
women@spinifexpress.com.au